NARRATIVE STRATEGIES
IN SCIENCE FICTION

Borgo Press Books by BRIAN STABLEFORD

Against the New Gods, and Other Essays on Writers of Imaginative Fiction
Algebraic Fantasies and Realistic Romances: More Masters of Science Fiction
Alien Abduction: The Wiltshire Revelations
The Best of Both Worlds and Other Ambiguous Tales
Beyond the Colors of Darkness and Other Exotica
Changelings and Other Metamorphic Tales
A Clash of Symbols: The Triumph of James Blish
Complications and Other Stories
The Cosmic Perspective and Other Black Comedies
Creators of Science Fiction
The Cure for Love and Other Tales of the Biotech Revolution
The Devil's Party: A Brief History of Satanic Abuse
The Dragon Man: A Novel of the Future
The Eleventh Hour
Exotic Encounters: Selected Reviews
Firefly: A Novel of the Far Future
The Gardens of Tantalus and Other Delusions
Glorious Perversity: The Decline and Fall of Literary Decadence
Gothic Grotesques: Essays on Fantastic Literature
The Great Chain of Being and Other Tales of the Biotech Revolution
The Haunted Bookshop and Other Apparitions
Heterocosms: Science Fiction in Context and Practice
In the Flesh and Other Tales of the Biotech Revolution
The Innsmouth Heritage and Other Sequels
Jaunting on the Scoriac Tempests and Other Essays on Fantastic Literature
Kiss the Goat
The Moment of Truth: A Novel of the Future
Narrative Strategies in Science Fiction and Other Essays on Imaginative Fiction
News of the Black Feast and Other Random Reviews
An Oasis of Horror: Decadent Tales and Contes Cruels
Opening Minds: Essays on Fantastic Literature
Outside the Human Aquarium: Masters of Science Fiction, Second Edition
The Plurality of Worlds: A Sixteenth-Century Space Opera
Prelude to Eternity: A Romance of the First Time Machine
The Return of the Djinn and Other Black Melodramas
Salome and Other Decadent Fantasies
Slaves of the Death Spiders and Other Essays on Fantastic Literature
The Sociology of Science Fiction
Space, Time, and Infinity: Essays on Fantastic Literature
The Tree of Life and Other Tales of the Biotech Revolution
The World Beyond: A Sequel to S. Fowler Wright's The World Below
Yesterday's Bestsellers: A Voyage Through Literary History

NARRATIVE STRATEGIES IN SCIENCE FICTION

AND OTHER ESSAYS ON IMAGINATIVE FICTION

by

Brian Stableford

THE BORGO PRESS

An Imprint of Wildside Press LLC

MMIX

I.O. Evans Studies in the Philosophy and Criticism of Literature
ISSN 0271-9061

Number Forty-Nine

Copyright © 2002, 2006, 2007, 2008, 2009 by Brian Stableford

All rights reserved.
No part of this book may be reproduced in any form without the expressed written consent of the publisher.

www.wildsidebooks.com

FIRST EDITION

CONTENTS

About the Author 6
Introduction 7

Narrative Strategies in Science Fiction 9
Immortality in Fantastic Fiction.. 29
Why There Is (Almost) No Such Thing as Science Fiction........... 61
Perfectibility and the Novel of Future.. 74
In Search of a New Genre: Attempts to Categorize and
    Promote "Scientific Fiction" in France, 1902-1928................. 83
Ecology and Dystopia 102
Cosmic Horror.. 124
Growing up as a Superhero 155

Bibliography... 160
Index.. 180

ABOUT THE AUTHOR

BRIAN STABLEFORD was born in Yorkshire in 1948. He taught at the University of Reading for several years, but is now a full-time writer. He has written many science fiction and fantasy novels, including *The Empire of Fear*, *The Werewolves of London*, *Year Zero*, *The Curse of the Coral Bride*, *The Stones of Camelot* and *Prelude to Eternity*. Collections of his short stories include a long series of *Tales of the Biotech Revolution*, and such idiosyncratic items as *Sheena and Other Gothic Tales* and The *Innnsmouth Heritage and Other Sequels*. He has written numerous nonfiction books, including *Scientific Romance in Britain, 1890-1950*, *Glorious Perversity: The Decline and Fall of Literary Decadence*, *Science Fact and Science Fiction: An Encyclopedia* and *The Devil's Party: A Brief History of Satanic Abuse*. He has contributed hundreds of biographical and critical entries to reference books, including both editions of *The Encyclopedia of Science Fiction* and several editions of the library guide, *Anatomy of Wonder*. He has also translated numerous novels from the French language, including several by the feuilletonist Paul Féval and numerous classics of French scientific romance by such writers as Albert Robida, Maurice Renard, and J. H. Rosny the Elder.

INTRODUCTION

The title article of this collection was written in January 2007 in response to a request from James Gunn to contribute something to an anthology of academic articles that he was editing in collaboration with Marleen Barr. No word limit had been specified, but when I delivered the article he declared that it was far too long and asked me to cut it to 4,000 words (about half its original length). Gritting my teeth, I obliged. One of the things that had to go in order to achieve this Procustean feat was the explanation of what Alexander Baumgarten meant by "heterocosm", but I was prepared to assumed that, as I use the term frequently nowadays, and have even employed it as the title of a book, it could probably pass without definition.

When the book eventually appeared, alas, I discovered that someone—presumably Gunn—had decided that the term did need to be defined, and had therefore inserted into the middle of the abridged essay's first sentence a parenthetical definition that was stupidly incorrect and astonishingly inelegant, thus transforming the sentence in question into a hideous atrocity. Given that even the laziest of academics and students tend to read the first sentence of a text before deciding not to read any further, this seemed to me to be adding injury to insult. I wish I could say that such actions are untypical of academic publishing, but they are not. The version of the essay here included is the one that I actually wrote; I shall maintain a discreet silence as to where the butchered version appeared, in the faint hope that it might somehow vanish forever from human ken if references to its existence can be kept to a minimum.

Two of the essays here, "Immortality in Fantastic Ficton" and "Cosmic Horror" were written at the request of S. T. Joshi for an anthology entitled *Icons of Horror and the Supernatural*, published by Greenwood Press in 2007. Whether the versions included here bear any resemblance to the published versions I am unable to say because my complimentary copy of the two-volume work arrived shrink-wrapped and I did not have the heart to diminish its potential resale value by removing the wrapping, but my past experience with Greenwood Press copy editors does not fill me with optimism on that score, and I am probably better off not knowing.

Two other essays were written for *The New York Review of Science Fiction*, which is one of my favorite outlets because its editors very rarely make changes in submissions, always ask politely if they want me to do so, and usually conduct themselves like perfect gentlemen if I say no. "Why there is (almost) no such thing as Science Fiction" was originally published in issue number 219 (November 2006); "In Search of a New Genre: Attempts to Categorize and Promote 'Scientific Fiction' in France, 1902-1928" was originally published in issue number 253 (September 2009).

"Perfectibility and the Novel of the Future" was written at the request of a Canadian academic, Donald Bruce, for a special issue of the journal *Texte* on "Épistémocritique" that he was co-editing with Christine McWebb. It appeared in that issue—number 43/44 (2008)—in French translation; this is its first appearance in English. "Ecology and Dystopia" was written in 2007 at the request of Gregory Claeys for an *Oxford Companion to Dystopia*, one of a rash of such anthologies on related topics that have been published over the last few years; I delivered it in July 2007 and a copy-edited verson was returned for my approval early in 2009, but nothing more was heard of the project thereafter and I assume that it is defunct (although every reference-book publisher in the world, in the days before wikipedia drove them all to ignominious extinction, made it a matter of firm policy never to publish anything until it was way out of date, so one never knows). Neither essay was subjected to any editorial vandalism whatsoever, so things do sometimes proceed as one would wish, even in the autumnal and fungus-infested groves of Academe, although the occasional absence of tangible end-products does detract somewhat from the meager satisfaction to be gained from that knowledge.

"Growning up as a Superhero" was written at the request of one of the editorial consultants of the *New Humanist*, who apologized for the fact that the periodical was only able to pay me in bottles of champagne—although the value of the champagne exceeded the trivial sums offered for two of the essays here assembled, and far outweighed the nothing at all that I was paid for some of the others. The article appeared in the Autumn 2002 issue, retitled "Saving Mankind" and subjected to various other editorial adjustments, about which I was mercifully too drunk to care.

NARRATIVE STRATEGIES IN SCIENCE FICTION

The founder of modern aesthetic theory, Alexander Baumgarten, writing in the mid-eighteenth century, described the work of artists as "secondary creation" and drew a fundamental distinction between the kind of secondary creativity that attempts accurate simulation of the experienced world and "heterocosmic" creativity: the construction of secondary worlds that differ in some crucial respect from the experienced world. Baumgarten belonged to a school of German philosophy descended from Gottfried Leibniz, who contended that ours must be the best of all possible worlds, because a good God would not have countenanced any flaws that were not inevitably inherent in the creative process; this allegiance led Baumgarten to take it for granted that artistic simulation is intrinsically superior to heterocosmic creativity.

Baumgarten knew, of course, that the vast majority of prose fictions recorded from previous oral discourse or newly composed before the eighteenth century were heterocosmic, but that only served to demonstrate to him—as it had to many of his predecessors and would to many of his successors—that storytelling, especially in its popular forms, was unworthy of serious consideration as Art. This casual dismissal does, however, ignore a significant enigma: how had it come about that listeners and readers had long found it easier to relate to heterocosmic creations than naturalistic ones?

This question remains awkward today. One aspect of its awkwardness is highlighted by Farah Mendlesohn's essay "Towards a Taxonomy of Fantasy" (2002), which employs a fundamental set of categories differentiated according to narrative strategy. Although the categories are "fuzzy sets"—they are neither pure nor exhaustive—Mendlesohn identifies three principal types of fantasy fiction, which she calls intrusive fantasy, portal fantasy and immersive fantasy. In an intrusive fantasy, the fantastic element is introduced into a simulacrum of the experienced world, which it disturbs. In a portal fantasy, the central character passes from the experienced world into a heterocosmic milieu by means of a definite process of transition involving a journey, a vision or an explicit gateway. In an immersive fantasy, the story is set entirely within a heterocosmic milieu, which is the assumed quotidian reality of its characters.

Mendlesohn's taxonomy helps to underline the fact that most writers in the early decades of the century had taken it for granted that heterocosmic fictions would be more easily construed by modern readers if they employed intrusive or portal fantasy formats, both of which rely on readers' assumed ability to orientate themselves easily within naturalistic texts and use that initial linkage as a preliminary springboard for the careful and measured introduction of heterocosmic creations. The most spectacular development in late twentieth-century fantasy fiction was, however, a dramatic increase in the production and popularity of immersive fantasy, in the wake of the slightly-belated success of J. R. R. Tolkien's *The Lord of the Rings* (1954-55)—crude imitations of which formed the core texts of a new commercial genre of "fantasy" in the 1970s.

The fact that early twentieth-century readers apparently found it easier to relate to heterocosmic creations if they were introduced intrusively or reached by means of portals reflects the vast strides made between the eighteenth and early twentieth centuries in the education of readers in the skills necessary to orientate themselves within naturalistic texts. The history of the novel is largely the history of narrative techniques by means of which writers can provide readers with the means to feel "at home" within a literary text. Informing readers when and where the story is taking place, so that they can bring to bear everything they already know about that time and place, is merely step one in a much more complex process, which involves managing the narrative flow in such a way that it seems to simulate the flow of real experience, enabling readers to "enter" the text in such a way that they appear to be experiencing what is happening there along with the characters.

One of the key discoveries made by pioneering novelists is that authorial exposition—in which the writer offers elaborate accounts of time and place, objective descriptions of the characters' appearances and personal histories, and, above all, commentaries on the substance of the story—inhibits narrative flow and compromises the processes of "identification" that allow readers to enter into texts more wholeheartedly. Novelists therefore developed a set of short cuts that allowed readers to avoid overmuch confrontation with structured information and commentary, relying on subtle cues to evoke the appropriate aspects of understanding that readers already have of what the experienced world contains and how it works. Modern writers of all kinds of fantasy fiction are generally expected to work in the same way; it is routinely assumed by critics and advice books for writers that the cardinal sin of modern fantasy writing is the communication of heterocosmic detail by means of "expository lumps" or "info-dumps"—which is to say, providing straightforward and orderly accounts of the various ways in which the heterocosmic creation within the text differs from the reader's experienced world.

Within this context, writing and reading immersive fantasy seems implicitly more difficult than writing and reading intrusive or portal fantasy, because the narrative crutches supplied by the intrusive and portal methods are unavailable. Writing and reading an immersive fantasy is no mere matter of introducing a heterocosmic "element" into a simulacrum of the known world, or of venturing along with characters born and bred in the known world into a heterocosmic creation that is every bit as strange to them as it is to the reader. It is a matter of plunging readers head-first into a heterocosmic milieu, and into the thoughts and actions of characters who might never have dreamed of the readers' known world, or will inevitably have a very different view of it if it is somehow known to them.

The implicit difficulties that modern readers face in orientating themselves within fantasy worlds can be assuaged in several different ways, but this discussion began with the observation that there was a time when almost all prose fiction consisted of immersive fantasies, and naturalistic fiction was virtually unknown. The reason for this lies in the nature of oral culture, which—by definition—has no history. There is a logical sense in which all stories have to be located in the past, because the mere fact of telling them implies that they have already happened. In oral cultures, stories only survive and thrive if they are repeated by many tellers—with the result that the past in which orally-transmitted tales are set inevitably acquires a considerable narrative distance: a dutiful appearance of antiquity, which the devisers of new tales inevitably endeavor to simulate. Because oral cultures have no historical past, however, this appearance of antiquity is cultivated by their displacement into a mythic past, which is not related to the present by means of a calendrical time scale but by qualitative differentiation.

The past of folktales—the world of "once upon a time"—is one in which myths of creation and evolution are still in the process of being worked out: a world in which magic worked, the gods were liable to appear on the earth, animals might well have talked, and so on. The nature of the qualitative contrast between the mythic past and the experienced present is neatly summarized by one of the terms that John Clute invented in *The Encyclopedia of Fantasy* (1997): thinning. The basic assumption of folklore, legend and myth is that the world is now less magical, and hence "thinner", than it once was. Sometimes its mythic elements have simply been annihilated, but thinning is often imagined in terms of displacement—it is not so much that fairyland, the world of the gods and the world of the dead have ceased to exist, but that their separation from the everyday world has become much more definite, because any connective portals that remain are increasingly difficult to locate and open.

Even within closed cultures, and to a far greater extent in open ones, what people know about the mythic past is a more reliable basis for communication between storytellers and their audiences than what people know about the actual world. Culture is complex; it relies, even in its most primitive forms, on elaborate divisions of labor, and hence of quotidian experience—but everybody knows the same things about the mythic past. This, as Michel Butor points out in a classic essay "On Fairy Tales", is why it makes perfect sense for adults to tell their children fairy tales. What adults know about the real world, and the manner in which they experience it, is very different from what young children know about that world and how they experience it, but when adults tell children fairy stories they are on common ground; they both have the same understanding of how the world of fairy tales works.

With this advantage, fantasy fiction easily survived the corrosions of Baumgartenian disapproval as a form of children's literature, and found fierce defenders in the nineteenth-century when it came under attack both from scientifically-minded people, who thought that children should not be "encouraged to believe in fairies" because fairies do not exist, and religious believers, who thought that children should only be taught about the specific aspects of the mythic past that were still licensed by dogmatic faith. Familiarity with the essential features of the mythic past never died away in literate cultures, and remained available as a launching-pad for the kind of immersive fantasy that returned to the marketplace in force in the 1970s. The mythic past was then swiftly dusted off and strategically re-elaborated into a generic "fantasyland", whose stereotypy attracted some scathing satirization—as in Diana Wynne Jones's *Tough Guide to Fantasyland*—but which legions of readers nevertheless found very useful as a means of rapidly coming to feel at home within modern immersive fantasies.

Just as the skills that readers learned to bring to bear on naturalistic prose fiction improved steadily throughout the nineteenth and twentieth centuries, so the skills of readers of modern immersive fantasy have undergone a process of sophistication since 1970, and will presumably continue to improve in times to come. There was, however, another subgenre of modern fantasy fiction that had made very considerable strides in the development of immersive fantasy in the earlier part of the twentieth century, in spite of difficulties that genre fantasy did not have to face: science fiction. The gradual and awkward development of the artistry of writing and reading science fiction is a fascinating sidebar to the story of the rehabilitation of the mythic past within popular literature.

* * * * * * *

There is an important sense in which the heterocosmic constructions of science fiction stand in crucial and fundamental opposition to those of folkloristic fantasy. Folkloristic fantasy imagines heterocosmic motifs as things that existed "once upon a time" but have now been eroded into non-existence by thinning. Science fiction, by contrast, imagines heterocosmic motifs as innovations: things that have not yet been discovered or invented, but might be. Unlike folkloristic fantasy, science fiction does not assume that our thin world has long been getting thinner, but the reverse: that our world might even now be less thin than it seems—because it is pregnant with all manner of new possibilities—and will certainly get fatter in times to come.

Science fiction can, however, be categorized in terms of exactly the same taxonomic divisions to which Mendlesohn subjects the broader genre. It has its intrusive fantasies, in which the known world is disrupted by a technological innovation or an alien incursion of some kind. It has its portal fantasies, in which the protagonist sets off in a spaceship, or a time machine, or travels through some kind of interdimensional gateway, to arrive in a different world. It has its immersive fantasies, which plunge the reader directly into an imagined future, alien world or alternative history, whose characters are native to it.

Science fiction has also followed the same pattern of prehistorical and historical development as that of fantasy fiction in general, beginning with a nineteenth- and early twentieth-century phase in which intrusive and portal fantasies were dominant, while immersive fantasies followed a more gradual and problematic process of evolution. Because of the fundamental difference between science fiction and folkloristic fantasy, however, the significance of this pattern was markedly different within the science fiction subgenre.

Intrusive fantasy and portal fantasy both have a "natural" story-arc built into them. The heterocosmic element in intrusive fantasy functions, as Mendlesohn puts it, as a "bringer of chaos", so there is an obvious way to bring closure to such a story: the bringer of chaos must be banished again, and normality restored. The characters who deal with the intrusion may or may not be richer for the experience—although, in many comedies and horror stories, they are merely relieved that the disruption to their lives is over—but the bringer of chaos must be put away regardless. Similarly, the "natural" conclusion to a portal fantasy is the return home; far travelers have to come back to tell their stories, just as all visionary dreamers must eventually wake up. The characters in portal fantasies are almost always expected to be richer for their experience, no matter how relieved they are to have returned, but that wealth is usually the sort that has to be cashed in at home.

The fact that the natural tendency of both these kinds of story is towards closure is very convenient for storytellers, not only because it helps to keep the stories neat and tidy, but because storytellers' audiences have always loved satisfactory closure. A concluding "and they lived happily ever after" was once as standardized as an opening "once upon a time", and although its explicit formulation has grown tired, along with such brutal narrative moves as "and then I woke up", it is still by far and away the most convenient and popular way to end a story.

In folkloristic fantasy, the normalizing closure of the story-arc has a built-in propriety. Because the intrusion comes from the mythic past, and the milieu preserved in the portal fantasy is a relic of that past, there is a fundamental sense in which they do not *belong* in the thinned-out world. No matter how life-enhancing an intrusion might occasionally be, or how valuable the education might be that the world beyond the portal provides, their imaginary time is over; the world no longer has space to accommodate them, and never will again. In science fiction, by contrast, the opposite is true; the normalizing story-arc is intrinsically opposed to the notion of a world whose thinness is temporary and remediable, and the removal from stories of the heterocosmic innovations of science fiction is inherently inappropriate.

In early clashes between this inherent lack of propriety and the convenience of the normalizing story-arc, the normalizing story-arc was bound to win. Brian Aldiss argues in *Billion Year Spree* that the foundation-stone of the science fiction novel is Mary Shelley's

Frankenstein (1818), and that subsequent sf was typically cast in a "Gothic" mode. Although it proved controversial, this assertion is not without justice. The Gothic novel was an essentially combative arena in which the narrative apparatus of the mythic past offered flamboyant but ultimately futile rearguard resistance to the inevitability of its suppression and supersession by the narrative apparatus of the historical past; science fiction is still afflicted by an intrinsic conflict of interest between mythic story-structures and a rationalistic notion of historical development.

In structural terms, *Frankenstein* is no different from other Gothic novels, all of which—whether their denouements "rationalized" their supernatural apparitions or merely subjected them to ritual exorcism—tended towards normalizing endings. Victor Frankenstein, however, discovered his resurrection technology by mean of the scientific method; even though he and the "monster" he creates are both destroyed, the logic of the situation cannot help but proclaim that the technique will be rediscovered repeatedly, and applied repeatedly, until the resurrected dead are as significant a human population as the naturally-born. In order to preserve the immense convenience of the normalizing story-arc, however, that logical consequence had simply to be ignored—as similar consequences have been in countless *Frankenstein* clones in which inventions or alien incursions prove troublesome and are destroyed, often along with their facilitators.

Although this kind of "Gothic science fiction" is logically flawed, Aldiss was correct to observe that labeled sf was and is typically cast in this mould. In purely quantitative terms, the majority of works that warrant description as science fiction—including almost all of those in the fringe subgenre of "technothrillers"—are intrusive fantasies in which every technological innovation and every alien incursion is conceived as a horrid monstrosity crying out to be put away by the deadly-but-satisfying thrust of a normalizing story-arc.

One consequence of the convenience of the intrusive fantasy formula, with its built-in normalizing story-arc is, therefore, that if science fiction is seen as a collective entity—*i.e.*, as a fuzzily coherent subgenre—then its dominant voice loudly proclaims that all technological innovation, and everything not yet discovered, is inherently evil. This opinion, while by no means unrepresented in the real world, runs directly contrary to the fundamental assumptions of scientific and technological endeavor, one of which is that the world can be, might be, and routinely is improved by of new discoveries and technological innovations. Writers ambitious to employ fiction as a means of celebrating the intellectual achievements of science and the life-enhancing potential of technology have therefore found themselves in an embarrassing situation, summarized by Isaac Asimov's complaints about the social and literary prevalence of a neurotic anti-scientific "Frankenstein complex", outlined in such essays as the preface to *The Rest of the Robots*.

Portal sf stories are not as restrictive as intrusive sf stories, but they are more difficult to contrive, especially in respect of futuristic scenarios. The necessity of returning from the expedition through the portal reduced all futuristic fantasies to the status of dreams before H. G. Wells invented a time machine, and that was a device which soon generated a whole spectrum of new corollary problems, in terms of opportunities to change past history and the hazards of so doing. The necessity of the final return tends to rob all portal fantasies of the dynamic element crucial to progressive imagery; singular trips in spaceships also tend to resemble visionary dreams. As with intrusive sf, the logic of the situation is that, once a demonstration has been made by a portal fantasy of what the scientific method can reveal and produce in other circumstances, the mortality of the present's "normality" becomes obvious, and its entitlement to function as a privileged situation to which all story-arcs must lead is lost.

The problem of adapting the narrative strategies of intrusive and portal fantasy to science fiction could have been avoided if writers had been more easily able to write immersive science fiction, because immersive fantasy is not cursed with the same "natural" story-arc as intrusive and portal fantasy. The readability of immersive fantasy had, however, always depended on the fact that readers were at least as familiar with the mythic past as they were with the historical past and the experienced present. Science fiction stories set in hypothetical futures, alien worlds or alternative histories had no such recourse. Writers and readers of folkloristic fantasy could bring to bear a coherent series of assumptions about the likely contents and dynamics of a heterocosmic creation with a simple narrative formula like "once upon a time"—but those assumptions were not merely useless but actively antipathetic to what writers of immersive science fiction needed to do.

The simplest response to this problem, in practice, was not even to attempt it. Early in his career Jules Verne produced an immersive futuristic fantasy set in *Paris in the Twentieth Century*, but he accepted the advice of his publisher, P.-J. Hetzel, to lock it away, forget it, and never to attempt anything like it again—with the result that such potentially-transformative technological innovations as the submarine and the airship were placed in the hands of the misanthropic Captain Nemo and the megalomaniac Robur, in order that they could be banished from the world in the normalizing denouements of *Twenty Thousand Leagues Under the Sea* and *The Clipper of the Clouds*.

H. G. Wells was also wary of immersive scientific romance, at least in the phase of his career when he wrote most of his memorable scientific romances. With only one exception, all his early works in that vein were intrusive or portal fantasies, most of which made use of the usual fudges to conserve traditional patterns of closure. Wells was, however, ambitious to extend his narrative reach beyond that meager grasp; he accepted the necessity of introducing an outrageous *deus ex machina* to restore a belated normality to *The War of the Worlds* (1898), but he preferred to cut *The First Men in the Moon* (1901) rudely short in order to conceal the impossibility of any such restoration. In *The Food of the Gods and How it Came to Earth* (1904) he accepted the logic of his imaginary situation and, far from banishing the imagined intrusion, described the manner in which it would change the world irredeemably.

The first immersive scientific romance that Wells attempted remains the least well-known, and the most awkward, of his early endeavors in the subgenre. In "A Story of the Days to Come" (1897) he felt obliged to adopt the same intrinsically-awkward practice that had been employed in every other proto-immersive science fiction story written before 1900: he equipped the story with a "metanarrative preface"—an introductory essay explaining to readers what the writer is about to do, and providing a kind of imaginative "handle" that readers could use to get their bearings within the story. The body of the story continues to assume that the ideative apparatus required by readers for the navigation of the heterocosmic milieu requires continual supplementation by authorial intrusion.

In effect, the metanarrative preface that every nineteenth-century example of immersive futuristic fantasy carries serves the same function as a portal in a portal fantasy. It starts readers off in the familiar world, then leads them by the hand into a unfamiliar one. Because a manifest authorial voice is required to do the leading, however, such stories cannot take full advantage of the narrative techniques that had been developed by novelists for encouraging reader identification with characters, which had made authorial devices far more discreet, tending gradually towards invisibility. A metanarrative preface is, by necessity, a massive expository lump. As the twentieth century began, therefore, writers of immersive futuristic fiction found themselves at odds with broader patterns in the evolution of fictional technique. Writers of fantasies using the apparatus of the mythic past were not as far out of step, because they were free to develop intrusive and portal fantasies without running into any logical problems, but a writer like Wells was caught in an awkward trap.

Wells's own eventual solution, as illustrated by *The Food of the Gods*, was simply to accept the necessity of exposition—with the result that his subsequent speculative works bore a greater resemblance to essays or tracts than to novels, no matter how they were packaged. It was intrinsically easier to write about futuristic heterocosms from the distanced viewpoint of a hypothetical historian or a satirical commentator than it was to display them through the innocent eyes of its native inhabitants, and that was what Wells mostly did after the turn of the century. Other writers sought other compromises.

The formal metanarrative preface began to fade away after 1900, as writers increasingly attempted to embed the informational substance of such prefaces within the story rather than presenting it as something essentially extraneous. No matter how adroitly the "back-story" of the heterocosmic world within the text was woven into the narrative, however, the problems of initial introduction and periodic supplementation remained. Even readers who were tolerant of expository lumps of background information could not help having difficulty in orientating themselves within sciencefictional heterocosms; the principal costs of their being provided with the necessary guidance were awkward narrative flow and characters with whom it was difficult to identify.

The necessity of getting over the hurdle of the metanarrative preface was the principal reason for the unusually immense importance within the history of labeled science fiction of the sf magazine. The title of such a magazine functioned as a device to inform readers of what to expect—or, at least, what not to expect—when they began the immersive fantasies contained within their covers. The act of reading is intrinsically akin to stepping through a portal, and the packaging of books plays an important role in assisting readers to orientate themselves within the texts they contain; such packaging is more important with respect to heterocosmic texts than simulative ones, and much more important with respect to heterocosmic texts that cannot rely on universal assumptions about the mythic past. The portals provided by early sf magazines were decorated with illustrations and blurbs that helped enormously to point readers in the rough direction of each heterocosm they were about to enter. Such stepping-stones were invaluable in the tacit quest of those early sf magazines, which was the rough outlining of a "mythic future" that could take the place, to the extent that it was possible, of the mythic past of folkloristic fiction.

****

It was probably inevitable, although there is a certain perversity about it, that many aspects of the nebulous "mythic future" that came to be assumed by the writers and readers of early sf magazines are straightforward transfigurations of the mythic past. The groundwork for such transfigurations had already been laid by the late nineteenth-century occult revival, which had relabeled many varieties of magic in order to clothe them more respectably for a post-Enlightenment world. The new jargon of telepathy, teleportation, precognition and other items of "parapsychology" was avidly adopted into science fiction, such "wild talents" being represented as evidences of a latent superhumanity whose flowering was yet to come rather than mythic relics filtered out of everyday experience by thinning.

The deliberate transfiguration of mythic materials became such a frequent stratagem of sciencefictional plotting that sf magazine editors were soon afflicted with a deluge of what Brian Aldiss dubbed "shaggy God stories"—which had not abated by the century's end. No one can count the number of spontaneously-generated sf stories in which two survivors of a cosmic catastrophe turn out in the story's denouement to be Adam and Eve, because very few of them ever each print, but they must number tens of thousands by now. More sophisticated examples reached print in considerable numbers, and still do, but their development has been a sideline to the quest that early sf writers undertook for new substance with which to stock their imaginary futures.

Of all the futuristic technologies that early magazine sf writers imagined and attempted to integrate into a consensus view of the likely course of the future, one particular image gained a unique priority: the spaceship. Magazine science fiction rapidly developed an intimate relationship with the idea of space travel, and—more importantly—the idea that space travel was likely to provide the central theme of future history. Within a decade of the appearance of the first sf magazine in the U.S.A., the fundamental "mythic future" on whose ready-made understanding much magazine sf depended was the notion of a coming Space Age, in which the central story of the future would be the expansion of the human species to other worlds.

The myth of the Space Age became a handy container for other oft-used elements in sciencefictional futures. Earthbound futures, especially repressive ones, were routinely provided with literally uplifting endings by the iconic image of a "cosmic breakout". The notion that a galaxy-spanning society of Earth-clone worlds might ultimately be established—and often then collapsed, so as to re-isolate the imagined worlds—became a handy framework for all manner of exotic human and alien societies. Space travel became a kind of infinitely-elastic portal connecting all manner of possible worlds, so that stories beginning in relatively simple and familiar futuristic scenarios could make rapid progress into the unknown.

There were important parallel developments in magazine sf—the most significant involving the investigation of potential corollaries of the idea of time travel, whose ultimate extrapolation was the notion of an infinite array of alternative histories packaged in a multiverse of parallel worlds—but such developments never threatened the dominance of the Space Age as a mythic future. The multiverse of alternative histories was much more extensively used for retrospective analyses of the logic of past history than as a device for the projection of alternative futures.

The association of science fiction with the idea of space travel now seems so intimate and intrinsic that it is hard to imagine alternative histories in which it never happened. The European subgenre of scientific romance, however—which retained an independent existence and evolution until the end of World War II—always regarded space travel as a peripheral issue of little significance to the future of humankind. To the extent that scientific romance had a consensual image of the future, that consensus saw the future in terms of social and physical evolution, intrinsically earthbound, at least until the uninhabitability of the Earth would force a desperate interplanetary migration. There is not the least trace of a Space Age future in scientific romance.

Nor was the idea of a coming Space Age universally welcomed in the U.S.A.; the first anthology of fantastic fiction to feature a significant sample of stories from the sf magazines, Phil Stong's *The Other Worlds* (1941), deliberately excluded "interplanetary fiction" from the showcase and featured an editorial railing against the imbecility and intrinsic worthlessness of fiction of that sort. If the writers and readers of the magazines had agreed with Stong, American science fiction would have centralized very different themes, and would have remained much closer to the Vernian and Wellsian roots of which it proudly boasted, but which it viewed through highly selective lenses. Far from being the obvious and inevitable development that hindsight makes it seem, magazine science fiction's development of the mythic future of the Space Age actually requires closer examination and more detailed explanation.

The popularity of the spaceship as an iconic image of American sf was not so much a result of its likelihood as an actual technological development—although the first U.S.-launched moon landing did take place a mere forty years into the genre's history—but its resonance with more recent and more localized "mythic past" than the elastic fabrication of folklore.

Two thousand years after the invention of history in ancient Greece, "actual" history, as produced in Western Europe, was still extensively polluted by mythic elements. That pollution was by no means entirely the result of folkloristic residues that were incapable of replacement by accurate records, nor was it merely a consequence of the persistence of superstition among the religious chroniclers of the Middle Ages; it was still an active and continuing process. It had proved far harder for historians to compile objective records than it was for "natural historians", let alone physical scientists, because all kinds of people—especially powerful ones—had had reason to falsify documentary sources while they were actually being produced, and to falsify their interpretation thereafter. No matter how hard historians had tried to figure out exactly what happened and why—and many did not try very hard at all, being more interested in producing propaganda—the intrinsically deceptive nature of much of their evidence had been, and remains, bound to confound them and lead to confabulation.

As soon as history became the substance of naturalistic fiction, the tendency to distort it for literary as well as political reasons subjected it to the same pressures of intrinsic narrative form and audience appeal that had previously been exerted by storytellers on mythic history. History, in large measure, became a narrative in itself—or, more accurately, a series of narratives. The tentative mythic futures that are discernible in European scientific romance do not differ very much between Britain, France and Germany; in those nations, the history of the future is seen as a continuation of a long past history rooted in Classical Greece and Rome, extrapolating a pattern of clearly-perceptible social and technological progress, continually blighted and hindered by the tendency of neighboring nations to fight and invade one another. The U.S.A., on the other hand, saw its own past very differently: as something recently started, after a bold and conclusive break with European history, in which social and technological progress had been quite spectacular, relatively uninhibited by local conflicts. Although the U.S.A. had been involved in numerous wars since its founding in the War of Independence, such internecine conflicts as the Civil War and the Indian Wars had been easily construed as instruments and aspects of progress, while international conflicts had been (and still are) construed as attempts to spread progressive American Enlightenment to various dark continents.

Because it was a recently-founded nation on a recently-discovered continent, the U.S.A. had no residual folklore of its own; the folklore imported by immigrants from Europe had been set aside with other redundant aspects of the European heritage, and Native American folklore had been put away in a more definite fashion. The U.S.A.'s "mythic past" was, therefore, derived from—or, rather, imposed upon—its historical past, and its central narrative thread was a stirring tale of westward expansion, of pioneering and frontiersmanship, in which the magic of the European mythic past was largely replaced by weaponry, especially the talismanic Colt revolver.

Given all this, it is hardly surprising that American science fiction, unlike European scientific romance, developed a consensus image of a future of expansion, shaped by pioneers and frontiersmen, who would colonize the solar system and the galaxy as American immigrants had colonized the West. On the "final frontier" of space, the spaceship replaced the covered wagon, Mars and Earth-clone worlds orbiting other stars replaced Texas and California, the blaster replaced the Colt revolver, and all wars were wars of progressive social enlightenment.

In much the same way that magazine writers transfigured ancient myths into sf, they also transfigured Westerns—indeed, they routinely conflated the two processes, spaceships becoming not merely the constituents of interplanetary wagon trains but also chariots of the gods. Many writers felt embarrassed about this, much as they had felt embarrassed about yielding to the pressure of normalizing story-arcs, but their protestations often rang hollow. The first issue of *Galaxy*—which replaced *Astounding Science Fiction* at the core of the magazine subgenre in the 1950s—carried an advertisement featuring the opening paragraphs of a hack Western juxtaposed with a crude sciencefictional transfiguration, together with the headline *You'll never see it in Galaxy!*, but it only meant that *Galaxy* writers would never be quite so crude in contriving their transfigurations.

* * * * * * *

The U.S.A. was not the only twentieth-century nation that conceived of itself as the product of a recent, radical and irrevocable historical break; the U.S.S.R. also represented itself as a post-Revolutionary cauldron of progress. It did not develop science fiction of the same sort—although it might have, if its unionized writers had followed up the precedent set by Konstantin Tsiolkovsky in *Outside the Earth* (1916) instead of cleaving so narrowly to the artistic principles of socialist realism—but it did invest heavily enough in actual space technology to launch Sputnik into orbit in 1957, thus provoking the U.S.A. into a "space race", which was inevitably construed by American sf writers and readers as the first phase of a Space Age.

The early phases of the space race seemed to many sf enthusiasts to constitute a justification of the majority decision taken by their own founding fathers, but it was not without cost. When the actual moon landing took place, it quickly proved to be an end rather than a beginning, a small step after which no further step, let alone any giant leap, was practicable. Although euphoria clouded judgment at the time—the only sf writer who measured the contemporary significance of the space race with deadly accuracy was the British writer J. G. Ballard, some of whose accounts of post-space-race disenchantment are collected in *Memories of the Space Age*—the revelation that the moon landing was not the beginning of a Space Age at all provoked a crisis in the history of subgeneric science fiction, by making it glaringly obvious that its mythic future had little or nothing to do with potential patterns of technological and social progress, and had not, after all, escaped the fanciful toils of the broader genre of fantasy.

Although the exposure of the mythic future of the Space Age as a naked emperor seemed to its most fervent adherents to be a terrible tragedy, there remains a sense in which the dependence of science fiction on any kind of mythic future had always been a regrettable handicap. In much the same way that the sum total of normalizing intrusive science fiction stories suggests that all innovation is evil, so the sum total of stories set in the mythic future of the Space Age suggests that some such future is at least the most desirable, and perhaps the inevitable, shape that the future might take. A striking illustration of this effect is provided in Donald A. Wollheim's *The Universe Makers*, which supplements a detailed and comprehensive summary of the Space Age future—labeled a "Cosmogony of the Future"—with a comment to the effect that, because so many fine minds see the future in such terms, we are obliged to suppose that it will actually turn out that way.

Various strategies have been tried since 1969 to find new mythic futures, whose basic assumptions might assist readers to navigate a course through texts affiliated to such myth-sets. The most loudly-touted was cyberpunk mythology, which found a new final frontier in the wilderness of cyberspace, where nerds could become superpowered cowboys and to which artificial intelligences could provide bespoke pantheons. Almost as soon as they were manifest, however, the basic suppositions of cyberpunk were plundered to prove a rescue package for a New Space Age, hastily revamped as a posthuman project whose principal protagonists would be AIs and genetically-engineered cyborgs, the latter being conveniently freed from the unfortunate frailties of flesh that made a human Space Age no longer imaginable. Both of these developments, however, were able to take considerable advantage—in their variety as well as their rate of evolution—of the education that half a century of labeled science fiction had laid on for its readers.

Although the ability of a large population of readers to draw upon a ready-made understanding of a mythic past or a mythic future is a considerable asset to a writer desirous of drawing readers into a heterocosmic construction and assisting them to navigate comfortably within it, it is not an absolute necessity. Just as many nineteenth- and twentieth-century readers became gradually more adept at responding up the devices used by naturalistic novelists to create a a sensation of synthetic experience, so some twentieth-century readers of science fiction became gradually more adept at responding to the signaling devices used by sf writers, in such a way as to figure out exactly what kind of heterocosm, out of all the multitudinous possibilities, they might be dealing with. Writers and habitual readers of the subgenre quickly cultivated an expertise in the extrapolation of various standard premises, which allowed them to enter into increasingly complex collaborative explorations.

The initial effect of this process was to make science fiction into an esoteric subgenre accessible only to initiates, resulting in the growth of a manifest society of sf fans, whose communications were mediated through fanzines and conventions. As time went by, though, the relevant skills became far more generalized, especially when the imaginative produce of magazine sf began to be adapted for TV and the cinema in the 1960s. This adaptation was complicated by the fact that there was already a subspecies of cinematic "science fiction", also reflected on TV, which consisted almost exclusively of alarmist intrusive fantasies, but such productions gradually broadened their scope and were increasingly supplemented by immersive fantasies. As in the history of text-based sf, metanarrative prefaces and their customary supplements were held to be a necessity at first, but soon proved dispensable as audience expectations became more sophisticated. The pattern of initial cultish esotericism was also repeated, but its effects became far less noticeable as the twentieth century gave way to the twenty-first.

As the number of viewers capable of understanding immersive science fiction narratives on TV increased steadily, the number of readers capable of handling heterocosmic materials in text form with consummate ease became so large that the boundaries between genres and subgenres began to disintegrate, not only at the literary end of the marketing spectrum but in the sturdiest strongholds of genre marketing. Few habitual sf readers are nowadays in need of the crutch provided by a mythic future, and the number of genre fantasy readers who require the crutch of a mythic fantasyland is also in steep decline. Habitual readers in general are much more adept than they once were at following the logic of heterocosmic modifications of naturalistic scenarios, although the privilege afforded to dogmatically-faithful simulacra has too much historical inertia to die easily. On the other hand, the number of habitual readers is steadily declining in Europe and the U.S.A., largely because it is not being renewed in the lower deciles of the demographic spectrum.

The principal reason for the gradual erosion of the reading habit is competition from other media—which has a disproportionate effect on the young, whose consumption habits are still in formation and whose take-up of new media opportunities is therefore much more extensive. The phenomenon is undoubtedly exaggerated, however—although the proportion of the augmentation is inestimable—by the fact that reading fiction is nowadays a more difficult business than it used to be, simply because the skills it routinely requires are more elaborate. It is not surprising that many young people despair in advance of their ability to cultivate the skills required for the full appreciation of modern fiction, just as many adults despair in advance of their ability to cultivate the skills required to make full use of mobile phones. Although simple texts—especially simple heterocosmic constructions reliant on the mythic past or the mythic future of the Space Age—are by no means as difficult to obtain as simple mobile phones, the direction of the trend is obvious.

* * * * * * *

Although the overwhelming majority of labeled sf texts are normalizing intrusive fantasies or immersive fantasies, whose sophistication has increased markedly during the subgenre's history, there remain several significant residual categories. There have been numerous attempts to follow up the example H. G. Wells set in *The Food of the Gods*, which begins as an intrusive fantasy but resists normalizing closure. Magazine science fiction also provided a useful venue for this kind of exercise, which is more easily adaptable to story series than individual works. The most obvious example of such an extrapolative series is Isaac Asimov's robot series, which began with an intrusive fantasy introducing the robot motif, "Strange Playfellow" (1940), and continued into further and stranger futures for half a century, until the author died in 1992.

Intrusive fantasies that refuse the normalizing story-arc immediately acquire a problem that is endemic to immersive fantasies, which have no apparent "natural" story-arc built in. Normalization is not the only way to provide a sense of closure in a story, of course; there are at least two others, which are often combined with it, or with one another. One is the "surprise ending", but by far the more important is moral settlement, by which characters who have been good obtain material rewards, while characters who have been naughty are punished.

Secondary creations, unlike the primary one, are intrinsically morally ordered, because they have a manifest creator who is clearly in charge of distributing rewards and punishments; readers know this, and tend to be terribly disappointed if characters do not get their just desserts, although connoisseurs of the piquancy of literary disappointment flatter subversions of that expectation with labels like "tragedy", "irony" or "realism". Almost all secondary creators do make some attempt at moral settlement, though, if only by lamenting its failure in the cultivation of tragedy; the fundamental assumption of the vast majority of literary texts is that good characters are entitled to the climactic reward of a satisfactory intimate relationship and a practical means of earning a comfortable living.

Although normalization is intrinsically ridiculous as a means of providing a science fiction story with closure, moral settlement is not. It does, however, become much more problematic, especially when the time comes to decide exactly what sorts of rewards the good characters are to receive and what sort of punishments are to be visited upon the naughty ones. While rewards and punishments in naturalistic fiction inevitably reflect the known potentialities of their historical settings, and those of magical fantasy tend to be even more convention-bound, the possibilities of reward in futuristic and otherworldly heterocosms are vast, and the potentialities of punishment are at least marginally increased. It is sometimes argued that the fundamental subjects of fiction are sex and death, but it is conceivable, if not inevitable, that both those phenomena are local and transient; it is highly likely that the spectrum of human possibilities, in either case, might and probably will be shifted considerably, and almost inevitable that our attitudes to both will change with social circumstances.

The development and sophistication of narrative strategies is not the only progressive element in naturalistic fiction, nor is it entirely separate from the other main element of that progress, which is the negotiation of the fine detail of moral settlement. Although Percy Shelley was exaggerating when he argued that poets are the true legislators of the world (the true legislators of the world are, alas, the legislators) there is certainly a sense in which the real business of art is to investigate the failings of what is, after all, very far from being the best of all possible worlds—and, if possible, point the way to their correction.

Science fiction's investigation of the ways in which the presently-emaciated world might get fatter cannot help reassessing the possibilities and patterns of moral settlement—and ought not to refrain from such reassassment, even if it could. One of the problems of creating any kind of mythic future for use as a narrative crutch—which the myth of the Space Age demonstrates in no uncertain terms, especially in its reckless promulgation of the American theory of war—is that such constructions tend to be founded on, and hence to embody, stern moral prescriptions that become difficult, in consequence, to challenge from within.

There is one element of moral settlement that is particularly typical of science fiction, even though there is a subspecies of science fiction that specializes in formulations of the opposite proposition, which is that "there are things that man was not meant to know". The key item of reward that figures very large in science fiction is the reward of intellectual enlightenment, which is the unique selling point of science itself. This is the form that the great majority of sf's climactic epiphanies take, even though all of them have to be fudged, because science fiction writers—no matter how hard they wish that it were not so—cannot actually specify the hypothetical intellectual enlightenments they hand out.

This crucial limitation is the ultimate restriction of the principle that modern narrators should, whenever possible, prefer showing to telling. No matter how far science fiction writers may succeed in slimming down their expository lumps, they will never, under any imaginable circumstances, be able to *show* their readers what any newly-imagined intellectual epiphany gifted to their characters actually constitutes; all they will ever be able to do is *tell* the readers that such epiphanies been duly and justly awarded.

No reader can ever be truly satisfied with that assurance—but the best function of fiction, whether it is naturalistic or heterocosmic, is not to satisfy its readers but to dissatify them, and leave them hungering for something beyond normalization and beyond conventional patterns of moral settlement. That is surely what reading science fiction ought to be about, and what the narrative strategies of ambitious science fiction ought to be directed to produce.

IMMORTALITY IN FANTASTIC FICTION

INTRODUCTION

Awareness of inevitable death is one of the most awkward aspects of human self-consciousness; the consequent *angst* is the fundamental condition of human existence, in the reckoning of existentialist philosophy. The prospect of avoiding death forever seems, therefore, to be more suited to hopeful wish-fulfillment fantasy than the darker kinds of supernatural fiction. Religious believers committed to the idea of an eternal afterlife are, however, well aware that the notion can only function as a reward if the afterlife in question can be spent in an analogue of Heaven; if it has to be spent in Hell it becomes the ultimate deterrent. Reincarnation only functions as a reward if the fleshy envelope to come is preferable to the one presently occupied.

The attractiveness of the prospect of Earthly immortality—or of any degree of unusual longevity—is similarly dependent on one's assessment of the lodgings, both in terms of the utility of the carcass in which one has to spend eternity, and in terms of the pleasantness or otherwise of the surroundings. Literary images vary quite sharply in their estimates, especially on the first count. Optimistic images of hypothetical longevity envisage a corporeal habitation secure in the prime of life, permanently free of serious injury and chronic disease. One of several pessimistic alternatives imagines the infinite durance of worsening decrepitude, without the prospect of release or remission. The notion is illustrated by the Hellenic myth of Tithonus, the brother of the Trojan king Priam, who was granted immortality by the gods in response to the prayers of Eos, but did not obtain immunity to the aging process, and could only find release from eternal misery in being transformed into a cicada.

Other pessimistic alternatives are equally cruel. The prospect of life as an immortal babe-in-arms, a cripple or a leper is just as unattractive as infinitely-protracted dotage; it does not require much expertise in statistics to observe that random immortality would prolong far more miserable lives than happy ones. Given the manner in which human life is generally lived, it is perhaps surprising that there have not been more literary polemicists like T. F. Powys, whose religious fantasies routinely argue that the only credible argument for forgiving God the crime of Creation is that he has provided an inviolable escape clause.

Powys' *Unclay* (1931)—in which "John Death" is temporarily prevented from taking any further action—is more elegiac fantasy than horror story; its horrific component is an observation of extraordinary human sadism, to which only Death can bring a merciful end. The folktale whose most familiar modern version is the 1939 movie of L. E. Watkin's novel *On Borrowed Time* (1937), in which Death has to plead for release when he is trapped in a magical apple tree, takes an equally dim view of the prospect of a world in which all living things are immortal, as does S. Fowler Wright's *conte philosophique* "The Rat" (1929), but such sweeping condemnations are rare. The vast majority of treatments of the theme are confusedly ambivalent.

Literary attitudes to the prospect of human immortality are confused by the fact that the prerogative of death-avoidance, as represented in myth, legend and folklore, is promiscuously gifted to nonhuman individuals, while human beings are virtually defined as "mortals." Although gods and various fairy folk tend to be very variable in form and moral character, it is extremely rare for them to be credited with the slightest pang of regret for their immortality; it is simply their natural condition, which they take for granted. The same does not apply to humans, whose extreme reluctance to take mortality for granted is coupled with an intense paranoia regarding the unreliability of any gift of longevity, proffered or received.

Folklore is rich in such devices as the fountain of youth and the elixir of life, by means of which vulgar nature can be cheated; both devices usually involve judicious rejuvenation, the former by definition, but their discoverers rarely get much joy from their use. Such devices are routinely represented as as objects of obsession, worthy of a whole lifetime's endeavor as a tireless expeditionary or a reclusive alchemist, but the suspicion always haunts such fantasies that the objective will turn out to be a poisoned chalice, a bunch of sour grapes, or the prelude to some horrid reversal of fortune. This anxiety is easily translatable into horror fiction, and it is therefore unsurprising the iconography of the immortal in supernatural fiction is deeply troubled.

Attitudes to the idea of immortality are further confused by the fact that consciousness very easily falls prey to the delusion that its essence is merely a passenger in the flesh, which ought to be able, even if it is not actually destined, to move on when the body fails. This prospect too is afflicted by profound anxieties. The rich tradition of afterlife fantasy is far more abundant in images of Hell and its purgatorial subsidiaries than it is in images of Heaven, partly because it is so very difficult to imagine a Heaven that ex-mortals would really find pleasant, or even bearable. The standard summary formula of an uplifting narrative ending is "and they lived happily ever after," but the extreme rarity of detailed accounts of how that might be done is not entirely attributable to the insatiable narrative thirst for melodrama and dramatic tension. The principal problem that arises in using unearthly immortality as a reward for the virtuous in literary works is not that it is incredible—most narrative rewards are improbable in the extreme—but that its promise is nebulous and implicitly treacherous by comparison with property, money, or even marriage.

Most wish-fulfillment fantasies turn into cautionary tales sooner or later, because one of their key functions is to issue warnings against the vanity of human wishes. The powerful psychological attractiveness of the notion of immortality is sufficient guarantee in itself of a profoundly ironic and tacitly hostile press in folklore and literature alike, but further complications arise because immortality is quite unlike other, more easily measurable, wishes. Its essential vagueness and limitless scope render it uniquely vulnerable to ironic corrosion and perverse subversion—but a similar uncertainty afflicts the arguments leveled against it. The combination of these effects ensures that folkloristic and literary assaults on the utility of immortality or unusual longevity are often unclear and unconvincing, even when they are not flagrantly irrational.

Tedious Punishments and Accursed Wanderers

Classical mythology is rich in images of unbearable immortality. As punishment for delivering the metaphorical fire of the gods (technology) to humankind, Prometheus was sentenced to be chained to a rock for all eternity; every morning an eagle was sent to tear open his breast and eat his liver, and every night that organ would grow again so that the torture might be repeated on the following day. The story became the subject of one of the most indignant Greek tragedies, although the two elements that once preceded Aeschylus' *Prometheus Bound* in the trilogy have been lost. *Prome-*

theus Bound is a particularly poignant story, from the viewpoint of a human audience, because Prometheus is not condemned for any selfish act of greed or violence, but for his altruism in enabling humankind to make mortal existence a little more comfortable.

Other torments inflicted in Greek myths are slightly gentler, but similar in their repetitive quality. Ixion, who invited a creditor to dinner and caused him to fall into a fiery pit, was bound to a wheel that was set to roll forever round and round the underworld's perimeter. Tantalus betrayed secrets confided to him by Zeus, and was placed in the shallows of a lake whose waters receded every time he lowered his head to drink, beneath a fruit-laden branch, which similarly retreated out of range whenever he reached upwards. Sisyphus, the details of whose bad character and dissolute life remain uncertain, was condemned to roll a rock up a hill, which always rolled back down again as soon as it reached the summit. The common factor in all these afflictions is not pain but tedium, in recognition of the fact that one might grow accustomed to ceaseless agony, but not to the sheer relentless of an eternity without opportunity. The ultimate enemy, in this existential philosophy, is not boredom but frustration—the frustration that converts passive *ennui* into seething *spleen*.

It is not surprising that Christian legendry, born out of the ideological ashes of Graeco-Roman culture, wrought a complex fusion of the Hellenic attitude to the prospect of human longevity with the Judaic attitude intrinsic to the Old Testament. The Hebrew scriptures have no more to say about the prospect of Earthly immortality than they have about the possibility of an afterlife—although they wax lyrical on the subject of the longevity of the patriarchs—but Jewish legend was not so closely confined. The most notable recipient of legendary immortality was Cain, whose punishment consisted in being cursed to wander eternally, without any possibility of settlement, by virtue of a stigmatizing mark that made his fellow men recoil from him in horror.

It is from these tangled roots that the establishment of the immortal as an icon of supernatural fiction mostly proceeded, although the myth of Tithonus also played its part, its most famous literary extrapolation being the depiction of the Struldbrugs of Luggnagg in Jonathan Swift's *Travels into Several Remote Nations of the World in Four Parts...by Lemuel Gulliver* (1726), better known as *Gulliver's Travels*, which offers a calculatedly unappealing account of the tribulations of an inconclusive old age:

"When they came to fourscore years, which is reckoned the extremity of living in this country, they had not only all the follies and infirmities of other old men, but many more, which arose from the dreadful prospect of never dying. They were not only opinionative, peevish, covetous, morose, vain, talkative, but incapable of friendship, and dead to all natural affection, which never descended below their grandchildren. Envy, and impotent desires, are their prevailing passions. But those objects against which their envy seems principally directed, are the vices of the younger sort, and the deaths of the old. By reflecting on the former, they find themselves cut off from all possibility of pleasure; and whenever they see a funeral they lament and repine that others are gone to a harbour of rest, to which they themselves never can hope to arrive. They have no remembrance of anything but what they learned and observed in their youth and middle age, and even that is very imperfect; and for the truth or particulars of any fact it is safer to depend on common traditions, than upon their best recollections. The least miserable among them appear to be those who turn to dotage, and entirely lose their memories; these meet with more pity and assistance, because they want many bad qualities which abound in others....

"At ninety, they lose their teeth and hair: they have at that age no distinction of taste, but eat and drink whatever they can get, without relish or appetite; the diseases they were subject to still continuing, without increasing or diminishing." (pp. 218-9)

By the time Swift's satire appeared, however, a rich literature had already grown up in Europe in which the immortal—or, at least, one particular immortal—was held up for the specific purpose of inspiring horror-stricken awe.

Given that the Israelites were a nomadic tribe who decided to settle down—whose religion was therefore obsessed with the divine allocation of, and their eventual acquisition of tenure in, a land flowing with milk and honey—it is perfectly understandable that the punishment inflicted on Cain should be the curse of eternal restlessness. It is equally understandable, in consequence, that Christian legend's archetypal image of the Jew who refuses to accept Christ as the messiah should be the *Wandering* Jew, cursed to roam the world until the opportunity might arise to settle his account. It was the Wandering Jew who became the most important image of immortality in Christian fiction, although opinions as to his original identity were somewhat various.

George K. Anderson's comprehensive account of *The Legend of the Wandering Jew* asserts that the legend first began to circulate in written form in the thirteenth century, although it presumably flourished as an item of oral tradition for some time before then, and there is an earlier reference in a sixth-century manuscript. In some versions of the legend, the Wandering Jew is apparently Judas, in accordance with a scriptural warrant provided by *John* 21:20-22, in which Peter, having heard "the disciple whom Jesus loved" (John) ask Jesus who would betray him, adds "And what shall this man do?" Jesus replies: "If I will that he tarry till I come, what is that to thee? follow thou me." The next verse of the gospel comments that the disciples took this to mean that John would not die, but suggests that they were mistaken—thus encouraging the inference that it would be Jesus' betrayer who would tarry indefinitely.

Another version of the legend took its inspiration from *John* 18:22, which states that when Jesus was questioned by the high priest after being arrested in the garden, one of the officers who had brought him slapped him. The thirteenth-century legend of the Wandering Jew is a descendant of this version; a Latin chronicle from Bologna dating from 1223 tells of a Jew encountered by pilgrims in Armenia, who had taunted Jesus as he was going to his martyrdom and was told "I shall go, but you will await me until I come again." Since then, the Jew in question had been rejuvenated, to the apparent age of thirty, at hundred year intervals. Shortly afterwards, the English monk Roger of Wendover, one of a sequence of writers working at the Benedictine monastery at St. Albans, claimed that his monastery had been visited by an Armenian archbishop, who was questioned on the subject of rumors about an immortal man. The archbishop replied that he had actually met the man in question, who had been a hall-porter in the service of Pontius Pilate, named Cartaphilus. Cartaphilus had struck Jesus as he was being removed to be crucified, urging him to move faster, whereupon he was condemned to wait until Jesus returned.

Roger of Wendover's account was reproduced by his successor as chronicler at St. Albans, Matthew Paris, who augmented later versions with endorsements by other supposed witnesses who had visited or come from Armenia. Matthew's versions of the St. Albans chronicle were copied and distributed abroad, but their early distribution was subject to the limitations of the manuscript medium; the advent of printing allowed its proliferation on a larger scale. It was translated into German for a printed version in the 1580s, at a time when plague was running riot in parts of Germany.

In 1602, fifteen years after the publication of the pamphlet that popularized the legend of Faust, a pamphlet performing a similar function for the Wandering Jew appeared; both items were elements of an *angst*-ridden flood of popular Millenarian literature anticipating an imminent apocalypse. The 1602 pamphlet calls the Wandering Jew Ahasuerus, claiming that he had been a shoemaker in Jerusalem who cried out in anger when Jesus, carrying his cross, had stopped for a moment to rest against the wall of his house. Its contents were very widely reprinted, translated and paraphrased, continually bolstered—after the manner of modern urban legends—with news of more recent and local sightings of the immortal wanderer.

The German legend acquired a new lease of life during the German Romantic Movement. J. W. von Goethe planned to make Ahasuerus the subject of an epic poem, to complement his *Faust*, but found the project even more difficult to complete, only producing a few fragments of the projected poem in 1774-75. Christian Schubart similarly set out to produce an epic that he never completed, but a section of it published in 1783 was widely circulated and translated, helping to inspire further exercises in the same vein. Schubart's wanderer has often been driven by his misery to seek death, but even though he has thrown himself into the mouth of a volcano he has been unable to find oblivion. Later Romantic writers produced dozens of further versions, whose profusion inevitably gave rise to many new variations. Clemens Brentano added an element of quest fantasy by promising the wanderer release if he could locate a series of magical artifacts, while other German works credited Ahasuerus with an assortment of superhuman powers to increase the dramatic potential of his interventions in present-day events. Sometimes he appeared as a Satanic figure of menace, but in other works he played the hero, his struggle against his fate becoming a noble attempt to claim and assert human rights in the face of divine persecution.

THE POPULARIZATION OF THE WANDERING JEW

The German pamphlet of 1602 was translated into French in 1605, and a *complainte*—a lyric lament—was attached to reprints from 1609 onwards. The *complainte* spawned numerous descendants, the most important of which was a Belgian version recounting an alleged sighting of Ahasuerus in Brussels on 22 April 1774. This "Brabantine ballad" was spread far and wide throughout France by means of an *image d'Épinal*: a pictorial print illustrating the Jew's confrontation with the burghers of Brussels, captioned by the 24 stanzas of the ballad. Another lyric composed in 1831 by Pierre de Béranger, initially intended to be sung to a familiar tune, was provided with new music by Charles Gounod. Béranger's poem was given a further lease of life in 1856, in an expanded version illustrated by a series of woodcuts by Gustave Doré. In the meantime, the literary career of the Wandering Jew took vast strides in France.

The Wandering Jew became a popular figure in theatrical melodramas, but was elevated to a higher level of literary significance in Edgar Quinet's *Ahasvérus* (1834), an epic verse drama that presented an entire history of the world, with a frame narrative set in Heaven three thousand years after the Day of Judgment. Quinet's eponymous protagonist is equipped with an immortal horse, and is eventually joined by an angel named Rachel, who has been expelled from Heaven because she has taken pity on him; their eventual marriage is followed by a witches' sabbath held in Strasbourg Cathedral. In the futuristic fourth act—which offers an account of the apocalypse very different from the *Revelation of St. John*—Ahasuerus becomes a representative of all mankind in facing divine judgment. (In the epilogue that concludes the frame narrative, God dies in His turn and His limited Creation is swallowed by the abyss of cosmic time.)

Quinet's symbolic Wandering Jew was like none that had gone before, and bore little enough resemblance to any that were to come after him, but he was the immediate inspiration of two spectacular attempts to adapt the character to popular fiction: Eugène Sue's *Le juif errant* (1844-45) and Alexandre Dumas' *Isaac Laquedem* (1853). Sue's was by far the more successful; *Le juif errant*'s serialization in a daily newspaper, following directly after the groundbreaking success of *Les mystères de Paris* (1842-43; tr. as *The Mysteries of Paris*), firmly established the credentials of popular fiction as a circulation-builder and medium of mass entertainment. Dumas intended *Isaac Laquedem* to be his masterpiece, begun in the heady years following the Revolution of 1848, to whose ideals he was firmly committed. Unfortunately, its serialization was rudely interrupted by Louis Napoléon's censors following the *coup d'état* of 1851. Like Sue, Dumas was exiled from Paris; although he took advantage of an amnesty to return, he was not permitted to resume work on *Isaac Laquedem*—the extant text only offers tantalizing hints of the nature and extent of the panoramic view of European history that Dumas had intended his protagonist to provide.

Sue's Wandering Jew makes only fleeting appearances in the text; rather than representing all mankind he is symbolic of the specific predicament of the working class; he is provided by a female counterpart, Herodias—the wife of Herod who procured the death of John the Baptist, as related in *Matthew* 14:3-12—who symbolizes the plight of women in a male-dominated world. The curse of restlessness that afflicts them is augmented by a further penalty, in that wherever Ahasuerus goes, plague follows. His attempts to pass on a fortune (accumulated by the effects of compound interest over the centuries) to the descendants of a man who once befriended him are eventually damned—after more than half a million words of pettier frustrations—by the fact that his presence brings cholera into Paris, with devastating effects on the poor and downtrodden.

Dumas presumably read Sue's novel, and decided to make his Wandering Jew as different from Sue's as he could. His character is literal rather than symbolic, and his story includes a long biography of Jesus. Once the curse has been pronounced on the eponymous antihero, however, the story takes off in a very different direction. Isaac takes up with the neo-Pythagorean philosopher Apollonius of Tyana, who had acquired a posthumous reputation as a magician and miracle-worker by virtue of an extremely fanciful account of his life by Philostratus. Dumas' Apollonius, in company with Isaac, encounters various witches, and their journey becomes progressively more phantasmagoric as they recruit the aid of a sphinx to seek out Prometheus, then raise the spirit of Cleopatra from her tomb—at which point the narrative breaks off.

The third-ranking member of the company of *feuilletonists*, after Dumas and Sue, was Paul Féval, who doubtless felt obliged to produce his own Wandering Jew story, making sure that his was different from both of theirs. He re-emphasized the differences by making his version a comedy rather than a melodrama. Initially serialized as *Vicomte Paul* (1864; aka *La fille du juif errant*; tr. as *The Wandering Jew's Daughter*) it pays wry homage to the proliferation of images by introducing an entire company of Wandering Jews. Féval's Ahasuerus is a more orthodox figure than Sue's or Dumas' equivalents, but his sufferings do not prevent him operating as a kind of superhero, locked in combat with his eternally-unrepentant adversary, Ozer. The other immortal wanderers featured in the novella are accumulated from various fragments of legend and literature, and from reports of impostors who claimed to be the Wandering Jew—who were not uncommon in the nineteenth century.

The Wandering Jew made headway in high culture as well as popular culture—an opera was premièred in Paris in 1852, with music by Fromental Halévy and a *libretto* by Eugène Scribe and Jules-Henri Vernoy de Saint-Georges—but it was the extensions of the legend in popular fiction that stressed the horror of his plight most fervently. That horror was, however, usually intended to arouse sympathy; straightforward figures of menace cast in the mold of Féval's Ozer were rare. The accursed wanderer of French popular culture was, in effect, a counterpart to Christ, embodying the old saying that if one cannot be a shining example, one can always serve, with similar effect, as a horrible warning. Because the horrific aspects of his plight were used to evoke sympathy, the Wandering Jew was usually redeemed by his literary employers; Sue eventually delivered him conclusively from his punishment, as Quinet had, and Dumas probably intended to. Even Féval allowed him the consolation of putting an approximate date to the termination of his—and humankind's—trial by ordeal.

A similar but patchier process of popularization occurred in England, where the Wandering Jew was adopted into the flourishing genre of Gothic romance. He plays a cameo role in Matthew Gregory Lewis's *The Monk* (1796), in which he exorcizes the malevolent spirit of the Bleeding Nun by means of the image of a burning cross emblazoned on his forehead. Percy Shelley wrote a verse soliloquy on his behalf in 1810 and further popularized the legend's substance in "Queen Mab" (1813) and "Hellas" (1822). Henry Neele's "The Magician's Visiter" must have been written in the same period, although its first publication remains obscure. George Croly's novel *Salathiel* (1827; aka *Tarry Thou Till I Come*) used the character as a witness to history, tracking his exploits from the pronouncement of the curse until the destruction of Jerusalem by Titus. New variations originated in Britain included the revelation of Robert Buchanan's narrative poem *The Wandering Jew: A Christmas Carol* (1893) that its protagonist is Christ, condemned to take a dose of his own medicine in recompense for the awful catalogue of crimes committed in his name.

In America, the Wandering Jew was employed satirically in Nathaniel Hawthorne's "A Virtuoso's Collection" (1846), in which Ahasuerus is a guide in a museum of absurd antiquities, and "Ethan Brand" (1851), in which he is one of the experts consulted by the eponymous seeker of the Unpardonable Sin. David Hoffman planned a major work, but only completed two of six projected volumes of *Chronicles Selected from the Originals of Cartaphilus* (1853-54). The legend was also summarized in Mark Twain's *The Innocents Abroad* (1869). Moncure Daniel Conway produced the first major study in English of the legend and its literary versions,

The Wandering Jew (1881), after which several other novelists took up the theme, including H. M. Bien, a rabbi who transformed the legend into the tale of the Wandering Gentile in *Ben-Beor: A Story of the Anti-Messiah* (1894). Eugene Field put a definitive account of the Wandering Jew's plight into the character's own mouth in "The Holy Cross" (1893):

> "Then of a sudden (quoth the old man) a horror filled my breast, and a resistless terror possessed me. So was I accursed forevermore. A voice kept always saying to me: 'Move on, O Jew, move on forever!' From home, from kin, from country, from all I knew and loved I fled; nowhere could I tarry,—the nameless horror burned in my bosom, and I heard continually a voice crying unto me: 'Move on, O Jew, move on forever!' So, with the years, the centuries, the ages, I have fled before that cry and in that nameless horror; empires have risen and crumbled, races have been born and are extinct, mountains have been cast up and time hath levelled them,—still do I live and still I wander hither and thither upon the face of the earth, and am an accursed thing. The gift of tongues is mine,—all men I know, yet mankind knows me not. Death meets me face to face, and passes me by; the sea devours all other prey, but will not hide me in its depths; wild beasts flee from me, and pestilences turn their consuming breaths elsewhere. On and on I go,—not to a home, nor to my people, nor to my grave, but evermore into the tortures of an eternity of sorrow. And evermore I feel the nameless horror burn within, whilst evermore I see the pleading eyes of him that bore the cross, and evermore I hear his voice crying: "Move on, O Jew! Move on forevermore!" (pp. 9-10)

Anderson's study describes hundreds of literary examples additional to those cited, testifying to the fact that the legend was one of the most popular and the most infinitely mutable of all the motifs that written literature inherited from oral tradition. As Anderson's record reaches the end of the nineteenth century, however, it grows much thinner; the motif had become over-familiar by then, and its apparent credibility had waned with Romanticism. Many late-nineteenth-century works—including George MacDonald's *Thomas*

Wingfold, Curate (1876) and Arthur Quiller-Couch's "The Mystery of Joseph Laquedem" (1900)—took the trouble to cultivate the possibility that their enclosed stories might be tall tales inspired by the legend rather than continuations of it. The character did hower, remain available for twentieth-century use in horror stories such as Bernard Capes' "The Accursed Cordonnier" (1902), explicit delusional fantasies such as O. Henry's "The Door of Unrest" (1911) and moralistic melodramas such as E. Temple Thurston's *The Wandering Jew* (1920), which enjoyed great success on the stage before being filmed in 1933, with Conrad Veidt in the lead.

OCCULT PRACTITIONERS AND FAUSTIAN IMMORTALS

The legend of the Wandering Jew was not the only source of impostors who posed as survivors from earlier eras of history. Anyone who posed as a successful alchemist was likely to feel obliged to support the contention that he was in possession of the philosopher's stone by claiming that he was much older than he seemed. One such poseur who made a particular point of emphasizing his antiquity was the Comte de Saint-Germain, who appeared in Paris at the end of the eighteenth century, following in the footsteps of Count Cagliostro.

By this time, alchemy had been absorbed into a more general "occult science" descended from neo-Platonic philosophy, which had taken on a powerful syncretic thrust under the sway of Iamblichus. The Jewish mystical tradition of the Kabbalah had also been adopted into this new synthesis, which came to be called the Hermetic tradition because of its alleged origins in the works of the legendary Hermes Trismegistus. The *Corpus Hermeticum*, fabricated in the 15th century, became very popular among Christian mystics, and the tradition's hospitality to further elaboration was exploited by such opportunists as Paracelsus and J. V. Andreae, the presumed author of the Rosicrucian pamphlets published in 1615-16. Would-be heirs to this great tradition routinely sought—and sometimes became convinced that they had found—teachers whose mastery of occult wisdom had allowed them to live covertly for hundreds of years.

The cannibalistic tendencies of the occult tradition led to its posthumous co-option of various Renaissance philosophers and scientists, especially those who taken an interest in alchemy, such as Albertus Magnus and John Dee. Legendary figures seemed even fairer game, so Faust was added to the list as soon as the pamphlets celebrating his pact with the Devil appeared in 1592-93. Given that the modern renewal of the legend of the Wandering Jew emerged from the same source, it is not surprising that the literary usage of the two characters overlapped. In parallel with the proliferation of characters explicitly identified as the Wandering Jew or Faust, a significant tradition arose of stories in which immortality—or, more usually, protracted longevity—was the price exacted by a diabolical bargain.

Unlike witchcraft, alchemy was never considered by orthodox Christian dogma to imply a diabolical pact, but it was treated with considerable suspicion nevertheless. The notion that immortality won by means of the philosopher's stone was the result of a tacit or explicit diabolical pact assisted legend-mongers and literateurs desirous of representing it as a deeply frustrating existential state. Diabolical pacts and alchemical adventures both became staple motifs of Gothic fiction, and it was in this context that the most memorable early images of "Faustian longevity" appeared. In William Godwin's *St. Leon: A Tale of the Sixteenth Century* (1799) a dying stranger imparts the secret of the philosopher's stone to the eponymous wastrel, who is enabled to enrich himself materially by making gold, although the corollary gift of extended life estranges him from his fellow men, isolating him from all amity and making him an object of permanent suspicion.

St. Leon's "immortality" is significantly different from the Wandering Jew's. Living under Christ's command, the Wandering Jew is forbidden to destroy himself—even volcanic fire spits him out, unharmed—but St. Leon merely has the *potential* to live forever, without aging, provided that no fatal violence intervenes. When he falls into the hands of the Spanish Inquisition, he is very nearly executed. This sort of potentially-infinite longevity—for which Alvin Silverstein coined the term "emortality" in *Conquest of Death* (1979)—is markedly different from true immortality. On the one hand, the everpresent option of suicide ameliorates the horror of infinite frustration; on the other, the effects of existential *angst* can be exaggerated into a continual paranoid dread of all possible agents of mortality. The literary development of emortal longevity tends, in consequence, to be somewhat different from contemplations of the Wandering Jew's predicament.

Some of Ahasuerus' nineteenth-century literary rivals were mere clones, like Ladurlad in Robert Southey's *The Curse of Kehama* (1810) and the protagonist of Caroline Norton's "The Undying One" (1830), but once the link with the original was broken such characters began to diversify, lending themselves to philosophical analyses untroubled by the Wandering Jew's ideological baggage.

Works featuring Faustian emortals are even more various. The most effective and influential Gothic image of Faustian longevity proved to be Charles Maturin's depiction of *Melmoth the Wanderer* (1820), whose function is to materialize when the subsidiary stories making up the novel reach their climactic moments, to offer characters *in extremis* the opportunity of exchanging their own imminently-dire fates for his protracted one. They all refuse, unwilling to traffic with the Devil, and in the end he has to meet his fate.

Melmoth the Wanderer is by no means emortal; his bargain with the Devil only entitled him to a fixed term of 150 years. His particular *angst* arises from the knowledge that he is doomed to Hell and the frustration of his continued failure to sell on his contract:

> "He dreamed that he stood on the summit of a precipice, whose downward height no eye could have measured, but for the fearful wave of a fiery ocean that lashed and blazed, and roared at its bottom, sending its burning spray far up, so as to drench the dreamer with its sulphurous rain. The whole glowing ocean below was alive—every billow bore an agonizing soul, that rose like a wreck or a putrid corse on the waves of earth's oceans—uttered a shriek as it burst against that adamantine precipice—sunk—and rose again to repeat the tremendous experiment! Every billow of fire was thus instinct with immortal and agonizing existence,—each was freighted with a soul, that rose on the burning wave in torturing hope, burst on the rock in despair, added its eternal shriek to the roar of that fiery ocean, and sunk to rise again—in vain, and—for ever!
>
> "Suddenly the Wanderer felt himself flung half-way down the precipice. He stood, in his dream, tottering on a crag midway down the precipice—he looked upward, but the upper air (for there was no heaven) showed only blackness unshadowed and impenetrable—but, blacker than that blackness, he could distinguish a giant outstretched arm, that held him as in sport on the ridge of that infernal precipice, while another, that seemed in its motions to hold fearful and invisible conjunction with the arm that grasped him, as if both belonged to some being too vast and horrible even for the imagery of a dream to shape, pointed upwards to a dial-plate fixed on the

top of that precipice, and which the flashes of that ocean of fire made fearfully conspicuous." (pp. 538-9)

The many variants and sequels inspired by Maturin's novel, however, routinely address the notion of spoiled immortality. One such supplement, by William Godwin's daughter, Mary Shelley—"The Mortal Immortal" (1834)—attempts to establish a paradoxical condition of "half-immortality." A similar move was made by Honoré de Balzac in "L'Élixir de longue vie" (1830; tr. as "The Elixir of Life"), in which a partial application of the balm in question is adequate to preserve its recipient's head while his body proceeds to die. In "Melmoth reconcilié" (1835; tr. as "Melmoth Reconciled"), however, Balzac turned horror into farcical comedy with the observation that Melmoth would have no trouble at all passing on his bargain in contemporary Paris, and that it would probably be traded from hand to hand with remarkable rapidity.

A pastiche of *Melmoth* was attempted by W. Harrison Ainsworth, who began serializing his novel *Auriol* in his own magazine in 1844 but abandoned it half way. Here, the immortality gained by means of the diabolical pact is conditional on a periodic human sacrifice—a device borrowed from modifications made to French stage adaptations of John Polidori's novelette "The Vampyre" (1819). There is a whole series of such texts, in which the focus is so decisively shifted from blood-drinking to the preservation of conditional immortality that they are more appropriately considered here than in an essay on vampires; the key examples are two versions of *Le Vampire* (1820), the first scripted by Charles Nodier, Achille de Jouffroy and the director of the Porte-Saint-Martin theatre, Jean-Toussaint Merle, while the second was penned by Alexandre Dumas for production in 1851. Others include Heinrich Marschner's opera *Der Vampyr* (1828) and Smyth Upton's prose version of its libretto, *The Last of the Vampires* (1845). Even in the days before serial-killer stories became the everyday currency of thriller fiction, however, it was as difficult to imagine that murder would exact too heavy a tax from the conscience of a dedicated immortal as it was to imagine that Melmoth would have found it very difficult to sell on his bargain.

The notion of rejuvenative immortality for which a price must be paid was often reinterpreted in the late nineteenth century in terms of "life-force vampirism," as in Sabine Baring-Gould's "Margery of Quether" (1884), J. Maclaren Cobban's *Master of His Fate* (1890), and Claude Farrère's *La maison des hommes vivants* (1911;

tr. as *The House of the Secret*). It lost none of its horrific force in transfiguration, and it was taken for granted that anyone possessed of such a leech-like ability would certainly use it. This subspecies of fiction gave birth to the rapid aging motif that was later to be transferred to the cinema with great effect in such movies as Frank Capra's 1937 dramatization of James Hilton's *Lost Horizon* (1933), becoming a standard means of subjecting emortal adversaries to rough poetic justice.

The most famous quasi-Faustian substitute for the Wandering Jew was the legendary Flying Dutchman, a sea captain who allegedly cursed God while attempting to round the Cape of Good Hope in poor weather and was damned to eternal frustration in consequence. Notable literary extrapolations of the story include Heinrich Heine's fragmentary "The Memoirs of Herr von Schnabelewopski" (1834), Captain Marryat's *The Phantom Ship* (1839), and W. Clark Russell's *The Death Ship* (1888), although none is as effective as the adaptation of the legend into an item of American "fakelore" in William Austin's account of "Peter Rugg, the Missing Man" (1824; exp. 1827), in which the story is transferred to land—specifically to the roads around Boston, along which Rugg and his luckless daughter are condemned to drive, pursued by a storm.

Nathaniel Hawthorne, who partnered Peter Rugg with Ahasuerus in "A Virtuoso's Collection," also toyed with an alchemical elixir of life in the allegorical "Doctor Heidegger's Experiment" (1837), and always intended to make more substantial use of it in a quasi-Gothic context. Like Ainsworth, though, he was unable to complete his romance, whose various fragments were published posthumously and patched together by his son Julian into *Doctor Grimshawe's Secret* (1882).

The difficulty so many writers found in completing their projected epics and romances of immortality afflicted those who took a positive view of the prospect as well as those dedicated to its darker extrapolation. Edward Bulwer-Lytton nearly joined their number when he abandoned the serial version of his Rosicrucian romance *Zicci* in 1841, but he started over and brought the story to completion as *Zanoni* (1842). The second version falters in a different way, though; the eponymous character, despite appearing to be as successful in his longevity as anyone could wish, gladly trades it in for the love of a good woman.

The occult quest for immortality also plays a key role in Bulwer-Lytton's other occult romances, "The Haunters and the Haunted" (1859; aka "The House and the Brain") and *A Strange Story* (1862), but direct confrontation with its implications is carefully avoided. This became the general trend in late nineteenth-century occult fiction; those works that placed the quest for the elixir of life centre-stage routinely consigned its eventual attainment—whatever the implications of that attainment might be—to the margin of the narrative or the undetailed hinterlands beyond. Alexandre Dumas' *Joseph Balsamo* (1846; tr. as *Memoirs of a Physician*), F. Marion Crawford's *The Witch of Prague* (1891), and Guy Boothby's *A Bid for Fortune* (1895) are typical in their use of this kind of evasion, although all three give the impression of having started out with more robust intentions. Bulwer-Lytton's hesitancy did not prevent *Zanoni* from becoming an enormously influential work, inspiring the lifestyle fantasists of the late-nineteenth-century "occult revival" as well as numerous literary imitators.

The occult revival moved into top gear in the 1880s, when the increasing popularity of spiritualism was supplemented by the advent of Madame Blavatsky's Theosophy, with its corollary popularization of "Eastern mysticism." This popularization encouraged the intricate entanglement of the imagery of immortality with that of reincarnation in such popular romances as H. Rider Haggard's *She* (1886), Edgar Lee's *Pharaoh's Daughter* (1889), Edwin Lester Arnold's *The Wonderful Adventures of Phra the Phoenician* (1891), Charles Godfrey Leland's *Flaxius: Leaves from the Life of an Immortal* (1902), and William Holt-White's *Helen of All Time* (1905). While Spiritualist fantasies fanned the flames of faith in an immortal afterlife, Haggardesque karmic romances helped to renew enthusiasm for the prospect of earthly immortality, and for its more frequent representation as a desirable possession.

The popular variant of reincarnation fantasy in which Egyptian mummies turn out to be emortals held in suspended animation—as in Theo Douglas's *Iras: A Mystery* (1896), Clive Holland's *An Egyptian Coquette* (1898), and Guy Boothby's *Pharos the Egyptian* (1899)—increased literary scope for bringing characters from the distant past, although the notion that immortality might be the prerogative of people frozen—often literally—into existential stasis also provided another telling instance of ironic frustration. The image of frozen beauty, whose preservation depends on the cessation of aging, became common in twentieth-century fiction, although almost all stories of this type involve the return of the object of desire to the stream of time.

The seeming impossibility of the dream of opposing time's ravages produced such agonized allegories as Oscar Wilde's *The Picture of Dorian Gray* (1891). Wilde's protagonist learns to count the cost of his own narcissism by observing the effects of his just desserts on the portrait hidden in his attic, and ultimately cannot abide the horror of that awareness. The most effective fantasy of existential arrest produced in the early twentieth century, on the other hand, made no attempt to traffic in horror, preferring to extrapolate a new kind of poignancy. The central character of J. M. Barrie's *Peter Pan* (1904; novelization as *Peter and Wendy*, 1911) was swiftly elevated to the status of a modern myth.

The costs of Peter Pan's indefinitely-preserved innocence are clearly manifest, in spite of their scrupulous understatement, but their revelation only excites pity and piquant regret for the inevitable loss of youth. Barrie's *Mary Rose* (1924), which features a far less radical temporal dislocation, threw the potential pain consequent upon remaining young while others age into much sharper focus, but that too was cast as a tragedy rather than a horror story. As in the case of the Wandering Jew, other supernatural immortals were increasingly employed in the twentieth century to claim sympathy rather than to excite distress.

LEARNING TO LOVE LONG LIFE

The occult revival was aided in its effect on the literary uses of longevity by rapid progress in medical science, which offered hope that material means of preserving mortal life might prevail where supernatural ones had not. This seemed to some literary observers to be an intrinsically horrific prospect—a thesis graphically dramatized in Georges Eekhoud's extravagant moral allegory of serial heart-transplantation "Le Coeur de Tony Wandel" (1884; tr. as "Tony Wandel's Heart"), and argued more earnestly in Walter Besant's *The Inner House* (1888). Its more obvious effect, however, was to introduce a more matter-of-fact attitude into such comedies of immortality as Frank R. Stockton's *The Vizier of the Two-Horned Alexander* (1899) and such Utopian romances as J. Emile Hix's *Can a Man Live Forever?* (1898).

As the twentieth century advanced, literary images of immortality were increasingly transferred from a supernatural context to a speculative one, although the ideological consequences of the shift were initially confused. The horrific aspects of hypothetical medical technologies of longevity were given a significant injection of repulsive potential in the 1920s, when Serge Voronoff proposed that aging was caused by a decline in the functionality of the endocrine system, which could be reversed by the transplantation of animal testicles (euphemistically known in press parlance as "monkey glands"). Literary responses to the prospect did include such squeamish horror stories as Robert Hichens' *Dr. Artz* (1929), but they also included cheerful farces such as Bertram Gayton's *The Gland Stealers* (1922) and Thomas le Breton's *Mr Teedles, the Gland Old Man* (1927), which refused to be intimidated by the notion. Gertrude Atherton's *Black Oxen* (1923)—in which the heroine's endocrine system is rejuvenated in a more palatable fashion, by X-rays—also took a dim view of the prospect, but could not muster much conviction in so doing.

Notwithstanding the customary effects of the "yuck factor" on medical fantasies, the inevitable trend of fiction that represented emortality as a realizable goal of technology was to encourage more welcoming attitudes. The process of transformation was slow, but it was definite. The Wandering Jew put in a guest appearance in Harold Scarborough's *The Immortals* (1924), to protest against a medical method of immunization against death, while E. Nesbit's *Dormant* (1911), George Allan England's "The Elixir of Hate" (1911), Martin Swayne's *The Blue Germ* (1918), and Aldous Huxley's *After Many a Summer Dies the Swan* (1939) all made similar cautionary recommendations, but the tide was running against reflexive negativity.

A vigorous ideological countercurrent to the cautionary tradition was established by such works as Marie Corelli's wholehearted wish-fulfillment fantasy *The Young Diana* (1915), George Bernard Shaw's propagandistic *Back to Methuselah* (1921) and C. J. Cutcliffe Hyne's amiable *Abbs: His Story Through Many Ages* (1929). Virginia Woolf's *Orlando: A Biography* (1928) and George C. Foster's *The Lost Garden* (1930) retained a sharper sense of irony, but still favored the view that the privileges of limitless opportunity would far outweigh the penalties. Shaw's polemical introduction to *Back to Methuselah* prompted Karel Čapek to add a preface to his own play, *Věc Makropulos* (1922; tr. as *The Macropoulos Secret*), arguing that immortality would be an unmitigated curse, but such diehard pessimism was already beginning to seem out of place, and the explanation put forward within the body of the play seems rather weak:

> "EMILIA: It's unbearable. You can put up with it for a hundred years, for a hundred and thirty years, but then...then you realise that.... And then your soul dies within you.
>
> "VITEK: What do you realise?

"EMILIA: Oh God, there are no words for it. And then there's nothing more for you to believe in. Nothing more. And that's what causes the boredom. You remember, Bertie, you said that I sing as if it froze me. Art, you see, has some point only as long as you haven't mastered it. As soon as you've mastered it, completely mastered it, then it becomes useless. It's just as idle, Krista, just as idle as snoring. To sing is the same as to keep quiet. It's all alike. There's not the slightest difference....

"VITEK: But allow me...surely there are...higher values...ideals....

"EMILIA: There are, but only for you. You cannot go on loving for three hundred years. And you cannot go on hoping, creating, gazing at things for three hundred years. You can't stand it. Everything becomes irksome. It is irksome to be good and irksome to be bad. Heaven and earth are equally irksome to you. And then, you see, nothing really exists. Nothing exists. Neither sin, nor pain, nor earth—nothing whatever." (pp. 202-4)

The camp that considered immortality to be a wholly desirable condition achieved a significant breakthrough when it produced its first best-seller in the 1920s. George S. Viereck and Paul Eldridge's *My First Two Thousand Years* (1928) brought the Wandering Jew back to centre stage yet again, morally rearmed with a far healthier attitude to his condition. The calculatedly procovative novel summarizes the memoirs of a Cartaphilus who has long relished his eternal conflict with the Great God Ennui and rejoiced in the opportunities afforded him by longevity, especially the search for the secret of "unendurable pleasure, indefinitely prolonged." His sometime companions, whose parallel stories were told in a similarly combative spirit in *Salome, the Wandering Jewess* (1930) and *The Invincible Adam* (1932), agreed with him wholeheartedly.

The casual salaciousness and determined irreverence of the Viereck/Eldridge trilogy succeeded in irritating the American audience it set out to offend, who were in the process of losing their long war against all kinds of self-indulgence, in spite of the temporary victory won in the battle for Prohibition. The series' mocking pretence of offering a serious philosophical allegory of the relations between the sexes increased its capacity to infuriate, and it provided a clamorous challenge to the contention that immortality must eventually become intolerably tedious.

The generic popular fiction that developed in the pulp magazines alongside the success of the Viereck/Eldridge trilogy mostly went along with the same ideological current. Its authors were mostly content to slot the idea of human immortality into the formulaic specifications of the thriller, and they were perfectly prepared to use immortals as menacing adversaries or puppets in ironic *contes cruels*, but they rarely struck an ideological pose that regarded immortality as an intrinsically bad idea. Variants of the fountain of youth and the elixir of life cropped up regularly as targets in quests featured in the new popular fiction. The quests were very often frustrated—and when they were not, the acquisition of the reward was usually used as a closing device rather than a topic for investigation—but such projects were usually represented as perfectly sane endeavors, conducted in a spirit of pragmatism that contrasted strongly with the Faustian ambience of their nineteenth-century antecedents.

The possibilities inherent in the experience of acquired emortality were rarely interrogated, but even the most self-consciously downmarket works of fiction are sometimes wont to dabble in philosophical rhapsody. Works of popular fiction from the pulp era that attempted some modification or consolidation of the iconic status of immortality included Jack Williamson's *Golden Blood* (1933), Robert Bloch's "Slave of the Flames" (1938), and "Yours Truly, Jack the Ripper" (1943)—both of which added extra turns of an ironic screw to the motif of immortality bought by murder—Jack Mann's *Maker of Shadows* (1938) and *The Ninth Life* (1939), and Wyndham Martyn's *Stones of Enchantment* (1948).

The pulp-originated subgenre of sword and sorcery fiction helped lay the ideative foundations for the eventual development of American generic fantasy, in which longevity is one of the standard rewards of magical power, though rarely entirely cost-free. The subgenre completed the long-ongoing absorption of the traditional image of the alchemist into the image of the all-round practitioner of the occult arts: the wizard. The stereotype of the wizard formulated by popular fiction of the period accepted a Tithonian component in his characterization; the most powerful and long-lived magicians usually manifest the appearance of extreme old age. The image of the witch was still handicapped by associations with diabolism that dated back to the days of the great European Witch-Hunt of the sixteenth and seventeenth centuries, but the witches of pulp fiction moved inexorably in the direction of becoming female equivalents of wizards. Witches, however, tended to make far more use of glamour in maintaining appearances, so that they could continue to function as *femmes fatales* as well as hagwives and wise women, no matter how old they might actually be.

Immortality was centralized as a key theme in some of the more upmarket works that assisted the evolution of sword and sorcery into generic fantasy—most notably Fletcher Pratt's *The Well of the Unicorn* (1948; initially bylined George U. Fletcher)—but it was more usually integrated into a much more elaborate magical fabric. The work that became the commodified genre's key exemplar, J. R. R. Tolkien's *The Lord of the Rings* (1954-55), included one of the archetypal images of ancient wizardry in the character of Gandalf. Although Gandalf was obviously modeled on the traditional figure of Merlin, he became a key model in a twentieth-century reconfiguration of Merlin's image, which was associated with the wholesale adoption of Arthurian fantasy into the body of modern generic fantasy. The integration of emortality into the standard pattern of magical attributes deployed within the genre was soon taken for granted, to the extent that Diana Wynne Jones' satirical *Tough Guide to Fantasyland* (1996) is able to induce the rule that "the longer a person marinades her/himself in Magic, the longer she/he lives."

The relegation of the emortal human being to this kind of standard and largely-uninterrogated role in supernatural fiction reflected a tacit acceptance that the rapidly-evolving modern genre of science fiction provided a more appropriate and convenient medium for direct approaches to the existential questions that arose in connection with the notion. Science fiction stories foregrounding the topic, and dwelling elaborately on its implications, increased in number as supernatural fiction doing likewise went into a relative decline. Some mid-twentieth-century works of supernatural fiction carried forward the evasive strategies developed in the nineteenth-century, after the fashion of Karen Blixen's neo-Gothic thriller *The Angelic Avengers* (1946, bylined Pierre Andrezel) and Vaughan Wilkins' sentimental fantasy *Valley Beyond Time* (1955), but such works already seemed quaintly old-fashioned at the time of their composition. There were, however, exceptions to the rule.

One significant group of exceptional texts was comprised of accounts of Biblical immortals akin to, and often including, the Wandering Jew. Like Viereck and Eldridge, several other writers decided that such figures were more easily adaptable to the priorities of modern narrative if they came in sets, and were prone to argue with one another. The stratagem was employed in C. E. Lawrence's

"Spikenard" (1930), which imagines that a company of accursed wanderers might one day inherit the Earth when the human race has had its day, and M. P. Shiel's *This Above All* (1933), in which various individuals supposedly gifted with immortality by Jesus—including Lazarus and his beloved John—while away the time in markedly different ways while awaiting his return. The lone wanderer still had some mileage left in him, though, as demonstrated by Pär Lagerkvist's version, introduced in *Sibyllan* (1956; tr. as *The Sibyl*) and brought into sharper focus in *Ahasverus död* (1960; tr. as *The Death of Ahasuerus*). Lagerkvist's immortal is far less happy with his plight than Eldridge and Viereck's Cartaphilus—he is sexually impotent—but he is defiantly unrepentant, considering his fate palpably unjust. Stefan Heym's *Ahasver, der Ewige Jude* (1981; tr. as *The Wandering Jew*) is even more assertive in reconsidering the notion in a post-holocaust context.

THE TWILIGHT OF THE GODS

Although twentieth-century supernatural fiction lost its monopoly on human emortals to science fiction, and was comprehensively overtaken in the quest to investigate the existential implications of the emortal condition, it kept its monopoly on an important spectrum of non-human immortals, and the philosophical initiative associated with that custody. While science fiction could invent undying aliens as easily as undying humans, it had great difficulty in taking aboard the traditional mythological images of immortal gods, godlings and fairy folk; they remained the near-exclusive property of supernatural fiction.

The manner in which supernatural fiction deals with non-human immortals is inevitably conditioned by the narrative status of the mythic past in any particular text, and by the situation of the mythical past in the text's literary-historical context. These matters are not as simple as they may seem at first glance, and the close affiliation of the concept of non-human immortality with the ambience of the mythic past makes literary representations of non-human immortality into a very effective indicator of the changing fortunes of that milieu.

The history of modern literature—particularly the recent history of prose fiction—is a narrative of the gradual displacement of the mythic past by the historical past in such genres as the novel. The historical novel first materialized in opposition to fiction dealing with the mythical past, and the Gothic novel can easily been seen as a battleground on which the virtuous historical past engages in a titanic struggle with the draconian mythical past, eventually triumphing in terms of literary prestige, while the mythical past retired to lick its wounds in the despised fields of children's fiction and horror fiction. Even in folklore, though, the mythical past is customarily represented as something dead and gone; the formula "once upon a time" does not signify mere historical distance, but the removal of a story into a world when everything was different. Even in oral traditions of myth and folklore, let alone their literary extrapolations, there is a marked dissonance between the world described within the text and the world in which the storyteller meets his audience. Long before the evolution of literacy, let alone the evolution of print, magic was seen as something that no longer worked, and miracles as events that no longer happened.

All fantastic fiction is conscious of this kind of implicit dynamic, but post-Enlightenment fantastic fiction exaggerates the consciousness into hypersensitivity. In consequences, all literary images of the mythical past represent it as a world in the process of what John Clute calls "thinning": a world whose inherent enchantment has been dwindling inexorably since time immemorial. This affects all the motifs and icons of supernatural fiction, but it has a very particular and somewhat paradoxical effect on the notion of immortality. When it is subjected to thinning, the taken-for-granted immortality of gods, godlings and fairy folk inevitably threatens to run to exhaustion, thus rendering them mortal in spite of the appearances of their existential state. Immortality cannot be gradually diluted, as most kinds of magic can; it is either absolute, or a sham. For this reason, all supernatural fiction—especially post-Enlightenment supernatural fiction—routinely deploys the paradoxical motif of the twilight of the gods: the notion of the fateful day when the immortals will vanish from a world that can no longer entertain magic and miracles.

The unprecedentedly loud and pretentious celebration of the twilight of the gods undertaken by Richard Wagner's operatic Ring cycle (1853-74) stands at the head of a rich tradition of elegiac supernatural fiction, in which the inevitable death of the ancient immortals, and the mythic Golden Age they symbolize, is mourned in much the same spirit of nostalgia in which adults tend to mourn their golden youth. It is no coincidence that the god of Arcadia, Pan, was the only Greek god whose passing was explicitly recorded in Hellenic mythology, nor that there was a very obvious resurgence of Arcadian fantasy—especially fantasies in which Pan is represented as a tragic figure—as the end of the nineteenth century approached and passed. When Pan was not personally present in such works his place was often taken by his trivial stand-ins, fauns and satyrs, or by their traditional female counterparts, nymphs. The outstanding items of this tradition include such passionately definitive accounts of the thinning of immortality as Richard Garnett's "The Twilight of the Gods" (1888), Anatole France's "Saint Satyr" (1895), and Justin Huntly McCarthy's *The Dryad* (1905), counterweighted with the occasional resistant fantasy such as Eden Phillpotts' *The Girl and the Faun* (1916).

Although the substance of pagan mythology is obviously more amenable to use in parables of thinning, the advancement of science ensured that Christian mythology was by no means immune to the process. God was highly resistant to thinning Himself, but the apparatus supporting Him—including His notorious adversary—was far more vulnerable. Marie Corelli's *The Sorrows of Satan* (1895) offers a wryly heartfelt portrait of a depleted Devil. Anatole France followed his earlier experiments in religious fantasy with a striking account of *La révolte des anges* (1914; tr. as *The Revolt of the Angels*), in which Satan eventually explains to a remustered army of rebel angels what long life has taught him about the wisdom of letting the decay of the mythic past take its natural course. Helen Beauclerk's *The Love of the Foolish Angel* (1929) countered Phillpotts' account of a conscienceless priapic faun with the first of an extensive sequence of twentieth-century narratives in which an angel voluntarily surrenders the privilege of immortality for the privileges of human love.

When the ancient gods did retain their immortality in twentieth-century fantasies, they became increasingly alienated from the world in which they found themselves. Even those who retained their function as incarnations of apects of human psychology were compelled to an awareness of threats to their traditional roles, as in such works as Stephen McKenna's *The Oldest God* (1926), Murray Constantine's *The Devil, Poor Devil!* (1934), John Erskine's *Venus, the Lonely Goddess* (1949), Susan Alice Kerby's *Mr. Kronion* (1949), George S. Viereck's *Gloria* (1952), and William Gerhardi and Brian Lunn's *The Memoirs of Satan* (1932). The last-named acquired considerable weight as its story unfolded, in spite of the fact that it had begun as an amiably farcical parody of *My First Two Thousand Years*.

Many works of this sort carried forward a tradition of literary satanism derived from Percy Shelley's polemical reassertion of William Blake's judgment that John Milton was "of the Devil's party without knowing it" when he wrote *Paradise Lost*. Novels that featured God and the Devil as characters routinely took leave to wonder whether the history recorded by the winners of the war in Heaven was entirely accurate, and attempted to offer the Devil the right of reply. Works such as Jonathan Daniels' *Clash of Angels* (1930), in which Lucifer becomes a heroic freedom-fighter rather than a vicious terrorist, rarely introduced the immortality of their protagonists as a specific topic for discussion or analysis, but it remained a significant aspect of their world-views.

The dissonance between the present and mythic past provides the fundamental parameters of one of the major subcategories of fantastic fiction, which Farah Mendlesohn calls "intrusive fantasy." In an intrusive fantasy some aspect of the mythic past intrudes into the present, where its incongruity inevitably makes it a "bringer of chaos." The chaos in question may be comic or horrific—or, of course, both—but its narrative value in either case is that it equips the whole generic subcategory with a ready-made story-arc aimed towards the restoration of order. Across the spectrum of intrusive fantasy, immortality functions as a narrative means of contriving intrusion: entities from the mythical past can only arrive in the present by virtue of unnatural endurance in a state of dormancy or by magical time travel; the former is the preferred option in the great majority of horror stories. The adversaries of intrusive fantasy, therefore, are almost always tacitly immortal—but the fact that they no longer belong in the world often licenses their eventual destruction, in spite of the seeming paradox entailed therein.

Many intrusive fantasies do not take advantage of this license, sometimes because it seems unsporting to do so, but often because there is an advantage to authors in retaining the option of returning adversaries to the fray so that the ritual of their defeat can be repeated—several times over, if necessary, as sequels generate series. For this and other reasons, a return to dormancy is routinely preferred to final destruction as a means of closure in intrusive fantasies. The non-human immortals of supernatural fiction, in consequence, are more likely to fall asleep than they are to fade away or meet actual destruction; while their immortality may remain absolute, their entitlement to consciousness and active authority is not—a circumstance that gives them something in common with those human immortals who can only retain their status and their beauty in suspended animation.

The second major category of fantastic fiction identified by Mendlesohn is portal fantasy, in which a mythic world continues to coexist with the historical past and present, but is displaced into another dimension, tentatively connected to ours by portals of some kind. One set of such portals—proverbially envisaged as a gate of ivory and a gate of horn—is said in folklore to separate the waking world from the world of dreams; another separates the world of mundane experience from the land of Faerie. Portal fantasy has no need of immortality as a means of narrative delivery, but immortality often features as a key attribute of folk who live on the far sides of portals.

Unlike the immortals of intrusive fantasy, the immortals of portal fantasy do not often fall asleep—there is no need of any such artifice to remove them from the world of the story, given that the portals can simply be closed again—but they are frequently prone to a different sort of suspended animation, born of the fact that time often flows at a different rate on the far side of a portal. The most familiar versions of this motif are derivatives of two Scottish ballads, which may be variants of the same tale: "Tam Lin" and "Thomas the Rhymer." Both tell of mortals beloved by the queen of Faerie, who are disconnected from their own world when she takes them into Faerie, because time flows much more slowly there. While the days and months of their lives pass, years and centuries pass in the world they left behind. By this means, mortality and immortality are confused—a confusion translocated into twentieth-century science fiction by means of the theory of relativity and the scope it generates for time-dilatation. Such narrative moves do not really make immortals of their mortal characters, although they may seem immortal to the descendants who glimpse them if and when they try to return, but it does make a considerable difference to the way the immortal characters are perceived within the narratives. The fairy queens who hold Tam and Thomas captive are prisoners of their own time-scheme, immune to progress in much the same way as any other victim of suspended animation, although they are blithely unconscious of the fact.

The transition from belief in a mythical past to knowledge of a historical past is by no means as smooth as the literary mechanism of thinning implies. The manufacture of the mythical past did not stop when history was invented, and it has not stopped yet. History often gives rise to its own myths, deliberately and accidentally—and literature is itself a prolific source of new myths, which renew the magicality of the past even while acknowledging the inevitability of its thinning. As the legends of Faust and the Wandering Jew readily demonstrate, immeasurably ancient immortals are not the only ones to wander from the mythic past into the narrative present, and they are by no means alone. All great literary heroes—and many of their adversaries—are granted a metaphorical immortality, which is very easily transmuted into literal immortality within works of supernatural fiction.

Consignment to dormancy is not only the preferred narrative option for ancient immortals but also for more recent heroes such as Arthur—the "once and future king," who is purportedly ever-ready come to England's defense whenever he is needed, and sometimes does return in modern Arthurian fantasies. Authors in search of witnesses who can see history as a historian does, panoramically, or observers who can look at a particular period with clinical objectivity, have a ready-made list of candidates, expandable at will. Heroes slot into such roles comfortably enough, as in Peter Vansittart's *The Death of Robin Hood* (1981) and *Parsifal* (1988), but monsters may serve just as well, precisely because they are distanced outsiders, as Frankenstein's monster does in Michael Bishop's *Brittle Innings* (1994) and Daedalus' minotaur in Stephen Sherrill's *The Minotaur Takes a Cigarette Break* (2000).

There is a considerable grey area between attempts to adopt the viewpoints of non-human immortals and accounts of human emortality, which is occupied by afterlife fantasies and posthumous fantasies. The second category is distinguished from the first by the fact that its viewpoint characters continue to exist on the margins of the real world—often not realizing immediately that they are dead—rather than proceeding to a further arena, but both types of story are, in essence, accounts of acquired non-humanity. Very few of the works in these subgenres are explicit studies of immortality, but again there is a sense in which that taken-for-granted circumstance colors everything seen from the narrative viewpoint—a fact that becomes obvious in such frankly existentialist examinations of the ghostly condition as Ashley Sampson's *The Ghost of Mr Brown* (1941) and G. W. Stonier's *Memoirs of a Ghost* (1947) and such sophisticated afterlife fantasies as C. S. Lewis's *The Great Divorce* (1945) and E. E. Y. Hales' *Chariot of Fire* (1977).

In the last decades of the twentieth century the philosophical contemplation of the emortal condition in supernatural fiction was dominated by the deployment of exotic "post-human" individuals, especially vampires. As in the nineteenth-century texts in which blood-drinking is replaced as the focus of attention by the conditionality of immortality, many late twentieth-century texts modify traditional versions of "undeath" in such a way as to place the issue of longevity centre-stage. A significant threshold was crossed in the mid-1970s when several striking works of this kind appeared, including Pierre Kast's *Les vampires d'Alfama* (1975; tr. as *The Vampires of Alfama*), Anne Rice's *Interview with the Vampire* (1976), and the first item in Chelsea Quinn Yarbro's extensive series chronicling the history-spanning exploits of her vampire version of the Comte de Saint-Germain.

Many such stories avidly exploit the sexual symbolism as well as the conventionally melodramatic potential of blood-drinking, but there is a sense in which they have more in common with the tradition of "psychic vampire" stories and stories of rejuvenative immortality renewable by human sacrifice, which were more explicitly echoed during the revisionist era in such works as Fred Mustard Stewart's *The Mephisto Waltz* (1969) and Whitley Strieber's *The Hunger* (1981). There is a sense in which fantasies of this sort constitute a reaction against the thinning process, some of the more extravagant examples hoping that a new dawn might follow the twilight of the gods. The fact that the ancient immortals have mostly retired to permanent slumber has created some scope for new ones to take their place—and whence can such replacements come, if not from the ranks of humankind, by means of death and transfiguration?

PROGRESS IN THE FLIGHT FROM FRUSTRATION

Most of the significant contributions to the further analysis of the narrative problems posed by the iconic immortal made in the last decades of the twentieth century were the produce of generic science fiction, but many of the most refined *contes philosophiques* produced in that context were hybrid or chimerical works. It does not matter much, in a tale whose primary purpose is philosophical argument, how its images are derived or supported.

Some science fiction writers were, in consequence, perfectly happy to adopt such supernatural archetypes as the Wandering Jew in order to facilitate their debates. He makes one of his classic cameo appearances in Walter M. Miller's post-holocaust novel *A Canticle for Leibowitz* (1960), where he is one of several symbolic figures lurking in the background while a reconstituted Church provides both the social solidarity necessary to rebuild civilization, and the dogmatic stubbornness that facilitates its repeated destruction. In J. G. Ballard's "The Lost Leonardo" (1964), Ahasuerus becomes a subtle retoucher of Old Masters, seeking some fugitive hope of redemption in reconstructing the representations that preserve the record of his sin. In Diana Wynne Jones' *The Homeward Bounders* (1981) he is one of a continually-augmented company of accursed wanderers, whose ultimate fate seems dependent on that of the imprisoned Prometheus.

Most of the new stories contained in the Dedalus anthology *Tales of the Wandering Jew* (1991) are seamlessly compounded from sciencefictional and supernatural motifs and methods, the most significant new twists on the myth being provided by Kim Newman and Eugene Byrne's ironic alternative history story "The Wandering Christian" and two stories that extrapolate the accursed wanderer's plight into the far future, Barrington J. Bayley's "The Remembrance" and David Langford's "Waiting for the Iron Age." The latter story is unusually uncompromising in its depiction of what literal immortality would actually imply in a universe that is not scheduled for closure by a Big Crunch, let alone Christ's imminent return.

A similar spirit is reflected in other sciencefictional *contes philosophiques* that borrow or reflect religious imagery, including Richard Cowper's "The Tithonian Factor" (1983), in which the beneficiaries of an early technology of longevity discover that they have cheated themselves out of the preferable kind divinely donated to the human soul. Robert Silverberg's long preoccupation with the themes of immortality, resurrection and rebirth extended from purely sciencefictional investigations through hybrid religious fantasies to surreal metaphysical fantasies; his most significant mediations on the central notion include *Son of Man* (1971), *The Book of Skulls* (1972) "Born With the Dead" (1974), and "Sailing to Byzantium" (1985). Natalie Babbitt's *Tuck Everlasting* (1975), though marketed as a children's fantasy, is similar in its narrative strategy. Another sf writer possessed by a similar preoccupation, Roger Zelazny, generated a series of hybrid immortal protagonists in such works as *This Immortal* (1966), *Lord of Light* (1967), and *Isle of the Dead* (1969).

The most extravagant hybrid account of the existential plight of immortals taking the fight against the Great God Ennui to its ultimate conclusion is Michael Moorcock's Dancers at the End of Time sequence, which includes the trilogy of novels comprising *An Alien Heat* (1972), *The Hollow Lands* (1974), and *The End of All Songs* (1976) and various supplementary items. Moorcock's immortals have the power to amuse themselves in any manner they choose, and exploit every opportunity with gusto, continually mining the past for inspiration as one fad succeeds another in infinite succession. Their lifestyles combine the ultimate extrapolations of decadence with a kind of innocent zest reminiscent of Peter Pan, who was able to engross himself in perpetual play because he had never grow up—"growing up" involving, of course, a grudging acceptance of the inevitability of mortality as well as a supposedly-healthy respect for the responsibilities of making a living and building an inheritance for the benefit of future generations. In Moorcock's world of immortals there is, of course, no future generation to come, and they need acknowledge no responsibility to anyone but themselves.

The end of the twentieth century saw a remarkable glut of sciencefictional images of immortality, including images of cyberspatial immortality such as those contained in Vernor Vinge's *True Names* (1981) and Greg Egan's *Permutation City* (1994), and images of immortality associated with Frank Tipler's revised version of Pierre Teilhard de Chardin's Omega Point, popularized in *The Physics of Immortality* (1994). Even in the presence of such extravagant imagery, however, supernatural fiction continued to produce *contes philosophiques* rooted in traditional ideas. The quest for the fountain of youth continued in such romances as Tim Powers' *On Stranger Tides* (1987). James Morrow's *Only Begotten Daughter* (1990) offered one of the most effective extrapolations of T. F. Powys' apologies in its depiction of Jesus toiling incessantly in Hell to bring the relief of oblivion to the damned, while *The Eternal Footman* (1999) offered a sophisticated allegorical analysis of death-anxiety against a background in which the terminus of thinning is represented by God's suicide.

Although it had become distinctly fugitive, the old cautionary tradition still persisted in such works as the movie *Death Becomes Her* (1992), which exploits special effects in a graphic re-emphasis of the truism that the rewards of immortality depend on the quality of the vessel, and Patrick O'Leary's *The Impossible Bird* (2002), in which humans gifted with immortality by kindly aliens fight for their right to annihilation. The tradition of literary Satanism moved on to new extremes of boldness in such revisionist fantasies of twilight-resistant immortals as Catherine Webb's *Waywalkers* (2003).

Although frustration is by no means absent from the images if immortality contained in texts such as these, it is never relentless; where modern equivalents of Tantalus appear, there is always an assumption that something might, and ultimately must, be done to relieve their plight. In the twilight of divine power, when the thinning process has juxtaposed the mythic past not with a degraded version of its former self but with a historical present rushing headlong into a future where progress is, at least, possible, Prometheus has long since won the right of appeal, if not release on bail.

Enlightenment has not dismissed all of the doubts and confusions surrounding the icon of the human immortal, or his various non-human antitheses, but it has weakened them considerably. When medical science delivers technological emortality—as it surely will, to our not-so-remote descendants—the nostalgia and poignancy in which so many twentieth-century images of immortality were steeped will be further amplified. John Death, and all his figurative brethren, will then be fully retired to the mythic past, from which they will only be able to return as intruders requiring banishment.

WHY THERE IS (ALMOST) NO SUCH THING AS SCIENCE FICTION

Some Observations on Rhetoric and Plausibility in Science and Science Fictcion

Rhetoric is the art, if not the science, of persuasion. It seems to have first been identified as a subject worthy of study and a practice worthy of careful development by the pre-Socratic philosophers who were subsequently labelled sophists. Socrates—according to his mouthpiece, Plato—affected to despise rhetoric, and his attacks upon it (delivered, of course, with considerable rhetorical flair) gave "sophistry" a bad name that it still retains. Plato's characterization of the rhetorician as a *logodaedalus* [speech-rigger] represented rhetoric as a form of cheating, deliberately making use of deceptive arguments to persuade an audience to accept a false conclusion.

Aristotle, who had been taught by Plato and subsequently made it a point of principle to disagree with him about absolutely everything, disagreed with him about the evils of rhetoric. Aristotle's *Rhetoric* insists on the essential neutrality of the art, and argues that the truth must have its own persuasive support if it is to prevail against falsehood. In a more fortunate world than ours, Aristotle's support for rhetoric as a means of supporting truth might have had better historical results, but in ours the enthusiastic adoption of rhetoric into the educational curriculum of the Roman Empire—where the art of oratory was highly esteemed—was carried forward into the Medieval curriculum of Christian education, where it became a key instrument of doctrinal defence, sternly protecting the dogmas of Christianity against skepticism. (Plato would presumably have appreciated the irony.)

We are nowadays so familiar with the relentless everyday use of rhetoric by gossips, advertisers and politicians that we are highly likely to sympathise with both Plato and Aristotle. We understand very well why it is that everybody is trying to tell us lies, and are acutely aware of the difficulties we experience in telling necessary lies of our own. We live in an era in which Logodaedalus rules as never before—and because of that, we understand how and why it is that the few honest defenders of truth we have left are among the most impassioned, desperate and beleaguered rhetoricians of our time. The truth certainly does need its own rhetorical support—and how!

We are, in fact, so very familiar with this situation that it is not easy to step back and see how ludicrous it is. How on earth does it come about that the truth is in such dire need of defence, and that its victories are so often Pyrrhic? How is it that evil rhetoricians flourish so abundantly, not merely in matters of political persuasion but in matters of empirical persuasion too, when their arguments are provably hollow and illusory? As the most cursory observation confirms, it is not merely stupid people who are gullible; clever people are, in fact, often more vulnerable to clever arguments simply because they *are* clever; great philosophers sometimes find it possible to believe absurdities that no idiot would ever entertain for a moment.

The problem can be restated, though not solved, by observing that the currency of argument is plausibility—a term that conflates and confuses two very different things: rational plausibility and psychological plausibility. The original meaning of the term, obviously, signified "worthy of applause" but one can become worthy of applause in more than one way, and the truth rarely attracts the loudest or more heartfelt plaudits. It is because there are different types of plausibility that rhetoric—the set of techniques by which plausibility is manufactured—is a double-edged sword, capable of lending support to both lies and truth. To observe this is, however, merely to supplement the terminology; the enigma remains as to why rational plausibility and psychological plausibility are so different that they seem almost incompatible.

This is not a recent problem, but it has got worse. Plato and Aristotle did not agree on many things, but they both thought that if they worked hard enough at refining psychological plausibility, then they would arrive at rational plausibility. That is in fact, the essence of their kind of "philosophy": they were armchair thinkers, who considered it unnecessary, as well as beneath their dignity, to make empirical enquiries regarding the composition and transactions of the world. Had they been right, we would not now be in a position to say, with total confidence, that virtually everything either of them believed about matters of fact was false. The progress of science has made that falsehood abundantly and incontrovertibly clear.

The scientific method can be regarded as something separate from rhetoric, even as something that cuts through rhetoric by providing *proof*, without which statements can have no justified claim of belief. On the other hand, the scientific method, and proof itself, can be considered as neither more nor less than one more persuasive strategy, one more rhetorical strategy. One thing that is certain, in either case, is that the actual historical progress of science has featured, and surely required, far more in the way of rhetorical support than mere statement and demonstration. From Galileo Galilei and Isaac Newton through Charles Darwin and Albert Einstein to James Watson and Stephen Hawking, the champions of science have had to be as innovative, versatile and adept in matters of rhetorical strategy as they were in their techniques of discovery.

Rhetorical theory divides the persuasive process into three basic components: ethos, pathos and logos (a combination that helps to explain how Alexandre Dumas named two of the three musketeers, but cannot account for Aramis). Ethos is an impression of trustworthiness cultivated by the orator or writer. Pathos involves the cultivation of a particular state of mind in the hearer or reader, by means of appeals to emotional or aesthetic sensibilities. Logos is the structure—the internal logic—of the argument itself. It is important to note that the importance of these three elements, and significant subdivisions thereof, varies considerably, not only between politics and science, but between speech and writing.

Ethos is divisible into personality and stance, the former being more relevant to oral discourse, in which an impression of warmth, friendliness, charm and status can be cultivated by tricks involving body language, eye contact and tone of voice, with the aim of making the speaker seem knowledgeable, competent and—above all—honest (as the saying has it, sincerity is the key; once you can fake that, you're made). Writing is intrinsically more impersonal, but such matters of personality as the vocabulary, tone and apparent authority of the discourse remain significant. The relative importance of stance—where the speaker or writer is "coming from," in terms of attitudes, beliefs and principles—is, however, considerably greater in written discourse than oral discourse.

Pathos is as vital to oratory as personality; the ability to influence the emotions of an audience is invaluable in face-to-face situations, the ability to create excessive moral indignation being particularly useful to polemicist "rabble-rousers." Writers have less scope in this respect, but manufacturers of popular fiction and newspaper reportage are routinely able to "push the buttons" that obtain a strong reader response to the predicaments of their characters. Aesthetic effects, on the other hand, are more suited to writing than oratory, being reliant on the cultivation of complex ornamentation.

Logos, which consists of the construction of logical or mathematical proofs and the marshalling and analysis of empirical evidence, is far more important in writing than in oratory, and writing is vitally necessary to the competent organization of complex data. Various techniques of presentation are involved in such organization, whose application has produced such formulas as the geometric theorem and the modern scientific paper. Various quasi-logical devices that are psychologically rather than rationally persuasive do, however, retain some significance in written discourse; the simplest include repetition, which exploits the crude psychological rule that what an audience is told three times it tends to take aboard, and the "Q.E.D. flourish," with which a chain of argument concludes by reconnecting its end to its beginning, as if closing a circle.

Although the logical component of an argument seems less hospitable to accidental and deliberate deception than ethos or pathos, there are several familiar strategies by which illusions may be constructed, including terminological obfuscation—"blinding with science", as the popular phrase has it—and, more significantly, the ordering of information so as to take advantage of psychological vulnerability to *post hoc ergo propter hoc* reasoning: the innate tendency of the human mind to suppose that if two events or two statements occur in sequence there is likely to be a causal connection between them. The exploitation of such strategies helps to ensure that writing can be just as deceptive as speech, and that written texts that pretend to be "scientific" can be polluted by various kinds of dishonesty.

The rhetoric of science has become standardized over the past two centuries; its basic strategy is to pretend to set aside matters of personality and emotion—so that its ethical component appears to be a purified stance of strict objectivity, and its pathetic component appears to be purely aesthetic, stressing values of neatness, economy and elegance—while maintaining strict scrupulousness in its logical component. The rhetoric of science, as embodied in the structure and presentation of the scientific paper, is supposed to be transparent and above suspicion, but it has not been without its detractors, even within the scientific community. The biologist Peter Medawar broadcast a talk on BBC radio in 1964 entitled "Is the scientific paper a fraud?" in which he suggested that the typical scientific paper of the time tended to imply an "inductive" model of discovery, whereby a general conclusion appeared to emerge spontaneously out of an array of reported facts.

Medawar argued, with supportive reference to Karl Popper's philosophy of science—that observations and experiments are invariably made with a hypothesis already in mind, and that the structure of the scientific paper tends to obscure rather than highlight this fact. Thanks to the increasing fashionability of Popperian philosophy, scientific papers have, in fact, moved in that direction since 1965, routinely specifying in advance the hypotheses that the reported observations or experiments were intended to support or refute—but that too can be artifice, which might not reflect the actual thought-processes of the scientist or the actual order in which methodological steps were taken. It seems highly probable that rational plausibility is more often the product of fudged afterthought than the Popperian rhetoric of science is prepared to allow.

Other forms of written discourse have similarly undergone a considerable evolution in the last two centuries. Storytelling has come a long way, changing its typical forms and methods dramatically as the novel and the modern short story have taken up all kinds of opportunities that oral storytelling could not provide. Poetry has survived, and continued an evolution of its own, while drama has undergone a spectacular metamorphic adaptation to the new media of film and TV, but the world of print is dominated nowadays by prose, and particularly by the kinds of prose facilitated by "reading by eye" rather than "reading by ear"—*i.e.*, by the direct translation of print into meaning, without the necessity of intermediary phonetic analysis.

It is perfectly possible to talk about "the rhetoric of fiction", even though the term has a certain oxymoronic quality. Defining rhetoric as "the art of persuasion" or "the manufacture of plausibility" implies that the goal of rhetoric is to persuade the hearer or reader that what he or she is being told is true, but there is more to truth than mere matters of fact. There are stories that are concocted deceptively, and whose effect is dependent on an insistence of their literal truth—urban legends, for instance—but even those instances are usually ironic, after the fashion of traveller's tales and fishermen's accounts of the one that got away, whose fervent claims to literal truth usually carry a tacit broad wink that accommodates them to the general category of "tall" tales. Most stories are, by contrast, "honest lies", which make no pretence at all to be *literally* true, but which nevertheless claim to reflect truthful observations about the way of the world. The fables credited to Aesop are among the most obvious as well as the earliest examples of this kind of literary endeavor—an endeavor that introduces a considerable confusion into the distinction between rational and psychological plausibility.

Plato's condemnation of rhetoricians appeared to some of his subsequent readers to extend to poets too; one notorious sequence in the *Republic* suggests that although the poet is a clever chap, fully entitled to applause after his fashion, he and all his kind ought to be driven out of civil society into the wilderness, because they nourish the well of the emotions when the rational man (and the rational society) out to be intent on achieving the *ataraxia* [calm of mind] necessary to see everything clearly. It is worth noting, however, that the *Republic* concludes with an allegorical short story: a visionary fantasy narrated by Socrates, usually known as the story of Er, which might be hesitantly advanced, at least by a logodaedalus with a point to make, as the first example of a protosciencefictional *conte philosophique*.

The *Republic* also includes the exemplary story of Gyges, which might similarly be considered ancestral to modern genre fantasy, and it is also worth noting that Plato went on, in the *Timeaus* and the *Critias*, to elaborate a fictional account of the island continent of Atlantis for exemplary purposes, thus leaving a rich legacy to clever men incapable of recognising a scholarly fantasy when they saw one (of which the world has never had any shortage). He was sufficiently interested in literary methodology to draw the key distinction between the *mimetic* (showing) and *diegetic* (telling) modes of discourse that has now become the foundation stone of practical and theoretical discussion of narrative technique.

Although Aristotle never stooped so low as to write a short story or invent an imaginary civilization, he did carry out a fairly extensive analysis of literary methodology in his *Poetics*, which examined the basic structure and customary narrative moves of Greek drama. Unfortunately, Aristotle's determined independence prevented him from integrating Plato's insights into his own account, and also resulted in his producing the ludicrous theory of catharsis to counter the argument for expulsion that Plato had put forward in the *Republic*. This unnecessary squabble helped to ensure that narrative theory made little or no progress for the next two thousand years, but it has gained considerable ground in recent years, especially in connection with analyses of the extent to which rhetoric and literary potential are intrinsically embedded in language.

The inherent logos built into the grammatical structure of language is pliable and supplementable in several ways; the multiplicity of choices inherent in the careful selection of words and their organization into comprehensible sentences is the space in which rhetoric operates, and which gives rise to literary endeavor. Flexible and expandable language is inherently prone to such celebrations of its own accidental qualities as wordplay and rhyme, which combine with such phenomena as wit and irony to encourage improvisation, innovation and invention. While rhetorical strategies that rely heavily on the component of logos tend to formulate special languages supposedly purged of such elements, the tendency of strategies that rely more heavily on ethos and pathos is to exaggerate them. The situation is, however, complicated by such factors as the double-edged nature of humor, which may be an asset in developing a personality but implies an unreliability of stance. Wit—especially when it plays with paradoxes—deliberately confuses meaning, thus creating a rhetorical uncertainty useful in satire, whose mockery of logos may be just as intense as its mockery of ethos and pathos.

The rhetoric of modern fiction appears to stand in stark contrast to the rhetoric of modern science in respect of its typical use of ethos and pathos, not merely in the extent of the emphasis placed on those rhetorical components but also in its nature. Where the rhetoric of science does makes use of ethos and pathos it tends to do so in a supposedly-impersonal fashion, whereas literary rhetoric is often intensely personal. Sophisticated *littérateurs* tend to strive for "originality" in the ethical and pathetic components of their work, routinely aiming to adopt distinct personalities and stances, and developing specific emotional and aesthetic effects. The logical component of literary work is not entirely immune to this kind of quest for originality, although works that deliberately set out to contrive "nonsense"—there is an entire school of such writing in England, pioneered by Edward Lear, Lewis Carroll, and W. S. Gilbert—are rare, and not entirely honest in their pose. In respect of its use of logos, however, most *littérateurs* are content to accept—at least in a vague and tacit sense—that fiction ought to be fundamentally "naturalistic" or "realistic" even when it dabbles in fantastic invention, accepting "common sense", if not science, as a "generative grammar" of secondary creation, defining *a priori* how characters may interact with their environment and one another.

Given this methodical overlap, it is not surprising that the evolution of fiction has been highly responsive in several ways to the parallel evolution of science, especially in the fields of psychology and forensic science, Nor is it surprising that scientific discourse has frequently found it possible and desirable of make use of exemplary fictions, even witty ones such as Maxwell's demon and Schrödinger's cat. Indeed, if one were to take a step back, it might seem to that ever-useful philosophical/literary device the Objective Observer that what is really puzzling is the near-non-existence of "science fiction".

The idea that "science fiction"—under that or some other label—is something that ought to exist has occurred spontaneously to numerous people in the last two centuries, and some have even gone so for as to identify examples of it or to found magazines that might contain it, but it would require a sophist of genius actually to convince anyone that any of the examples really qualify, or that any of the magazines, books and TV shows carrying the label actually deserve that description. As has been often pointed out, most labelled "science fiction" not only contains no science, but manifests a phobic antipathy towards science so intense that the tiny minority of works supportive of scientific endeavor and achievement tend to be regretful Jeremiads complaining about their own reader-unfriendliness.

Advocates of "hard" science fiction continue to claim that there is a core or fringe of authentic science fiction, which does adhere strictly to principles of rational plausibility and does celebrate the triumphs of the scientific method. This pretence is not necessarily undermined by the literary convenience of employing such facilitating devices as time travel, superluminal space travel and galactic empires, given that those can be "bracketed" and set aside from the serious speculative elements of the text. The undeniable truth is that such facilitating devices have a strong tendency to resist such bracketing, and to become central elements of the story, even in supposedly hard sf, but that is hardly a necessary condition of their existence. In historical terms, the extent to which hard sf has relied so heavily on the myth of the Space Age—a myth that no longer has the slightest claim to rational plausibility—to structure its future histories has devastated the argument that it ever had any convincing claim to authenticity, but that too might have been otherwise. The real problem with science fiction does not arise from the imaginative seductiveness of its facilitating devices or any accident of history; it arises from the fundamental relationship between rational and psychological plausibility, and the manner in which they have drawn further and further apart over the last two centuries, resulting in a situation in which they are implicitly—and perhaps irrevocably—antipathetic to one another.

The problem is, to some extent, age-old. Narrative plausibility is routinely associated with events that defy the calculus of probability, sometimes to the extent of being frankly but unrepentantly impossible. As Terry Pratchett is fond of observing, whenever a character in a story says "It's a million-to-one chance, but it might just work", the actual probability of it working is one, because what determines whether or not happens in a story is the requirement of bringing a plot to a satisfactory conclusion. However much it may be disguised, that is always a *deus ex machina*—a blatant disruption of the mathematical calculus of probability and material flow of causality. (Literary manifestos like the one allegedly cooked up for the British magazine *New Worlds*, which pretended to reject the fundamental "generosity" of the literary universe, are blatantly preposterous; writers can be as miserly as they please, but they cannot be ungodlike.) The existence, since time immemorial, of an extremely rich and various store of fantastic stories not only demonstrates that entities and events impossible or highly unlikely in the world of experience can be forcefully endowed with literary plausibility, but also illustrates the remarkable fact that such narrative devices often seem far more psychological plausible than everyday events: an awareness summarized in the dictum that "truth is stranger than fiction." Age-old as it is, though, this situation is not unchanging, and the simple fact is that what passes for truth nowadays is much stranger than it used to be, and is, in consequence, so much stranger than fiction that it beggars belief.

The history of actual beliefs testifies very clearly to the power of psychological plausibility, and the history of science can easily be seen as a series of hard-fought battles to overthrow idols whose shabby feet of clay were stoutly and comfortably booted by psychological plausibility. When Francis Bacon offered his stirring account of the ideological origins of such idols he was under the impression that, once they had been smashed, the simple truth would be plain to see, but he was wrong; the truth turned out to be amazingly complex and anything but plain. As science progressed from the seventeenth century to the twentieth, the progress of its understanding took it further and further into realms of psychological implausibility, whose capacity to challenge, defy and defeat "common sense" became starkly manifest with the advent of modern theoretical physics. However powerful the representations of such twentieth-century theses as relativity and quantum mechanics might be in mathematical and predictive terms, they are certainly not psychologically plausible—and yet, they are the foundation-stones of authentic knowledge, the bases of our understanding of the composition and transactions of matter, space and time.

There is a challenging imaginative gulf between modern science and the human mind's faculty of comprehension, the crossing of which many people are afraid even to attempt. Science fiction ought, in theory, to offer examples of bold attempts to cross it anyway; in fact, fiction bearing that label is—almost without exception—a monument to an entirely understandable but not entirely forgivable intellectual and imaginative cowardice. Whether the fault is in ourselves or in our stars is, however, a matter of perspective. If we were self-made, or the whimsical fancies of a ludicrously anthropomorphic God, then we would probably have to plead guilty; given that we were made by natural selection, however, we can legitimately plead insanity.

The principal reason for this increasingly-awkward dissonance between rational and psychological plausibility is the adaptation of the human sensorium to the necessities and vicissitudes of our immediate environment. The ingenious extension of that sensorium by such optical instruments as microscopes and telescopes and such measuring-devices as barometers, voltmeters and Geiger counters, has been a great boon to the refinement of rational plausibility, but the further such instruments take us into the realms of the ordinarily invisible and the ordinarily intangible, the more inadequate the assumptions that natural selection built into our senses become, and the less capable our powers of imagination are to "visualize" what we know is actually there. The universe of modern science, in terms of its vastness, its age and its fine structure, is an intellectual construct whose effect on the human mind is so profoundly unaccountable that the English language routinely refers to it by means of derivatives of the frankly nonsensical verb "to boggle".

The difficulties of imagining the world outside ourselves on the basis of the immediate objects of our perception pale into insignificance, however, when the "mind's eye" tries to look back on itself, following the introspective philosophical method of René Descartes. There are no objects of perception inside the mind except for thoughts, feelings and sensation, whose role as instruments of perception catches them in an awkward trap when they are perceived in their turn. The Cartesian mind—a ghostly entity of mental substance that sits in the pineal body, pulling the levers that control the body-machine—is easily revealed by rigorous Socratic criticism to be a sham, but it really is how we appear to ourselves when we attempt to examine ourselves from within. Cartesian dualism is not only seductively but quintessentially plausible; not only is it easy for us to "picture" ours minds as ghosts in fleshy machines, but it is difficult in the extreme to picture ourselves in any other way. This way of imagining the mind has numerous corollaries blessed with elementary psychological plausibility.

These corollaries include the notion that the ghost-mind might be able to exist—and seem not much different to itself—outside the body or after the body's death, and the notion that if another ghost-mind were to invade and take possession the body it might displace or enslave its native inhabitant. Because the ghost-mind can create mental pictures and thoughts formulated in words, it seems plausible that the pictures might be "seen" by other ghost-minds, or the verbalized thoughts overheard by mental eavesdroppers—and because the ghost-mind can pull the levers of the body machine, it seems plausible that it might extend its reach to more distant levers.

Moreover, because the ghost-mind is aware of the limitations of its own self-control, the authority of reason being compromised and undermined by the impulses and urges produced by appetites and emotions, it seems plausible that the self is a battleground between opposed forces—which might just as well be categorized as guardian angels and tempting demons as the Freudian *superego* and *id*—on which all kinds of alien forces might intrude, as magic spells ranging from curses to love potions.

Then again, because the ghost-mind is gifted with memory, it seems to be a traveler in time, capable by mental effort of bringing back yesterday or projecting itself into tomorrow—wishing all the while that it might have done something other than it did, or that events yet to come will actually work out as planned rather than suffering any of the myriad possible disasters conjured up by fear.

All these corollaries are easily recognisable, not merely as the building-blocks of mythical and magical fantasy, but also as the building-blocks of generic science fiction. They are not mere "mistakes" based in miscalculations of rational plausibility but something far more fundamental and corrosive. They really do represent an *antagonism* between psychological and rational plausibility, an active enmity rather than a failure born of mental indolence. If those of us who claim to be science fiction writers and readers are, almost without exception, thundering hypocrites, it is because of the way we are made rather than any superficial or easily-remediable treason.

The exterior universe revealed by scientific analysis is difficult to grasp, but there is much in it that can be convincingly described, even if it remains outside the scope of visualization, by the language of mathematics. The rational arguments that reveal the idolatrous nature of the Cartesian ghost-self, on the other hand, can put no other image in its place; the vacuum they leave is unfillable by describable possibilities, however implausible. There is not now and never will be an authentic science of psychology, no matter what future progress we might make in neurophysiology, because we have no language capable of representing thought and emotion but literary language, which cannot shake off the handicap of psychological plausibility.

By virtue of this void of potential understanding, the Cartesian attempt at rational self-confrontation remains unresolved, uneasy and fundamentally anxious. This anxiety is clearly reflected in all the constructive literary images built upon Cartesian plausibility: not merely the intrinsically monstrous notions of demonic possession and temptation, curses and lycanthropy, but those which might otherwise seem quite hopeful and exciting, such as life-after-death and out-of-body experiences, telepathy and psychokinesis, time travel and prophecy. The literature of the psychologically plausible is insistent and prolific, but by no means over-blessed with self-confidence. That is why so much fantastic fiction, and so much so-called science fiction, is horror fiction.

Literary plausibility is not solely a matter of exploiting Cartesian and other delusions. The innate moral order of worlds within texts creates a powerful desire in readers to see "poetic justice" done, and this routinely lends "poetic license" to improbable, impossible and even implausible events and actions, whenever they are invoked in good causes. The intrinsic generosity of worlds within texts extends further than merely providing resources for heroic characters to employ; it also the ability to perform extraordinary feats under extreme duress, thus creating a palpable narrative attraction towards the superheroic. Similar pressures assist in the conversion of literary love into an irresistible romantic force, readily likened to the pull of gravity, and in the detachment of literary luck from any vestige of restraint by the principles of probability.

Science fiction, if it really existed, would be bound to resist these forces, and to establish a Newtonian equal-and-opposite reaction, but generic science fiction, even of the hardest variety, never has. Hard sf has never shown the least sign of ungenerosity to its heroes, or the least reluctance to play fast and loose with their luck. The quasi-gravitational attraction of love has often been given slightly shorter shrift, but not by virtue of conscientious adherence to rational standards of plausibility.

It is worth noting that the extreme modern dissonance between rational and psychological plausibility is also reflected, to varying degrees, in the various fields of "non-fiction," ranging from reportage and scholarly fantasy through pseudoscience, history and conduct books to the popularization of science and formal scientific publication. Ironically, it is easier to cultivate psychological plausibility in "non-fiction" than in fiction, because the assertion that a statement is true—especially if it is insistently repeated—is itself one of the principal rhetorical devices used in the manufacture of psychological plausibility. Truth *is* stranger than fiction, but even conscientious fiction is stranger than the kinds of fake truth that deliberately set out to substitute psychological plausibility for rational plausibility. Because a serious work of fiction is an honest lie, devoid of mere delusion, the further-reaching honesty of the best fictional narratives easily outstrips the delusions of most popular non-fictional narratives. In a contest of cowardice, the true believers will always beat the science fiction fans hands down. That may be a small crumb of comfort, but it not without nutritional value.

Plato would presumably have appreciated the irony, and might even have applauded as we wander away into the wilderness.

PERFECTIBILITY AND THE NOVEL OF THE FUTURE

In his *Préface* to *Le Roman de l'avenir* (1834; tr. as *The Novel of the Future*), Félix Bodin issues a prospectus for a new genre called *le roman futuriste*, which begins by distinguishing between two fundamental patterns of anticipation: the *péjoriste* thesis and the *mélioriste* thesis. In the former case, anticipators "*plaçait l'âge d'or au berceau de l'humanité, et l'âge de fer à son lit de mort*" [placed the Golden Age in the cradle of humankind, and the Iron Age on its deathbed]; in the latter, "*l'avenir s'est offert aux imaginations tout resplendissant de lumière*" [the future is offered to the imagination entirely resplendent with light] (p. 16) Anticipators of the first sort, Bodin observes, tend to produce *apocalypses* when they adopt literary methods; anticipators of the second kind generate *utopies*.

Bodin admits that he has raced his book into print in the hope of claiming the honor of being the originator of the idea of writing a *roman de l'avenir*—a term that slyly conflates the idea of a novel set in the future with that of a novel of a sort that will be written in the future as a matter of course. In one of several appendices to the text of his own fragmentary sample of a *roman de l'avenir* he lists previous attempts to envisage the future in literary terms, but dismisses all the examples he cites as apocalypses or utopias: expressions of hope and/or fear rather than sober attempts to imagine the future as it might actually be and to describe the lives of people living in the future in the fashion of a novel, establishing them as interacting characters with various personal ambitions and problems.

It is possible that Bodin was being a trifle disingenuous in his summary of precedents. He gives Charles Nodier credit for mentioning to him the existence of one of those earlier works—Jean-Baptiste Cousin de Grainville's *Le Dernier homme* (1805; tr. as The Last Man)—and adds a fulsome note to the effect that "*si le Roman de l'avenir eût dû être fait par tour autre de moi, c'eût été certaine-*

ment à lui de faire" [if the novel of the future had been invented by anyone other than me, it would certainly have been him] (p. 398) but he does not mention the fact that Nodier had already published a two-part futuristic narrative of his own in the previous year in the *Revue de Paris*, comprising "Hurlubleu grand Manifafa d'Hurlubière ou la perfectibilité" and "Léviathan le long Archikan des Patagons de l'île savante ou la perfectibilité" (combined in translation as "Perfectibility" in *The Germans on Venus and Other French Scientific Romances*, ed. Brian Stableford). Although Bodin must have had time to become aware of Nodier's publications before his book went to press, he had probably written the non-fictional appendices some time before writing the exemplary fragment, and could not be bothered to update them when he hurriedly put the book together.

Nodier's two-part *nouvelle* is not a *roman*, but nor does it fit neatly into either of the categories to which Bodin had attempted to relegate previous futuristic fictions; it is, in fact, a parodic anti-utopia, which mocks the *méliorist*e pattern of anticipation mercilessly, while refusing to endorse the *péjoriste* position or even adopt a neutral one. In this respect, it is also bears an interesting relationship to Bodin's sample of a *roman de l'avenir*, which tries hard to adopt an enthusiastically *méliorist*e outlook but cannot quite manage the feat, although it sternly refuses to retreat to a *péjoriste* position, or even a neutral one.

The lack of neutrality in both narratives is conscious rather than merely accidental; Nodier and Bodin both take the trouble, in somewhat different ways, to pillory the procedural philosophy that the French government established in the wake of the July Revolution of 1830—which had placed Louis-Philippe on the throne—was actually employing in steering the nation forwards into the future: the quest for the *juste milieu*, which attempted to negotiate a compromise between the forces of reaction and reform by splitting the difference between them in as exact a manner as possible. Although they were in complete disagreement as to the direction in which the world ought to be going, Nodier and Bodin were equally convinced that the *juste milieu* was a road to nowhere, to be avoided if possible.

The futuristic speculations of Nodier and Bodin were similarly driven by an awareness that the path of progress—the idea of progress being the foundation-stone of *méliorist*e faith—had gone badly awry in France, but they adopted very different attitudes in consequence of that awareness. Nodier, who was still the doyen of the French Romantic Movement in 1833, took it as proof that the idea of progress had always been a silly one, and that the late-eighteenth-century philosophers of progress, led by Anne-Robert Turgot and the Marquis de Condorcet, had been a bunch of starry-eyed fools. Bodin, who had written a Romantic novel of his own in the 1820s but had made his name as a popular historian and political journalist before being elected as a *député* to serve in the post-July-Revolution government, took it as proof of the unfortunate strength of the various ideologies opposed to a noble and sacred cause whose eventual triumph was a consummation devoutly to be wished.

* * * * * * *

The protagonist of Nodier's *nouvelle* is Berniquet, a present-day philosopher of progress who entertains Hurlubleu, a tyrant ruling an Ottoman-style empire ten thousand years in the future, with the tale of how he set off on a quest with others of his ilk to discover the perfect man, who would be able, willing and delighted to live in the perfect world that technological and social progress is destined to forge.

Berniquet's journey is a terrible one, which costs the lives of all his companions; some fall by the wayside when their first vehicle, a high-powered steamboat, runs out of control and blows up; others die when their second, a vast and heavily-armed airship, is caught up in atmospheric turbulence and crashes. Both vehicles are symbolic, the former of the 1789 Revolution and the second of the Empire. After surviving the fall from the airship, poor Berniquet ends up buried neck-deep in a rut in the middle of the road: the dreaded *juste milieu*, from which the well-meaning philosophers of the utopian *île des Patagons* are unable to extract him, although the local children easily improvise a means of so doing.

Hailed as a hero by the Patagons, whose lives have been completely freed from the inconvenient demands of nature by science—they are fed and maintained in good health by advanced biotechnologies—Berniquet unfortunately falls victim to a medical error that puts him to sleep for ten thousand years. After waking up again, he conceives a nostalgic desire to return to Paris. His obliging hosts dispatch him to Europe by means of an electrically-powered flying-machine even more powerful and even more dangerous than his earlier means of travel, and he crash-lands in the court of the despotic Grand Manifafa of the empire whose capital has long replaced Paris. There he is recruited to the *collège des mataquins* [clown college] to serve as Hurlubleu's *grand loustic* [chief jester]—his new master finds his story quaintly amusing, and requests its recitation as a reliable means of lulling himself to sleep—until he incurs the potentate's wrath by being caught *in flagrante delicto* with a favorite concubine. In consequence of this heinous crime, Berniquet is exiled to the depths of a vast excavation, in order that he might continue his quest for the perfect man in the center of the Earth—where, it is rumored, a secret formula, by means of which the great sage Zérétochthro-Shah (Zoroaster) once made such a perfect man, was lost in the wake of a cataclysmic earthquake.

The central character of Bodin's fragmentary *roman de l'avenir*, Philirène, is also a philosopher of progress, but one who is in the much more fortunate position of having been elected president of the world-governing *congrès universel* in the late twentieth century. While he is addressing a meeting of that congrès held in Centropolis, the capital of the Central American republic of Benthamia, however, Philirène's fiancée Mirzala is kidnapped from her home in the rebuilt city of Carthage by agents of his great rival, Philomaque. Philomaque is about to make a bid for world conquest under the pseudonym of Aëtos, exploiting the great prestige he enjoys as a military leader among the relatively barbaric tribes of the Far East, and he wants Mirzala for his queen, although he has already married and deserted her adoptive sister Politée.

Philirène has to raise an army to combat Philomaque's planned invasion, aided by Politée, who is the heir to a heroic dynasty of technologists and capitalists—a crucial alliance that has secured the tremendous social and technological progress made in the previous century and a half. Unfortunately, the external threat posed to the *congrès universel* by Aëtos is supplemented by an internal threat posed by its dark counterpart: the subversive *association antiprosaïque universelle* or *association poétique*, which holds its own assemblies in subterranean caves. This loose alliance of dispossessed aristocrats, unreformed Churchmen and redundant military men is a parody of the opposition that Bodin faced on a daily basis in the chamber, in his capacity as a radical *député*. Bodin's narrative voice regretfully admits, however, that it also includes a great many artists and writers of a Romantic stripe, and the same narrative voice continually observes that his potential readers—especially his female readers—might well have more sympathy for that opposition than for the defenders of progress, and will probably find Philomaque considerably more attractive, as a fictitious hero, than Philirène.

Bodin's fragment comes to an end long before the climactic confrontation between Philirène and Philomaque can take place, although it does take the trouble to sharpen their contest by revealing that they are half-brothers, and drops enough hints for the reader to deduce that the battlefield on which they will meet will embrace the geographical location of Armageddon. The narrative voice offers no clear indication as to who will win that contest, but has established while introducing the story that the magnetically-induced visions permitting the story to be reconstituted in 1834 cannot recover any information at all about the twenty-first century—a suggestion that does not bode well for any readers hoping that Philirène and his *mélioriste* cause might triumph and that his victory will ensure that the long march towards *perfectibilité* can continue unchecked.

* * * * * * *

Because he had been born in 1795, Félix Bodin had not actually lived through the 1789 Revolution and the consequent Terror, as Charles Nodier—born in 1780—had. Nor had Bodin been persecuted on account of his political satires—many of which took the form of humorous *complaintes*—as Nodier had been for penning a few satirical verses about Napoléon in 1803. Such differences in experience cannot account for the differences in their attitude to the possibility of future progress, but they do help to explain the contrast between Nodier's stubbornly cantankerous certainty that progress is a myth and Bodin's querulously reluctant suspicion that, even if progress is possible, its cause might well be betrayed, not merely by the lurking forces of Reaction but the capricious seductions of Romance.

Like such pre-Revolutionary literary popularizers of the idea of progress as Louis-Sébastien Mercier, whose account of *L'an deux mille quatre cent quarante* (1776; tr. as *Memoirs of the Year Two Thousand Five Hundred*) is one of the utopian models from which he tries so conscientiously to distance his own *roman*, Bodin convinced himself that the principal means of social improvement lay in the elaboration of technology, carefully fostered by economic reform. He had great hopes for the steam engine and even greater ones for the future of aerial transport, once a method of steering airships could be devised. More rapid communications and more effective means of production, in his opinion, were bound to bring people closer together and ameliorate the economic causes of conflict between them—but he could not suppress a lurking suspicion that economic causes were not the only, or even the most important, sources of human conflict. While economic wellbeing might be a necessary condition of social improvement, Bodin doubted that it was a sufficient one.

Nodier, by contrast, regarded both steam engines and airships as hazardous contraptions more likely to prove destructive than constructive. This suspicion cannot be dismissed as ridiculous. When Richard Trevithick first developed the "Cornish Engine" that worked at much higher pressures than James Watt's original contraption—during the 1790s, while Nodier was in his teens—early models, including Trevithick's first steam locomotive, did indeed have a tendency to explode. The conquest of the air pioneered by the Montgolfier brothers in 1783 also demonstrated its hazards quickly enough, especially when highly flammable hydrogen was used as an agent of buoyancy. In Nodier's view, moreover, rapid communications and effective means of production were just as likely to reduce the quality of human life as to improve it, even if they did succeed in reducing conflict, because of the danger that they would gradually remake humans in the image of the machines on which they depended. Although he did not suppose that the whole world would ever be remade in the image of the *île des Patagons*, he did assume that the cost of avoiding that fate would be the persistence of crass dictatorships and all their attendant injustices.

Bodin's depiction of bird-like flying-machines in *Le roman de l'avenir* is extravagantly enthusiastic, but his airships, like Nodier's, are heavily armed, and the aerial battle he describes between Philirène's ship and a pirate vessel—by far the most dramatic incident in his sample text—costs several lives. Again, Bodin's narrative voice is uncommonly honest in admitting that it is the *romance* of flight that is attractive, not only to would-be readers and writers of *romans futuristes* but to the characters within them, and there is an obvious incongruity between that addiction to romance and the hypothetical Platonic ataraxia of a perfected world. Although Bodin did make the effort to imagine a world of routine commercial air travel, which does not contrast completely with the matter-of-fact world of contemporary air tourism, his own stubborn anti-prosaic tendencies would not allow him to leave it untroubled by pirates, or even to regret the fact. As a would-be *mélioriste*, he was his own worst enemy—considerably worse, at any rate, than Nodier, whose *loustic* tendencies blunted the force of his own attempts to shoot down the buoyant airship of progress. (Nodier's successor as the doyen of French Romanticism, Victor Hugo, was prepared to take a very different view in "Plein ciel", the element of the *Légende des siècles* that celebrates the future conquest of the air as the ultimate achievement of the Romantic imagination.)

Interestingly, the most striking difference between Nodier's anticipations of technology and Bodin's is not in their anticipations of the future development of steam-powered industry and transport but in their starkly contrasted depictions of the artificiality of everyday life. When Philirène spends a brief sojourn in the Loire valley, after his skirmish with the pirates, he describes a rural idyll that might almost be Rousseauesque were it not for the fact that the valley now has a railway line and much of the river traffic consists of steamboats. The fact that Mesmeric "magnetism" has become the chief form of domestic medicine further enhances the general atmosphere of rustic simplicity. Evidently, Bodin would have been just as antipathetic as Nodier to the latter's depiction of the life of the everyday life of the Patagons, whose island utopia has been cleansed of all other living organisms and whose food is manufactured—albeit with consummate culinary artistry—in chemical factories from raw materials. It is not entirely obvious, however, why Nodier finds this prospect so intrinsically appalling, given that it reproduces the same gustatory and nutritional effects as animal flesh, without the need for callous butchery. On the other hand, it is all too obvious that Bodin's affection for conventional rural productivity stems from the same romantic wellspring as his infatuation with flying machines, providing further tacit support for his anxiety that readers and voters alike will never be able to forsake their anti-prosaic tendencies sufficiently to embrace reason and progress wholeheartedly.

There is a sense in which Bodin, like Berniquet, set off in search of the perfect man when he sat down to write his *roman futuriste*—and there is a sense in which, like poor Berniquet, he got lost *en route*. It is not only Bodin's narrative voice but Philirène himself who wonders whether he really can pass for perfect, even in a dim light. Is his calm, reasonable and reliable love for Mirzala really superior to the violent, irrational and unreliable passion of a Philomaque? He cannot, in all honesty say so—and neither can his loyal friend Politée, when he consults her on the matter. If perfection really does involve drying up the well of the passions—as Plato assumed when he decided that Romantics would have to be expelled from his ideal Republic—is the prize really worth the cost? Bodin and Philirène, although by no means as certain in their own minds as Nodier and Hurlubleu, are desperately anxious that it might not be—and that desperation, in itself might be enough to demonstrate the hopelessness of their quest.

* * * * * * *

The explicit and tacit arguments raised by Nodier and Bodin continued to run through all the *romans futuristes* produced after

1834, and continue to do so today. The scathing sarcasm that Nodier employed as a weapon against the *mélioristes* was further refined by Émile Souvestre in *Le Monde tel qu'il sera* (1846; tr. as *The World as It Shall Be*), and further darkened with tragedy by—of all people—Jules Verne in *Paris au vingtième siècle* (written 1863; pub. 1894; tr. as *Paris in the Twentieth Century*). Verne's publisher, P.-J. Hetzel, who was very much a *mélioriste* cast in Bodin's mold, refused to publish the latter item and contrived to bury it for more than a century, but he could not stem the dystopian tide; nor could he prevent Verne from maintaining Bodinesque anxieties throughout his own career, even though Professor Lidenbrock triumphantly outdid Berniquet in returning from the center of the Earth in *Voyage au centre de la terre* (1864; tr. as *Journey to the Centre of the Earth*).

It is hardly surprising, given the compromises to which Bodin was forced, that very few of the minority of subsequent literary images of the future that have pledged allegiance to the *mélioriste* perspective have ever lent any but modest and hesitant support to the cause of *perfectibilité*, while very many of them have accepted the Romantic opinion that passion is indispensable to human wellbeing. Although *mélioristes* have continued to disagree with *péjoristes* on the question of whether the advancement of technology, and economic reforms that foster it, are inimical to that wellbeing, their apologetic cases are routinely haunted by anxiety. As *romans de l'avenir* have gradually displaced Merciereseque utopias, they have brought all the weighty baggage of Bodin's uncomfortable fragment with them.

There is no shortage of modern Nodiers, avid to scoff and satirize and proclaim that only fools believe in progress; nor is there any shortage of modern Bodins, eager to suggest that progress has much to be said for it but conspicuously hesitant by virtue of recognizing their own ideological frailties and weak-kneed Romantic proclivities. Nor, it must be said, has any attempt to apply the philosophy of the *juste milieu* seemed likely to unstick us from that morass of confusion.

There is little in either of the two works under consideration here that might be deemed "prophetic" in the vulgar sense of anticipating actual future developments. Bodin's flying machines bear hardly any resemblance to twentieth-century flying machines and Nodier's Patagonian food-technology bears little resemblance to twentieth-century food technology, but such prosaic quibbles are of no real relevance to either exercise. In their fundamental contentions, however—remarkably enough, given their contrasted opinions—both writers were absolutely right. The quest for the perfect man has, thus far, failed dismally, and without him, the prospect of a perfect world seems quite ridiculous; while we remain fallible, the social contract can only pander to our fallibilities. On the other hand, it is manifestly obvious that the world has made considerable progress since 1834, and that much of that social progress has been due to technological progress and its economic facilitation. To the extent that social ills have been magnified, so have social cures—and the fact that modern literary endeavors often refuse to acknowledge or applaud these facts merely serves to confirm Bodin's observation that the vast majority of *littérateurs*, whether they are trying to flatter their audience or only themselves, owe an entirely natural allegiance to anti-prosaicism, and hence to the enemies of progress.

Bodin comments in his preface that *melioriste* views seem to have replaced *pejoriste* ones, at least in large measure, and evidently regards this as a sort of progress in itself—which it is. *Péjorisme*, which locates the Golden Age in the past and views the dynamics of social change in terms of deterioration, is intrinsically linked to the kinds of mythical past acknowledged by oral cultures, which have no history and therefore imagine the past as a magical era, relative to which the unmagical present is bound to seem a trifle jejune. *Méliorisme*, by contrast, is a product of historical perspective and the awareness of a measurable improvement of technical and social means that can be tracked across time by means of written records and archaeological excavations. If writing and scientific enquiry represent progress, therefore—and it is hard to deny that they do—then the idea of progress is indeed a self-evident symptom of progress.

The notion that future progress can be estimated simply by extrapolating the curve calculated from the measurement of past progress, all the way to "perfection", is clearly false, however, even if the notion of its likely extrapolation to some degree is not quite as silly as Nodier thinks it is. Because that curve was the product of human effort rather than any kind of external destiny, it can only be extrapolated as far as human effort is willing to take it—and that, as Bodin quickly realized when he began to explore the notion by the only technical means at his disposal, is probably not very far. As Bodin wisely observed, and dramatized as best he could, this is not so much because the world is too abundantly supplied with ambitious Philomaques and power-crazed Hurlubleus (although it is), or even with sarcastic Nodiers (although it is), but rather because its Philirènes are sane enough and conscientious enough to doubt the grandeur of their own merits, and to avoid going to ridiculous extremes.

IN SEARCH OF A NEW GENRE

Attempts to Categorize and Promote "Scientific" Fiction in France, 1902-1928

The problems associated with attempts to identify and label a new genre of fiction that seemed to numerous writers and critics in Britain and the U.S.A. to be nascent in the final decades of the nineteenth-century are well-known to modern exponents of "science fiction studies". H. G. Wells, who was universally considered to be responsible for many of the key exemplars of the new genre, disliked the popular designation "scientific romance", considering that what he was actually doing was producing "novels of ideas" (as contrasted with "novels of character"), although he was eventually forced to capitulate and accept the label. In the U.S.A., Edgar Fawcett's advocacy of calculatedly-oxymoronic "realistic romances" had no result, and Hugo Gernback's far more successful promotion of "scientifiction" was abandoned and replaced when he lost market control of that label. Many of the practitioners of work subsequently marketed under the "science fiction" label came to dislike it just as much as Wells disliked "scientific romance" but various campaigns to substitute "speculative fiction" came to nothing. We are still living with the accumulated legacy of a century of terminological dissatisfaction, in which the satanic horrors of "sci-fi" are proving difficult to exorcize.

In the French language, the problem proved just as awkward, for much the same reasons, although it is not easy for an English historian to describe the problems because of the additional difficulties that arise in translation. The term *roman scientifique*—that being the first label for the nascent genre to be suggested in an arena that might have led to the term being more generally adopted—could, in principle be translated in three different ways, as "scientific novel", "scientific romance" or "scientific fiction", by virtue of the flexibility of the French noun *roman*. In order to convey the awkwardness of the French debate in an intelligible fashion, it is therefore necessary to vary the translation of the phrase *roman scientifique* slightly, according to its context.

It is also necessary to beware of pitfalls inherent in the translation of other French terms that inevitably got dragged into the quest for new labels, most notably *fantastique* and *merveilleux*. Although these terms can be transcribed directly into English as "fantastic" and "marvelous", the French terms do not have identical ranges of meaning, the former being primarily applicable to a tradition of psychological horror fiction whose key exemplars were translations of Edgar Allan Poe and E. T. A. Hoffmann and the latter to a more venerable tradition whose key exemplars included Antoine Galland's version of *Les Mille et une nuits* and *contes des fées* [literary "fairy tales", as distinct from the *contes populaires* of folklore]. (The further complications introduced into the meanings of the latter terms by the perverted operational definitions forced upon them by Tzvetan Todorov are mercifully irrelevant to the considerations of the present essay.)

* * * * * * *

French writers and critics first became conscious that it was possible to discern a genre of "scientific fiction" at much the same time that British writers and critics became conscious that it was possible, and perhaps desirable, to designate a genre of "scientific romance", and for exactly the same reason: the crucial series of exemplars provided between 1895 and 1901 by H. G. Wells, which were rapidly translated into French by Henry Davray. One of the first French writers to take notice of this new literary category and its potential significance was Alfred Jarry, who wrote a "Commentaire pour servir à la construction pratique de la machine à explorer le temps" [Observations to assist in the practical construction of a time machine] for the *Mercure de France* in 1899 and produced a novel of his own in that vein in *Le Surmâle* (1902; tr. as *The Supermale*). Not long after the publication of the latter item, Jarry wrote a brief essay for *La Plume*, entitled "De quelques romans scientifiques" [On Some Scientific Novels], which appeared in the October 1st and 15th issues of that periodical.

So far as I know, Jarry's is the first essay on the Wellsian protogenre to have appeared in French—although there had, of course, been numerous previous essays on the subgenre of Vernian *voyages extraordinaires*. The latter subgenre was, however, generally seen as a species of adventure story in which elements of scientific speculation were by no means necessary and, if present, were essentially peripheral. Verne flatly rejected the notion that there was any literary kinship between himself and Wells—whose work he considered excessively fanciful—and most French critics and writers agreed with him. They recognized that, in moving ostensibly plausible hypotheses to center-stage, and using narrative as a means of extrapolating them, Wells was using fiction in a fashion that echoed, or perhaps even simulated, the scientific method, rather than drafting scientific and technological apparatus to the imaginative reinforcement of adventure stories, as Verne and his many imitators were sometimes wont to do.

The difficulties in characterizing the new genre's relationship to previous forms of fiction, in terms of kinship and contrast, are evident in the first two paragraphs of Jarry's essay. While the first states flatly that "the scientific novel descends, in a direct line, from the *Mille et une nuits*, many of the tales in which are alchemical, and the *Cabinet des fées*", the second offers a very different, and perhaps contradictory, viewpoint: "The novel of manners studies what happens *when* certain elements are brought together. The scientific novel—which could be just as accurately described as the hypothetical novel—images what would happen *if* certain elements were brought together. That is why, in the same way that certain hypotheses will be realized one day, some of these novels will be found to be, at the time when they were written, futuristic novels."

The tension between these two views is sustained through the remainder of the essay. The first example Jarry offers of a "scientific novel" is Cyrano de Bergerac's *Histoire des états et empires de la Lune et du Soleil* (1657-9; tr. as *Other Worlds*), which he congratulates for its anticipation of "montgolfiers" [balloons] and for its "neo-Darwinian" suggestion that "birds are more advanced than humans in evolutionary terms" but he jumps thereafter to a consideration of H. G. Wells: "the present master of this literature, by virtue of his exceedingly unexpected creations", whose "admirable sang-froid in the description, not of the absurd but of the possible, in a mathematical sense, is more comprehensible if one considers that he writes in the language of Lord Kelvin." He fills in the gap between the two by citing two "more recent precursors of Wells": Villiers de l'Isle Adam, the author of *L'Ève future* (1886; tr. as *Tomorrow's Eve*) and Didier de Chousy, a belated reading of whose *Ignis* (1883) appears to have been the spur that prompted Jarry to write the essay.

Unfortunately, after a brief summary of the contents of *Ignis* (a satirical farce about an attempt to draw energy from the Earth's hot core, which also features a revolution of newly-intelligent machines against their human masters) Jarry, not untypically, simply trails off, abandoning the initial argument. He never returned to it in the five years he still had to live, although he did leave behind a series of notes and sketches for a subversive *roman scientifique*, which were published posthumously as *Gestes et opinions du Docteur Fauustroll, 'pataphyscien* (1911; tr. as "Exploits and Opinions of Dr. Faustroll, 'Pataphysician") and which founded the imaginary and paradoxical "science of exceptions", 'Pataphysics.

Like everything Jarry wrote, his essay on *romans scientifiques* is blithely tongue-in-cheek, and it is not surprising that he was particularly entranced by the humor in Didier de Chousy's satire. He had, however, read Lord Kelvin's essays and Henri Bergson's "neo-Darwinian" *Évolution créatrice*, as well as many other scientific works, and we know from his other writings that he was familiar with other earnest items of scientific fiction than those penned by Wells; one of J. H. Rosny's Xipéhuz makes a cameo appearance in his first novel, *Les jours et les nuits* (1897; tr. as *Days and Nights*). Several of the brief essays Jarry wrote for various periodicals in the early years of the century involve absurd technologies and items of speculative science—including advice to aircraft pioneer Alberto Santos-Dumont about the simulation of the flight of birds and a proposal to control the weather by "inoculating" the sun—in much the same spirit as contemporary vignettes by Alphonse Allais and later ones by Gaston de Pawlowski. Jarry was, therefore, in as good a position as anyone to comment on the advent of the new genre, and the fact that his essay was published in *La Plume* is of some significance with respect to the early development of French scientific fiction.

The proprietor of *La Plume* was "Willy"—Colette's husband—who had significant social links with several writers who were to go on to make significant contributions to the genre identified by Jarry. Jean de La Hire, who became one of the first popular *feuilletonists* to specialize in that genre, had been his secretary. Théo Varlet, who wrote poetry and criticism for *La Plume* while he still had independent means, also became a specialist in the genre when circumstances eventually forced him to make a living from his pen. Gaston de Pawlowski, who took up where Jarry left off as a writer of humorous scientific fiction, was also a close friend. In the years before the Great War, once the genre had begun to make significant progress, Willy and Colette, although separated by then, became regulars at a literary salon hosted by one of its most important domestic pioneers, Maurice Renard; the other regulars included J. H. Rosny, the leading French "Wellsian", and Charles Derennes, who had also been inspired by the examples of Wells and Renard to try his hand at such fiction.

While it lasted, *La Plume* was one of the bastions of the Symbolist Movement, the most important anchorage of which was the *Mercure de France*, edited by Jarry's close friend Alfred Vallette—who, like Willy, had a more talented and much more spectacular wife in Colette's fellow "Amazon" Rachilde. Henry Davray, Wells's translator, was on the staff of the *Mercure*, Rosny was a regular contributor, and two of the most significant calculated attempts to produce French *romans scientifiques*, Derennes' *Le peuple de la pôle* (1907; tr. as *The People of the Pole*) and Renard's *Le Docteur Lerne, sous-dieu* (1908; tr. as *Doctor Lerne, Subgod*) appeared under its imprint. There was, therefore, a strong affinity between the French Symbolist Movement and the attempt to found a distinctive variety of French *romans scientifiques*, further enhanced by such ex-Symbolist recruits to the new genre as Gustave Le Rouge, who had been part of Paul Verlaine's clique before turning his hand to commercial fiction, and Guillaume Apollinaire, who had hailed Renard's first novel as the prototype of a new genre of "subdivine fiction". Rosny had directly influenced the work of several other contributors to the nascent genre while he was in regular attendance at Edmond Goncourt's salon, including Louis Mullem and Léon Daudet.

Of all these interested parties, the one who took up the new genre's cause most determinedly, and the one who took up the analytical and promotional mission that Jarry had left off so abruptly, was Maurice Renard. Renard followed up his earliest venture in the genre, "Les Vacances de Monsieur Dupont" (1905; tr. as "Monsieur Dupont's Vacation") and *Le Docteur Lerne, sous-dieu* with an essay-cum-manifesto—published in the Octobre 1909 issue of a Symbolist periodical that had a formally-declared interest in literary theory, *Le Spectateur*—entitled "Du Roman merveilleux-scientifique et de son action sur l'intelligence du progrès" (tr. as "On Scientific Marvel Fiction and its Effect on the Consciousness of Progress").

* * * * * * *

The *Spectateur* essay was not the first item of non-fiction in which Renard had tackled the issue of re-categorizing modern imaginative fiction. Earlier that same year he had published his second collection of short stories, *Le Voyage Immobile suivi d'autres histoires singulières* [The Motionless Voyage and Other Strange Stories] (Mercure de France, 1909; tr. in *A Man Among the Microbes and Other Stories*), in which he attempted to arrange the stories according to their position in a spectrum contained within a contemporary subgenre of *le merveilleux*. The introduction to the collection claims that: "The following stories are not assembled at hazard; they constitute deliberately-disparate parts of the same whole, and are grouped in methodical succession. Their totality forms a study of what I shall call the *logical marvelous*: a study whose object is the recognition of the limits of the genre and a proof of its flexibility."

This suggestion is a product of whimsical afterthought attempting to add an element of coherency to a remarkably heterogeneous collection, but the claim that all the fantasies contained in the collection—ranging from a deft combination of Greek myth and Christian legend that allegedly "only includes the indispensable minimum of logic" to the title story, which "contains the maximum dose of science"—belong to the same "strange ambiguous domain" is by no means uninteresting or irrelevant to Renard's work as a whole. The notion that ancient and modern notions of "the marvelous" are routinely confronted with one another in modern imaginative fiction, and that a particular kind of narrative energy can be drawn from their conflict, is highly relevant to any consideration of Alfred Jarry's work as well as to Renard's, and to Symbolist fantasy in general as well as to *romans scientifiques*. Even so, just as the second paragraph of Jarry's essay had jarred somewhat with the first, so Renard's extended essay on the "roman merveilleux-scientifique" adopted a position markedly different from that of the preface to *Le Voyage Immobile suivi d'autres histoires singulières*.

In translating the central term of Renard's essay I have rendered *roman* as "fiction" rather than "novel" or "romance" because his paradigmatic examples include short fiction as well. Once the adjective is sited before the noun, as is conventional in English, "scientific marvel" reads better than the crudely literal "scientific-marvelous", but I have used "scientific marvelous" when the phrase is employed as a noun rather than an adjective. The term is conspicuously awkward, but that is a dutiful reflection of the awkwardness of the task. (American labelers struggled in similar fashion when they came to invent such substitutes as "Science Wonder Stories" and "Marvel Science Stories" in the early days of the pulp genre that eventually settled—not without a struggle—for "[adjective optional] Science Fiction".)

Renard asserts that scientific marvel fiction is "the inevitable product of an era in which science predominates—without, however, extinguishing our eternal need for fantasy" and affirms that "it is a genuinely new genre...of which Wells's *The Island of Doctor Moreau* and Derennes' *Le Peuple de la pôle* can furnish use with two adequate type specimens." He re-emphasizes his insistence that the genre is new by stressing the originality of Wells's work therein:

> "...prior to the author of *The War of the Worlds*, the rare practitioners of what might later be called the 'scientific marvelous' only devoted themselves to such work at rare intervals, occasionally, and, it seems, playfully. All of them treated it as inconsequential fantasy; none of them specialized in it and most of them combined it with other elements. Cyrano de Bergerac used it to support utopias; Swift used it as a framework for satires...Camille Flammarion has recruited it to make certain metaphysical ideas that are too abstract for the ordinary reader a little more concrete [while] Edmond About...approaches it from the opposite direction, turning it into comedy, thus contriving in advance of its existence parodies of a genre to come."

The reference to About, in preference to Jarry, reflects Renard's conservative taste in humor.

Renard goes on to built up a more elaborate history, crediting Edgar Poe with the foundation of the modern scientific marvel story, and naming Villiers de l'Isle Adam, Robert Louis Stevenson (for *Doctor Jekyll and Mister Hyde*) and H. G. Wells as his most celebrated "apostles". He is careful, though, to say that "by no means all of [Wells's works] are specimens of it". He lists five novels and a few short stories that qualify unambiguously, but marginalizes several others as hybrids of one sort or another, and recalls his earlier essay in mentioning others "in which it is not science but logic alone, considered not as science but as a habit of mind, which intervenes in the marvelous", retaining the term "logical marvelous" for such fables as *The Wonderful Visit*, while "reserving 'scientific marvelous' for those which present us with the adventure of a science extrapolated to the point of a marvel, or a marvel envisaged scientifically."

Unsurprisingly, as Renard was very ambitious in 1909 to be a significant exponent of the new genre he characterized by means of these examples, he felt no need to be modest in his claims for its importance: "Scientific marvel fiction is...the form of contemporary literature that embodies the most philosophy...and it appears to us, in fact—with its noble instructive and moralistic tendencies, and its immediate or eventual educative effects—to be one of the finest creations of the human mind: a great work of art, which only seems small to those who are to distant from it by virtue of an optical illusion, and which can only appear childish to puerile minds."

As an active practitioner, he is inevitably concerned with the imaginative method of the new genre, and sees the fundamental problem arising out of its seemingly-paradoxical character in that light. "We are," he says, "forced to seek our Romantic themes in the unknown and the uncertain. As we are concerned with *scientific* marvels, however, how can we reconcile the seemingly contradictory demand that we take our subject matter from both within science and from that which is not science? We act exactly as the scientist does who wishes to tackle the problems of the unknown; we apply the methods of scientific investigation to the unknown and the dubious."

Having elaborated this point, he employs it as a means of limiting the new genre, digressing to remark that because "it is a matter of launching science *into the heart of the unknown* and not of imagining that it has finally accomplished some project or other that is in fact in the process of execution" the new genre excludes such writers as Jules Verne, who "merely anticipated discoveries in the process of gestation" and Albert Robida, "who has only supposed that some of our least redeeming and most superfluous desiderata have been fulfilled, without bothering to obtain that result in a coherent fashion, or to draw the slightest consequence therefrom." While these judgments are a trifle excessive as descriptive statements—both Verne and Robida produced some works that certainly qualify as "scientific marvel fiction"—the excess is excusable in terms of prescriptive zeal, and the essay continues with further commentary on the methodology and aesthetics of narrative extrapolation before returning to propagandizing.

Eager to persuade potential writers and readers of the merits of the new genre, Renard is enthusiastic to stress the educational advantages of scientific marvel fiction, but he only mentions straightforward didactic merits in passing, being more concerned with the argument that supplies the second half of his title: "Having noticed in a large number of people, after reading such a work, a sort of meditative astonishment, having interrogated them about the cause to which they attribute it, and having questioned by own sentiments,

I had been led to this conclusion: that, after reading *The Invisible Man* or 'In the Abyss', for example, we no longer see things from the same angle. And, having asked what relationships have been modified, what proportions changed, I have perceived that the confused disturbance of our judgments comes, in the final analysis, from the effect of the scientific marvelous on the consciousness of progress."

The remainder of the essay is devoted to the question of what we ought to mean by "progress", and what effect the reading of "scientific marvel fiction" might or will have on our consciousness of that phenomenon. Renard is insistent that scientific marvel fiction has the potential to be more than a mere reflection or anticipation of the pattern of technological progress, or even a commentary upon that advancement, but might become an active participant in human intellectual progress. Because he was writing in 1909, Renard was particularly keen to identify an important new phase in technological innovation, which seemed to him to have opened up (in the sense of demonstrating its potential) in that year. Unlike previous technologies—which had, he argues—merely magnified and extended physical and sensory capacities that humans already had, "the addition of wings, realized by the invention of dirigibles, and especially of airplanes, seems to us to be the acme of progress, because its introduces an entirely novel means of displacement.... Aerial navigation projects us into an element previously inaccessible, for whose access we have no natural motor...."

According to Renard, the advent of aviation altered our intellectual horizons very profoundly, and shifted the limits of the human imagination once and for all:

> "It finally answers our millennia-old desire, exacerbated by the eternal temptation exerted above our foreheads and the feverish expectation of a more profound knowledge capable of its satisfaction. It makes us sovereigns of a space vaster than the surface of the globe, so beautiful in its blueness and purity—further enhanced in being a zone forbidden *but promised*, in that our ancient myths already celebrate the flight of mortals through the sky—that we have lodged our divinities and our paradises there, and the shoulders of our seraphim and the ancient genies of Egypt deploy the wingspans of a swan or an ibis.... It therefore symbolizes the acme of *progress*."

It is by means of this notion of a crucial threshold in the process of being crossed—a small step that is also a giant leap—that Renard attempts to set up his notion of scientific marvel fiction not only as a genre whose time has come but one whose advent is highly desirable. "With a force of conviction drawn from reason itself," he argues "[scientific marvel fiction] brutally unveils for us everything that the unknown and the doubtful might perhaps hold in reserve, everything in the depths of the inexplicable that might become disagreeable or horrible to us, everything that the sciences are capable of discovering and extrapolating beyond the accomplished inventions that seem to us to be the terminus, all the *lateral* consequences, all the unexpected and possible consequences of those same inventions, and also all the new sciences that might emerge for the study of previously-unsuspected phenomena, *which might create new needs for us in creating in advance the means to nourish or pander to them*. It shows us our petty way of life upset by the most natural and yet the most unexpected cataclysms. It reveals to us, in a new and gripping clarity, the instability of contingencies, the imminent menace of the possible. It infects us with the nauseous malaise of doubt. Finally, by its means, all the horror of the unknown appears to us with a terrible intensity. It uncovers for us the incommensurable space to be explored outside our immediate wellbeing; it pitilessly detaches from the idea of science any afterthought of domestic usage and any sentiment of anthropocentrism. It breaks our habits of thought and transports us to other points of view, outside ourselves."

This ringing manifesto was not, of course, fulfilled. "Scientific marvel fiction" never became established as a significant genre in early twentieth-century France, and the relatively few examples of it revealed to us by hindsight remained far more peripheral to the aggregate of French literary culture than Vernian fiction had been in the late nineteenth century. Renard's subsequent essays on the subject attempt to analyze the reasons for that stillbirth as well as expressing his own lamentations for the death of his hopes.

* * * * * * *

In personal terms, although he did not realize it at the time, the rot had already set in before Renard published his 1909 essay. The novel with which he followed up *Le Docteur Lerne, sous-dieu*, which was intended to be his first masterpiece of the nascent genre, *Un Homme chez les microbes*, was completed in that year but could not find a publisher. Disappointing as that was, it might have been dismissible as a temporary glitch, and he did manage to publish his next scientific marvel story, which was something of a *tour de force* in its own right—*Le Péril bleu* (1911; tr. as *The Blue Peril*)—but the revised version of *Un Homme chez les microbes* that he prepared thereafter met the same fate as the first—although it might conceivably have fared better had it not been for the outbreak of the Great War in 1914.

The Great War changed everything, not merely for Renard but also for the genre for which he entertained such high hopes. Renard was immediately mobilized as a cavalry officer in August 1914 and did not return to civilian life until January 1919; he survived, but the war took a heavy toll on him both personally and financially; the invading Germans had destroyed all the property his family owned in the Champagne region, whose income had previously insulated him from need. In spite of his tribulations, Renard returned to his literary work with great determination, apparently having lost none of his literary ambition. His prospects were enhanced by the publication of new editions of *Le Docteur Lerne, Le Voyage immobile*, and *Le Péril bleu* and all three volumes advertised new works "en préparation", including *Un Homme chez les microbes, Les Mains d'Orlac, Le Maître de la lumière*, and *L'Homme truqué*. These publication plans, however—like those Renard had made immediately before the war—went sadly awry.

The ingenious and rigorously logical, but only peripherally marvelous, mystery novel *Les Mains d'Orlac* (1920; tr. as *The Hands of Orlac*) duly appeared, but the other three—all of which were identified as novels—fell by the wayside. A truncated version of *L'Homme truqué* (tr. as "The Doctored Man") appeared as a novella in the March 1921 issue of *Je Sais Tout* but the third version of *Un Hommes chez les microbes*, fared no better than its predecessors, and nor did a fourth produced in 1923, although a fifth version did reach print in 1928. A novel entitled *Le Maître de la lumière* (tr. as *The Master of Light*) finally saw the light of day as a feuilleton serial in 1933, but it was probably very different from the novel that had originally been planned; like its two predecessors, its belated appearance presumably reflected Renard's stubbornness in trying to improvise something salable out of previously-written materials.

One highly significant factor in the extirpation of Renard's ambitions, and those of scientific marvel fiction in general, was that the brief fashionability of Wellsian scientific romance—which had already been waning before the Great War, as publishers realized that many readers found it too alien—was wiped out by the conflict. The experience of war concentrated minds very forcefully on the vicissitudes of the immediate and the material, at the expense of the imaginative and the hypothetical, and that legacy lasted for at least a decade afterwards in both France and England. Although British scientific romance eventually enjoyed a new period of energetic endeavor and modest commercial success after 1930, its French equivalent remained longer in the doldrums.

A more specific legacy of the war, derived from the extraordinarily rapid advancement of technologies of destruction, had considerably darkened attitudes to technological innovation. Before the war, the development of the automobile and the advent of winged aircraft had seemed to many observers—including Renard—to be a marvelous adventure, extending the range of human capability in a positive fashion, but the development of aircraft as fighters and bombers, and the development of automobiles into tanks, not to mention the military deployment of high explosives and poison gas, set the march of science in a very different light. To many people, technological "progress" seemed in the wake of the Great War to be an inherently destructive and potentially apocalyptic process. Fiction dedicated to the extrapolation of "scientific marvels" inevitably suffered the toxic effects of that antipathy. Renard was not the only writer forced by the circumstances of the new literary environment to redirect his attention crime novels, but he was, inevitably, the one who most bitterly regretted and lamented the dismal and ignominious failure of the genre for which he had entertained such high hopes. One of the expressions of that regret was a despairing rejection of the label he had coined, which had proved sadly unnecessary.

In the spring of 1923 Renard was interviewed by the Belgian writer Jean Ray, who asked him to write an essay on the *fantastique* to accompany the interview and an overview of his work to be published in the 15 Juin issue of *L'Ami des livres*; the resultant article, "Depuis Sinbad" (tr. as "Since Sinbad") updated and revised his manifesto for the *roman merveilleux-scientifique* and gave clear expression to Renard's disillusionment with the genre' prospects.

In the new essay Renard addressed the matter of definition in the following terms:

> "I think that the first thing to do is to limit the domain of the word 'fantastic', an adjective evocative of devilry, the supernatural, crazy dreams, even nightmares; an epithet too exclusive of thought, method and knowledge, which is not at all adaptable to the work of a Wells [or] a Rosny aîné. The application of the word 'fantastic' to stories like *The Time*

> *Machine* or 'Un Autre monde'—or, more accurately, the confusion of genres revealed and consecrated by that application—makes a considerable contribution to the laborious slowness with which the public moves toward distractions that are, however, quite new and delightfully educational. It is because the public sees them only as simple fantasies. It classifies them in the same family as the tales of *The Thousand-and-One Nights*. It takes them for 'Ali Babas' arbitrarily accommodated to present-day tastes— which is to say, seasoned with science. It tells itself that Scheherazade's imagination is not of a kind to support the parasitic invasion of electrical or chemical modernities. In its view, science and imagination, thus combined, are reciprocally harmful. The former, in departing from the truth, loses all its value; the latter, touched by reason, creases to sparkle."

Renard, of course, thought that "the [reading] public" was looking at things the wrong way, and thus missing out on a valuable opportunity. "The truth is," he proposed, "that in the nineteenth century, the state of science and the progress of knowledge have put writers in the position of manipulating hypotheses in the speculative field. By virtue of that fact, the physical world has become the object of conjectural, 'parascientific' studies, which are not less captivating for arising essentially from philosophy—with the condition, nevertheless, of being considered as what they are, and not being taxed as 'fantastic'."

Having identified the cornerstones of the genre of the *fantastique* as the works Hoffmann, Poe, and Erckmann-Chatrian, and having failed to see any significant contemporary followers in the footsteps but Hanns Heinz Ewers (who had enjoyed a brief vogue in France prior to the Great War), Renard concludes that the *fantastique*, in some essential sense, "not French". He still hopes, however, that the genre of "parascientific fiction" he is attempting to distinguish from it might be salvageable as a French genre if only readers can be persuaded on its value, and that is what he sets out to do:

> "The majority of 'parascientific' novels and stories (I resolutely proscribe the term 'scientific marvelous') also present the merit of being instruments of human observation which in the unusual light of suppositions, cause certain normally-imperceptible

interior reliefs to stand out. But what clearly distinguishes the parascientific from the fantastic is that the fabulation of the former must, in itself, possess a 'value'—a rational value—in being the development of a logical and fecund hypothesis, while we demand nothing similar of the latter; it is sufficient for us that its subject should be charming, burlesque or terrible, and that there should be something subhuman in it. Now, the postulate of a parascientific novel can itself embody such a treasure of novelty, possess such a power of evocation, that its exposure, taken for what it is, constitutes an infinitely seductive and fruitful work. That which, in the fantastic, is merely a form, merely an expression, can here become the very foundation, the substance. And if the conceptions that emerge from it are not always related to humankind, or if the psychological element is absent therefrom, I say that no great harm is done."

In making that last remark, Renard is of course, keenly aware of the fact that his new genre has run into trouble with editors and readers because alleged lack of "psychological" interest:

"People have been persuaded that no novel exists in which no psychology is manifest," he remarks, "and that the quality of a novel is in direct proportion to the dose of psychology that it contains. I do not approve of that, because it makes me see readers as monkeys crouched in front of mirrors. I recall what was said, thirty years ago, about the first performances of the works of Claude Debussy. People said, disdainfully, 'That's not music'—and the moment that it 'wasn't music' it became worthless! Well, let people cease to call stories stripped of psychology 'novels', if they insist—but please allow people, from time to time, to interrupt their self-contemplation in order to raise their eyes above their navels, to accept that there are a few other objects in the universe that are not without interest…and to approach the parascientific novel without arguing about its psychological nature or lack of it, or its ambiguity or lack of it. Let them abandon that 'accurate, subtle, powerful' and benevolent fictive opium in order to discover new points of view."

Although he bravely continues this argument for several more paragraphs, it is obvious that Renard is convinced that he is fighting a losing battle, not only on his own behalf but that of the entire genre he is attempting to defend. In the end, in spite of his argumentative efforts, his conclusion is bleak: "There is no point in searching any further for the reason for the discouragement that led Wells to stop working in the vein of *The War of the Worlds* and why Rosny aîné so rarely publishes works like "Les Xipéhuz" or *La Force mystérieuse*. To earn a living by addressing oneself to intelligence—that, indeed, would be truly fantastic!"

* * * * * * *

When he wrote "Depuis Sinbad", Renard was still optimistic that the fourth version of *Un Homme chez les microbes* might get into print later in 1923—he told Jean Ray in May that it was tentatively scheduled for October publication—but, having written the essay, he probably felt that the fact that the novel failed to appear yet again was merely one more inevitable failure of his disappointed expectations. He did, however, manage to get a version into print in 1928—conscientiously, if falsely, advertising it as the "fifth edition"—and that success seems to have prompted him to make one last attempt to promote the genre to which is belonged, in an essay entitled "Le Roman d'hypothèse" (tr. as "Hypothetical Fiction") which appeared in the 15 Decembre 1928 issue of *A.B.C.*

This time, Renard began his essay with an attempted explanation of the fact that French readers simply do not "get" certain kinds of fiction, including what he now elected to call by the alternative label (*roman hypothétique*) that Alfred Jarry had suggested in his 1902 essay. He uses the analogy of an iron gate that bars the way into a park, concluding that:

> "The person who sets out to read a hypothetical novel without reading between the lines, without glimpsing, beyond the story, certain conceptions that it is impossible to translate, or the exposure of which would necessitate the employment of a forbidding language contrary to the principles of the novel, is also only seeing the grille, neglecting the park, and will

answer with reference to the lock when you talk to him about the flowers."

He goes on:

> "I have taken the trouble to clarify this point before saying what I think about the genre of fiction that is often identified as 'scientific marvel fiction', to which I now prefer the appellation 'hypothetical fiction'. There would, in fact, be no point in writing it—or, at least, in publishing it—if everyone read as everyone calculates, coldly and flatly. The imagination of the writer of hypothetical fiction requires that readers are willing to 'dance with him'. J. H. Rosny aîné's *La Force mystérieuse* and *La Mort de la Terre*, or H. G. Wells's *The Invisible Man* and *The Island of Doctor Moreau* are as many invitations to the waltz of worlds. If the reader remains passive and inert, if he does not perceive the profound rhythm of the universal jazz that is the music of the spheres, he is done for; he will not enter into the mentality of the hypothetical novel—which mentality consists, by means of a story that is ingenious and attractive in itself, of supposing that which is not, in order to acquire an idea of that which might be, of that which might perhaps happen in future or that which might exist beyond the range of our senses; and also in order to gain a better understanding of that which we know, whether by studying that which our world is not, or by adopting unusual viewpoints in order to look at it."

The argument continues by considering the importance of the "zone of hypotheses" that firms "a sort of phantasmal halo" on "the fringe of science" and the consequent, or at least potential, importance of fiction that communicates "the delightful illusion of obtaining some slight understanding of the inexplicable". Renard is still prepared to make big claims for this kind of fiction. He states:

> "In the nineteenth and twentieth centuries, hypothetical fiction has replaced the eighteenth-century *conte philosophique*…. Without a doubt, if Voltaire and Swift were to reappear among us, the former

would not have failed to import into *Micromégas* and the latter into *Gulliver* a series of issues descendant from the scientific knowledge that we have acquired in the century of Edison and the Curies—and, scant as our belief might be in the possibilities of metempsychosis, it is easy enough to imagine that the soul of Voltaire nowadays animates our great Rosny, and that Swift's has passed into the body of Wells."

This remark is particularly pertinent, given that *Un Homme chez les microbes* had explicitly taken its imaginative warrant from Voltaire's *Micromégas*, not merely in playing games with magnitude but in taking up Voltaire's contention that human understanding and imagination are direly limited by the partiality of our senses; the novel attempts to depict a society whose members are possessed of a sixth sense, dominant over the five that we possess—a notion that Renard had tried to extrapolate again, much more modestly, in "L'Homme truqué", but had been similarly unable to follow through to the extent that he wished. Inevitably, the essay goes on to lament the fact that such modern *contes philosophiques* cannot find an audience in contemporary France—although it adds a qualification that modern exponents of "science fiction studies" might find surprising:

"It follows from this, necessarily, that the most enthusiastic lovers of the hypothetical novel are to be found on the far side of the Rhine. We...do not understand it any better than the people of central Europe. The Latin peoples already show us much more indifference. The English consider works like *The Food of the Gods* or *The First Men in the Moon* to be secondary within the oeuvre of their Wells. As for the Americans, they are still a trifle young, and it was surely by virtue of an error that Edgar Poe was born in Baltimore more than a hundred years ago."

Renard probably did not know, in 1928, of the existence of Hugo Gernsback's *Amazing Stories* and other examples of "scientifiction", but if he had, he might well have considered them to be products of German rather than American enterprise. He was probably better acquainted with the success in the 1920s of the German *zukunftsroman* [futuristic fiction], whose technophilic practitioners included the best-selling Hans Dominik, but his plaintive comment about hypothetical fiction being better appreciated on the far side of the Rhine might have more to do with his familiarity with Fritz Lang's movie *Metropolis* (1926) and the fact that his own modestly hypothetical novel *Les Mains d'Orlac* had been filmed in Germany in 1925—the American version, *Mad Love*, was not made until 1935.

As to whether Renard found out about the existence of American scientifiction after 1928 we can only guess, although he probably did, given that Gernsback printed an abridged translation of "Le Voyage immobile" as *The Flight of the Aerofix* as a pamphlet in 1932. He died in 1939, however, before *Thrilling Wonder Stories* printed another version of one of his "scientific marvel stories", "Le Brouillard de 26 Octobre" (1913) as "Five After Five" (1941; it is more a summary paraphrase than a translation). He must have been aware of US translations of *Le Docteur Lerne, sous-dieu* (1923, extensively bowdlerized, as *New Bodies for Old*) and a novel he had co-authored with Albert Jean in 1925, *Le Singe* (1928 as *Blind Circle*), but their fortunes had obviously had not given him a higher opinion of the American public than he had of the French public. There is also no way of knowing whether he was aware of the renaissance of British scientific romance after 1930, or what he thought of it if he was. We do know, however, that the few items of scientific marvel/parascientific/hypothetical fiction he published in the thirties were all calculatedly trivial, and imbued with a curious kind of nostalgia for what he might have done with their central ideas had he only been given freer rein ten or twenty years before.

We also know that French fiction of the type that Renard attempted to identify and promote never did acquire a label of its own, but was eventually content to import the American one when post-World-War-II "coca-colonization" flooded France with American cultural produce. There had, of course, been numerous novels published in France between the wars that qualified as scientific marvel/parascientific/hypothetical fiction, but the vast majority were crude items of popular fiction in the *feuilleton* tradition, indistinguishable in imaginative ambition from the dregs of US pulp science fiction. Only a handful of Wellsian (or Renardian) works contrived to get into print, and none won much in the way of critical praise or commercial success. In the meantime, the German *zukunfstroman* flattered only to deceive, having been hijacked by the Nazis before perishing along with them in the war. British scientific romance fared better than the parallel French tradition in the short term, but it too was virtually drowned by post-war coca-colonization and was subsequently replaced by science fiction on the American model. As the twenty-first century staggers along, however, the most intriguing thing about looking back at Renard's sequence of essays is how extraordinarily familiar their initially-flamboyant rhetoric and eventually-bleak pessimism seem, even to students of the supposedly-victorious genre that eventually filled the gap whose emptiness depressed him so much.

ECOLOGY AND DYSTOPIA

INTRODUCTION

The terms "ecology" and "dystopia" were first improvised from their Greek roots in the mid-nineteenth century. The former was used by Henry David Thoreau in 1858 before being formally defined as a branch of biology seven years later by Ernst Haeckel, while the latter was by employed by John Stuart Mill in 1868.

A basic awareness of ecological relationships had been a necessary concomitant of agricultural endeavor since the first crops were sown and the first animals domesticated; farming is, in essence, a matter of creating, sustaining and improving artificial ecosystems. The application of the scientific method to agricultural practice had made considerable impacts long before Haeckel identified a science of ecology, but Thoreau's usage was more closely connected to an increasing sensitivity to the complexity of natural processes, which changed the significance of the word "nature" in philosophical discourse and popular parlance, where it was often rendered, with a degree of personification impregnated with mystical homage, as "Nature". Thoreau was continuing a tradition summarized in Ralph Waldo Emerson's *Nature* (1836), which owed a good deal to the Romantic Movements of Europe; Romantic poets often elaborated their responses to Nature and celebrated supposed communions therewith.

In addition to its scientific definition, the term "ecology" retained these mystical connections throughout the twentieth century. It was the mystical rather than the scientific aspects of ecology which forged a crucial bond with the history of utopian thought, helping to redefine notions of eutopia (and hence of dystopia) and eventually necessitating the coinage of the term "ecotopia"; the notion of "Nature" was central to that bonding process.

The personification of Nature was begun by the exponents of "natural theology", who attempted to employ the study of Creation as means of cultivating a better understanding of the mind of God. As doubts about God's existence spread in the nineteenth century and theories of evolution provided an alternative to Creation as an explanation of the ecosphere's richness and complexity, it became possible—and, indeed, increasingly popular—to see Nature not as a means of reading the divine mind, but as a sort of divine mind in its own right. This was not welcome news to everyone, as exemplified by Alfred Lord Tennyson's reference in *In Memoriam* (1850) to "Nature red in tooth and claw", but the idea of an implicitly cruel Nature was always in competition with the notion of an essentially benign Mother Nature—who was proverbially supposed to know best, however mysterious her ways of movement might be. The notion that Nature was blessed with an inherent "balance" or "harmony" became commonplace, and ecological representations of the complex relationships identifiable within ecosystems were routinely invoked as alleged proof of that contention.

The mystical aspect of ecology retained the concept of sin, tacitly if not explicitly, although its adherents were forced to reconceive sin as a trangression of "laws of Nature" rather than Mosaic commandments. Whereas *Genesis* had explicitly established the natural world as something specifically made for human exploitation, and thus subject to human dominion, mystical ecology reversed that priority, making human beings part of Nature and subject to its imperatives. This inversion was bound to have an effect on utopian speculation, particularly in terms of the ways in which eutopian ambitions might run into trouble.

The alteration of perspective was dramatically illustrated by the arguments employed in Robert Malthus' *Essay on the Principle of Population as it Affects the Future Improvement of Society* (1798), which suggested that debates regarding the precise political shape of a future utopian state were pointless, because *all* futuristic dreams of universal peace and plenty were impossible of achievement, on ecological grounds. Malthus argued that food supply can only increase arithmetically, while population tends to increase exponentially. The logical result of this imbalance, he contended, is that human societies always require numerical restriction by war, famine and disease, formerly notorious as Horsemen of the Apocalypse but scientifically re-labelled as "Malthusian checks".

Malthus provided a stern challenge to the philosophy of progress developed in pre-Revolutionary France by Anne-Robert Turgot and the Marquis de Condorect, whose fundamental thesis was that technological advancement and social advancement went hand-in-hand: that increasing scientific knowledge and technological sophistication favoured and facilitated the growth of liberty, equality and fraternity. The specific formulation of the thesis inevitably generated a shadowy antithesis in the form of fears that at least some advances in technology might actually be detrimental to the ends of social justice, inhibiting rather than furthering the ideals in question; although a superficial inspection of the broad sweep of history seemed to favour the thesis, Malthus lent imaginative fuel to the antithesis.

Malthus was forced to modify his argument in subsequent editions of the *Essay* to take aboard criticisms made by William Godwin and other English philosophers of progress. He accepted that voluntary restriction of population might be possible by the exercise of "moral restraint"—but he clearly had no faith in the likelihood that future generations might exercise such moral restraint. He was not alone in this suspicion—and it was in order to assist consideration of the darker aspects of future possibility, including Malthusian anxieties, that the word "dystopia" was eventually coined.

In Malthus's time, the most apparent cutting edge of progress in "applied ecology" was the calculated transplantion of crops in the development of colonies. Joseph Banks, as president of the Royal Society, played a leading role in defining the scientific missions of British naval expeditions; it was he who commissioned William Bligh to transplant breadfruit from Tahiti to the Caribbean colonies, and made sure that the *Providence* completed the mission in 1793 after the *Bounty*'s crew mutinied in 1791. Banks's immediate motive for augmenting the collection of plants held at Royal Gardens at Kew, for which he assumed responsibility in 1798, was to discover and develop resources for the use of the colonists of Australia. In the wake of the American War of Independence, Thomas Jefferson, George Washington and John Quincy Adams similarly recognized the naturalization and cultivation of useful plants as a vital economic necessity for the success of the new nation.

The establishment of "plantations" of every kind was the heart of colonial endeavor, and it is hardly surprising that a keen appreciation of the problems involved in their maintenance developed in the nineteenth century. The branches of biology that grew rapidly in that period tended to be guided by those imperatives, as evidenced by such works as Thaddeus William Harris' pioneering entomological study *Treatise on Some of the Insects of New England Which are Injurious to Vegetation* (1842). The primary function of the US Entomological Commission, established in 1877 under the directorship of Charles V. Riley, was to co-ordinate endeavors in pest control. The first textbooks of ecology were produced in this context, and were thus of considerable interest to utopian experimenters, whose endeavors were very often formulated as colonial settlements.

Colonial adventurism was routinely justified, in moral terms, by the notion that the native societies of colonizable lands were intrinsically bad because they were "savage"—innately inclined to brutal violence of every sort, including human sacrifice and cannibalism—and thus direly in need of progress towards civilization. Eighteenth- and nineteenth-century fiction lent robust ideological support to this notion, especially in the adventure stories featured British "boys' books" and the fledgling American genre of the Western. As civilized society came under attack by such eighteenth-century philosophers as Jean-Jacques Rousseau, however, a contrarian anthropological myth was born which conceived of unspoiled tribal societies as innocent, peaceful, happy and paradisal—a model to which some French commentators attempted to accommodate the actual islands of the remote Pacific Ocean, especially Tahiti. This idea, too, became a staple of nineteenth-century romance, albeit a far less obvious one; it eventually spawned an entire subgenre of quasi-nostalgic "lost race stories", because it had to be admitted that very few actual tribal societies provided convincing candidates of paradisal innocence, peacefulness and happiness.

The Rousseauesque notion of technological development as a process of intrinsic spoliation of primal innocence was further augmented by nostalgic contrasts between rural life and life in the new industrial towns that were springing up all over Europe. Although such towns were sometimes allowed, like the curate's egg, to be "good in parts", the idea took deep root that they had archetypally bad places within them. The coal mines where the fuel to drive steam engines was produced became, in the eyes of some commentators, the core of a modern Dantean Hell, whose outer circles were formed by the "slums" that grew up in the vicinity of factories where steam engines were used in the production of goods. Some commentators refused to be selective; the English reformer William Cobbett wrote off the whole of London as "the Great Wen", neatly encapsulating the horror that early nineteenth-century sceptics felt as they observed the unfolding of the industrial evolution. William Blake might not have meant his reference in "Jerusalem" (1804) to "dark satanic mills" to be taken literally, but it was frequently read that way.

Cities had always had a dystopian aspect of this sort; the first laws to abate smoke production and restrict garbage disposal in London had been enacted by the English parliament in 1273 and 1388. The dramatic growth of cities in the nineteenth century amplified the problem alarmingly, however; the modernization of London's sewer system was inspired by the "Great Stink" of the 1850s, which made the citybound banks of the river Thames—including the stretch on which the Houses of Parliament stood—quite unendurable. Futuristic images of eutopian cities, from Louis-Sébastien Mercier's pioneering account of Paris in *L'an deux mille quatre cent quarante* (1771; tr. as *Memoirs of the Year Two Thousand Five Hundred*) onwards, were often optimistic that technological progress would enable cities to become much cleaner, but it is hardly surprising that the Great Stink generated a certain scepticism in that regard.

The original meaning of the word "pollution" had a moral and spiritual context, referring to defilement or desecration rather than common-or-garden uncleanliness, and the increasing use of the term "environmental pollution" with reference to problems of industrial waste disposal retained a plangent echo of that implication. In effect, pollution became the first and foremost of the deadly ecological sins. The idea of dystopia was infected with this consciousness at birth, and the history of the idea has, inevitably, seen a gradual and inexorable increase in its elaboration within the context of ecological mysticism and science. The idea of ecology was similarly infected; the historical development of the science has been haunted by the imagery of disaster and the festering anxieties that lie at the core of dystopian romance and satire.

IMMISERATION, POLLUTION, AND ALIENATION IN EARLY SPECULATIVE FICTION

The narrative of the first significant dystopian satire, Émile Souvestre's *Le monde tel qu'il sera* (1846; tr. as *The World As It Shall Be*), makes only passing reference to the extent of industrial spoliation, but the illustrations accompanying the text—which are reproduced in the English translation of 2004—were more explicit, the cityscapes being notable for their murky atmospheres. The same is true of the illustrations of the city of Stahlstadt in the first edition of Jules Verne's *Les cinq cents millions de la bégum* (1879; developed from a first draft by Paschal Grousset; tr. as *The Begum's Fortune*), which are similarly reproduced in early translations issued by Sampson Low *et al*. Verne's textual description of life in the "City of Steel"—hypothetically located in Oregon—depicts the extreme regulation of time and effort within the vast factory-complex and its associated mine in a much more earnest fashion than Souvestre, and its awareness of the effects of environmental pollution is correspondingly grim.

Even in Verne's Stahlstadt, however, let alone its eutopian counterpart Frankville, technology enables pollution to be held at bay where required; the centre of Stahlstadt is a privileged enclave centred on a beautiful tropical park, populated with plants and animals transplanted from distant parts of the globe. The most obvious impact of nineteenth-century reality on literary imagery of this sort was the lesson of social division: the notion that bad places were for the abandonment of the poor, while the rich and privileged could and would build exclusive eutopian microcosms. In naturalistic and speculative fiction alike, eutopia and dystopia often sat side by side, as two sides of the same coin, the eutopia of the few being built at the expense of the dystopia of the many.

Striking instances of this pattern of thought can be found in many alarmist futuristic fantasies. In the first significant American dystopian romance, Ignatius Donnelly's *Caesar's Column* (1890, initially bylined Edmund Boisgilbert), the dystopia of the masses proves to be a fertile breeding-ground for an unprecedentedly vengeful revolution; the titular column is erected from the skulls of its victims. In H. G. Wells's *The Time Machine* (1895) the imagery of social division attained a new extreme in the contrast between the effetely eutopian society of the Eloi and the nightmarish dystopian underworld of the Morlocks.

The immiseration that takes place in such conventional dystopian locations as Stahlstadt is, to a large extent, a straightforward representation of the actuality of nineteenth-century slum life; it is a matter of living in squalid conditions in a spoiled environment with barely enough to eat. There is, however, another significant element to which Verne and Grousset pay particular attention: the fact that the lives of the factory-workers are excessively regulated by the nature of their labour and their shift-patterns, to the point where they become mechanized themselves. This was a well-established nineteenth-century anxiety, dating back to the Romantic Movements. When Thomas Carlyle suggested, in "Signs of the Times" (1829) that the modern era ought to be characterized as an "Age of Machinery" he complained bitterly that "mechanical genius" had not restricted itself to the management of physical and external factors, but had invaded the internal and spiritual aspects of human life.

Carlyle's essay elevates Mechanism to the status of a satanic counterpart to Nature, similarly personalized as an elementary force of malevolence—and this was the status it assumed in much dystopian fiction. The most obvious corollary of this opposition, in the context of literary didacticism, is the mechanization of time. One of the principal defining features of Nature is its relationship with the temporal cycles of the day and the year, while one of the key features of technological society is its domination by clocks.

The oppressive regulation of time is responsible for much of the distress of the downtrodden citizens of Verne's Stahlstadt, and was increasingly seen as a fundamental defining feature of dystopian existence. It was given striking visual representation in Fritz Lang's film *Metropolis* (1926) after extensive literary development in such novels as H. C. Marriott-Watson's *Erchomenon; or, The Republic of Materialism* (1879), Owen Gregory's *Meccania* (1918), and Evgeny Zamyatin's *Myi* (1920; tr. as *We*, 1924). In *Les condamnés à mort* (1920; tr. as *Useless Hands*) by "Claude Farrère" (Charles Bargone) the misery of mechanized labour reaches breaking-point when the process of automation achieves its logic end-point, but the enclosed eutopia of the élite is well-defended by heavy artillery. In Karel Čapek's *R.U.R.* (1920) the artificial "robot" labourers who support a similar eutopian élite find a means of overcoming their own enforced automatism once the oppressive élite has been exterminated, but that merely takes the whole historical process back to square one.

The notion that the division between the major classes of society would inevitably become wider, the condition of the rich tending towards eutopia and freedom while that of the poor tended towards dystopia and mechanization, had been widely popularized by Karl Marx. The first volume of *Das Kapital* (1867; tr. as *Capital*) had made free use of ecological analogies in representing the essential relationship between the classes in terms of parasitism, predation and vampirism, as well as giving a new meaning to the term "alienation" in speaking of the relationship between workers and their produce. The latter term was, however, already confused by another new meaning, which gave that term a quasi-ecological context, in speaking of human alienation from Nature by virtue of the Carlylean mechanization of every aspect of everyday life.

Marxism offered a potential solution to the immiseration of the proletariat in terms of revolution, while other socialists—including H. G. Wells—preferred to pin their hopes to evolutionary reform, but the record of literary commentary gives little evidence of widespread faith in either solution. Literary accounts of hypothetical societies did, however, become increasingly suspicious of the eutopian qualifications of the idle existence that social élites already led, which were often presumed to be in the process of a gradual exaggeration towards absurdity. Enclaves of the sort found in the heart of Stahlstadt and taken to their extreme in the lifestyle of the Eloi were routinely judged by literary commentators to be false eutopias, symptomatic of morbid social stagnation. That notion could easily be detached from the imagery of social division; Walter Besant's *The Inner House* (1888), which extrapolates the consequences of a technology of longevity, imagines an entire society that has fallen victim to spiritual stagnation, while James Elroy Flecker's *The Last Generation* (1908) looks forward satirically to a near future in which the human race, having become too keenly aware of the ineradicable dystopian aspects of its existence, refuses to perpetuate itself any longer.

Early speculative fictions based in a conscious ecological awareness sometimes went to extremes in rejecting the notion that an ideal society could ever be based in the artifices of civilized luxury. A graphic extrapolation of Cobbett's notion of London as a Great Wen is featured in Richard Jefferies *After London; or, Wild England* (1885), in which the capital has been reduced to a bleak scar of ineradicable pollution and the quality of English life has been restored by a technological retreat. W. H. Hudson's *A Crystal Age* (1887) is an extreme extrapolation of the principles of ecological mysticism, in which harmonious ecological relationships become a frankly supernatural means to the establishment of a peculiar matriarchal eutopia. Hudson's best-selling exotic romance *Green Mansions* (1902) is equally wholehearted in its assertions, maintaining that all extant human societies, from the most savage to the most civilized, are equally alienated from ecological harmony and uniformly dystopian in consequence.

Early fantasies of runaway future pollution usually took the form of moralistic disaster stories rather than dystopian romances; W. D. Hay's *The Doom of the Great City* (1880) and Robert Barr's "The Doom of London" (1892)—both of which feature catastrophic smogs—are ringing accounts of richly-deserved punishment. On the other hand, the traditional link between cleanliness and godliness came to seem rather dubious if God were replaced by Nature, because—however well-balanced its harmony might be—Nature did seem to have a sort of essential dirtiness. The early development of dystopian romance and satire showed as much evidence of fear of excessive cleanliness as fear of spreading pollution. Excessive cleanliness was frequently seen as a manifestation of the excessive orderliness of Mechanism, construed in opposition to the beautiful untidiness of Nature.

Writers involved in the Decadent movements of the *fin-de-siècle* defiantly celebrated artificiality in all its aspects, but they were working in conscious opposition to a perceived majority whose members considered technological artificiality to be somehow intrinsically awful, even while they drew extravagantly and enthusiastically on the particular opportunities it presented. *Fin-de-siècle* Romantic literature made much of the symbolism of Pan, the Graeco-Roman god of Arcadia, who was widely employed as a figurehead of Nature, and Romantic utopianism routinely favoured the nostalgic imagery of Arcadian pastoral existence over that of eutopian city-states.

In consequence of these lines of thought, most futuristic fantasies of the late nineteenth and early twentieth centuries, irrespective of whether they featured exaggerated social division or wholesale social reform, accepted the notion that the most fundamental social evil—the essential seed of dystopia—was the abstraction of human beings from a supposedly-harmonious relationship with the natural environment and its inherent rhythms: a pernicious form of alienation that was equally corrupting in its effects on the rich and the poor.

ENEMIES OF THE RATIONAL STATE

The argument that the severance of human beings from Nature is a kind of ultimate folly is strikingly exemplified by the futuristic horror stories collected in S. Fowler Wright's *The New Gods Lead* (1932), which offer a scathing indictment of the values of technocracy and the perversity of the worship of the "new gods", here named as Comfort and Cowardice. Fowler Wright's argument is that eutopians who see the good life in terms of a leisurely existence supported by all the luxuries of modern technology are woefully mistaken, and that the quality of human life depends on their engagement in a healthy struggle for existence against the vicissitudes of Nature—a Nature whose redness in tooth and claw is an essential component of its harmony, to be celebrated rather than regretted. He went on to recapitulate James Elroy Flecker's image of a future society that becomes literally suicidal by virtue of its own existential sickness in *The Adventure of Wyndham Smith* (1938).

The novel that now has the reputation of being the first great dystopian satire of the twentieth century, Aldous Huxley's *Brave New World* (1932), is fully conscious of the incipient hypocrisy of this kind of nostalgic Romanticism, and was enabled by that acute consciousness to set a new standard in black comedy. Huxley had sketched out an earlier ambiguous utopia in the unashamedly nostalgic *Crome Yellow* (1920), whose later chapters feature an enthusiastically ominous description of a coming "Rational State". In *Brave New World* that model is greatly elaborated, and considerably enriched by input from an alternative prospectus for the future offered by J. B. S. Haldane in *Daedalus; or, Science and the Future* (1923).

Haldane's essay looks forward optimistically to a day when biotechnology has secured the food supplies of an expanding population and "ectogenetic" children born from artificial wombs can be biologically modified at will; in *Brave New World* Huxley combined the latter notion with technologies of socially conditioning to form a system ensuring that all the citizens of his rigidly stratified future society are content with their various stations and capabilities. This was to become a central motif of much late-twentieth-century dystopian fiction: the notion that future inhabitants of a bad society might be conditioned gladly to celebrate their own alienation added a vital element of insult to injury.

Haldane was careful to preface the image of the future contained in *Daedalus* with a cautionary observation that there is always extreme initial resistance against "biological inventions," because they are invariably perceived, at first, as blasphemous perversions. He was certainly right about that, as the literary response to his essay clearly demonstrated. Huxley's was not the first, and was certainly not the last dystopian satire based on its anticipations; Julian Huxley—a fellow-biologist and close friend—got in ahead of his younger brother with "The Tissue-Culture King" (1926), which describes the nightmarish use made of Haldanian biotechnologies by a taboo-laden African tribal society. As if the skepticism of his friend were not hard enough to bear, Haldane's sister, Naomi Mitchison, produced grim futuristic fantasies based on the essay's key motifs in *Solution Three* (1975) and *Not by Bread Alone* (1983), although she diplomatically waited until he was dead before publishing them. Muriel Jaeger's *Retreat from Armageddon* (1936) offered a more even-handed response, although the optimistic side of the case is somewhat undermined by the fact that the dialogue takes place between intellectuals hiding in a bunker from the threat of a potentially-apocalyptic world war.

Brave New World is a more ambiguous text than many of its modern commentators assume; final judgment in the debate between Mustapha Mond and John Savage regarding the merits and limitations of the future it depicts is delivered by the latter's suicide, when he realises that he cannot resist the seductions that the world of artifice has to offer. A similar ambiguity is reflected in E. M. Forster's criticism of technological eutopianism, "The Machine Stops" (1909), which concentrates its criticism on the essential precariousness of an overprotective technological environment.

Huxley's suggestion that the inhabitants of a future dystopia might be conditioned to like it was an extrapolation of an anxiety common among the literate middle class that the fondest ambitions of society's ill-educated "masses" were inherently dystopian, judged by the tastes and preferences of literate and literary people. John Stuart Mill's father, James Mill, had been a Utilitarian eutopian who believed that the universalization of literacy would drive bad fiction to extinction, but the first prophet of dystopia had observed the falsification of that prediction; by the time Huxley wrote *Brave New World* its absurd naivety was painfully manifest. By that time, the appeal of "pulp fiction" was incontestable.

Although the American genre of pulp "science fiction" was established by its founder, Hugo Gernsback, as a propagandistic medium for the calculated celebration of the advancement of technology, it was rapidly infected by anxieties regarding the ultimate results of the worship of Fowler Wright's "new gods". Laurence Manning and Fletcher Pratt produced a striking account of "The City of the Living Dead" (1930), in which civilized humankind gladly retreats into synthetic experience, preferring life in what would nowadays be called "virtual reality" to the vicissitudes of natural existence.

The demands of popular melodrama ensured that pulp science fiction writers would be more interested in representations of rebellion against evil futures than peaceful accommodation to pleasant ones, but that imperative cannot entirely account for the anxieties manifest in the sf genre from its inception, regarding the "decadence" that might overtake human societies addicted to the comforts of technology. The fear of creeping decadence is, however, intrinsically muted, and has an obvious solution. John Savage could not, in the end, escape the seductiveness of Mustapha Mond's corrupt world, but when E. M. Forster's Machine stopped, its minions had no alternative but to return to the challenging wilderness, and Fowler Wright's Wyndham Smith was eager to do the same, in the hope that his descendants might learn to belong there again. Such dystopian societies are not manifestly or actively evil; their worst feature is, in fact, the hollowness of their eutopian pretence. Wholehearted dystopian imagery, in the first half of the twentieth century, required the kind of active vindictiveness in the deployment of technology and authority that was only displayed in political fantasies that set out to stigmatize some particular party as an incarnation of evil.

There was no shortage of such political fantasies in the first half of the century, their production being greatly encouraged by such actual instances of outrageous tyranny as Josef Stalin's regime in Russia and Adolf Hitler's in Germany. The tradition eventually culminated in George Orwell's *Nineteen Eighty-Four* (1949), whose careful excesses only served to emphasize the assumption that technological development unaided by tyrannical brutality could not plausibly be seen as an intrinsic road to hell. In spite of its tight focus on the politics of tyranny, however, *Nineteen Eighty-Four* retains an element of nostalgic Nature-worship in its depiction of Winston Smith's brief escape to an enclave of rural harmony.

Orwell's classic borrowed much of its narrative energy from anxieties left over from World War II, and the decade following the end of the war produced other memorable dystopias provoked by the same anxieties. Those with an ecological component to their anxieties included several accounts of extreme pollution in the wake of atomic warfare; Aldous Huxley's *Ape and Essence* (1948) is, in this respect, a much more contemptuous comedy than *Brave New World*. The most successful Orwellian fantasy, save for the original, was Ray Bradbury's *Fahrenheit 451* (1953), which brought the literary man's fear of the illiterate masses into uniquely sharp focus in its portrayal of future "firemen" whose job is to burn books and thus prevent the spread of the kinds of grief that, according to *Ecclesiastes*, inevitably stem from wisdom and the kinds of sorrow produced by the increase of knowledge. Here, too, a nostalgic regard for Nature is carefully conserved, and it is the wilderness that ultimately provides a refuge for the last custodians of literary value.

Orwellian political dystopias continued to appear for some thirty years, but they gradually faded from view. Ecological concerns were never irrelevant to these works, which routinely employed notions of alienation and pollution as well as conserving a certain Romantic nostalgia, but ecological issues rudely barged their way into the foreground of futuristic fiction in the 1950s and 1960s, with the result that the political issues central to Orwellian novels were gradually forced out to the margins. The disenchantment with political systems fostered by Orwellian dystopias helped to feed the conviction that the essential problem afflicting eutopian ambitions lay outside the arena of party politics, arising from such ecological problems as population expansion and environmental pollution, whose potential ill-effects put those of tyranny somewhat in the shade. The perception gradually grew that politicians of every stripe, however well-intentioned they might be, were all hirelings of the Rational State, unwitting slaves of Mechanism and hapless instruments of dystopia, impotent even to perceive, let alone to contend with the impending ecological crisis.

THE RESURGENCE OF MALTHUSIAN
ANXIETIES IN SPECULATIVE FICTION

Anxiety regarding the possibility of ecological disaster was sharpened in the U.S.A. between the two world wars by the emergence of the Midwestern "Dust Bowl", which received considerable literary attention in contemporary novels. These anxieties were extrapolated in the sf magazines by such alarmist fantasies as Nathan Schachner's "Sterile Planet" (1937) and Willard E. Hawkins' "The Dwindling Sphere" (1940), while more respectable novels foregrounding the potential problems of soil exhaustion included A. G. Street's *Already Walks Tomorrow* (1938) and Edward Hyams' *The Astrologer* (1950). In spite of such hiccups, though, the expansion of food supply had kept pace with the actual expansion of global population throughout the nineteenth and early twentieth centuries, soothing the anxiety that Malthus had tried to spread. Food-producers were still showing considerable enterprise in mid-century, participating in a "green revolution" based in the selective breeding of crop-plants which increased their yields markedly.

In parallel with the success of food production technologies, on the other hand, dramatic improvements in hygiene and the treatment of bacterial infections had lessened the impact of the most powerful of the Malthusian checks, facilitating an increase in global population that was increasingly likened in popular parlance to an "explosion". In the spring of 1955 a number of interested parties formed the Population Council, whose eleven-strong committee became a significant disseminator of propaganda regarding the dangerous rapidity of world population growth. The March 1956 issue of *Scientific American* carried an alarmist article on "World Population" by Julian Huxley, which assisted the Council's efforts.

The successes of modern technology in augmenting food production and reducing mortality rates seemed, in this context, merely to be postponing an inevitable disaster, which would be all the more catastrophic for its postponement. In the meantime, it seemed, society's attempts to sustain a vast population, or interrupt its expansion by draconian means, might be forced to become desperately ingenious. Anxiety was further heightened in the following decade, widely popularized by a best-selling account of *The Population Bomb* (1968) by Paul Ehrlich. Ehrlich dramatized his warnings in a fictionalized futuristic vision of "Ecocatastrophe" (1969), and similar images of future social collapse became commonplace. Literary accounts of desperate holding actions multiplied with equal rapidity, producing a rich spectrum of dystopian satires and futurological horror-stories.

Literary accounts of "the population problem" had begun to appear in some profusion in the sf magazines before the Population Council was formed. Stories addressing the idea as a problem requiring ingenious solution were already commonplace in 1954. In that year Isaac Asimov's *The Caves of Steel* offered a conscientiously even-handed analysis of the kinds of living conditions that a huge population would have to adopt and learn to love, while Damon Knight's gentle satire "Natural State" (revised for book publication as *Masters of Evolution*) provided a modest account of the biotechnological improvisations that might be necessary to sustain and overcrowded world, and Kurt Vonnegut Jr's brutal black comedy "The Big Trip Up Yonder" re-emphasized the hopelessness of the expectation that any such situation could long endure. The Council's propagandizing familiarized the idea, assisting earnest projections to push further and further ahead in dramatizing the search for imaginative solutions and satirical projections to become increasingly bitter.

The dystopias produced in this context were not all despairing. Robert Silverberg's *Master of Life and Death* (1957) maintains a certain pragmatic optimism in its depiction of a day in the hectic life of the bureaucrat responsible for the difficult organization of Malthusian moral restraint. Lester del Rey's *The Eleventh Commandment* (1962) tries to find some compensation for the continued harassments of the Malthusian checks in terms of the logic of natural selection. James Blish and Norman L. Knight's *A Torrent of Faces* (1967) bravely attempts to identify the advantages of the explicitly Fascist organization that a vast population might require. John Brunner's *Stand on Zanzibar* (1968) conscientiously dissects its overpopulated global society to expose its hopeful and heart-warming elements as well as nasty and frustrating aspects in multitudinous vignettes of everyday existence.

On the other hand, blackly comic projections published in the same period became increasingly sharp. The bureaucrats in Frederik Pohl's "The Census Takers" (1956) are more coldly methodical in meeting their targets than Silverberg's. In C. M. Kornbluth's "Reap the Dark Tide" (1958; reprinted as "Shark Ship") members of tribal societies exiled to the oceans by virtue of population pressure on land return to shore to discover the relics of the inevitable ecocatastrophe. The effects of inexorable inevitability in the vignette of everyday existence featured in J. G. Ballard's "Billennium" (1961) are all the more telling for their careful understatement. Harry Harrison's *Make Room! Make Room!* (1966) adapts Jonathan Swift's "modest solution" to the alleged problem of overpopulation in eighteenth-century Ireland to a twentieth-century near future. Robert Sheckley's "The People Trap" (1968) adapts the American improvisation of the Land Race to the acquisition of scarce property in the smogbound Jungle City of future New York.

As Malthusian anxieties began to play a leading role in popular debate, a US pressure group calling for Zero Population Growth attempted to make strategic use of dystopian fiction by promoting a science fiction anthology, *Scenarios for a Ship Called Earth* (1971) edited by Bob Sauer, and a movie named for its own acronym, *Z.P.G.* (1971; novelized as *The Edict* by screenwriter Max Ehrlich). 1971 was a particularly fruitful year for overpopulation dystopias; it also saw the production of Robert Silverberg's *The World Inside*, in which huge Urban Monads accommodate the population of an entire city on every floor while the surrounding fields are subjected to ever-more-intense agricultural exploitation, T. J. Bass's *Half Past Human*, in which decadent Nebishes have had to adopt a troglodytic existence while the world surface is entirely devoted to agricultural production, and Gordon R. Dickson's *Sleepwalker's World*, in which the broadcast energy that keeps food factories running at full capacity also maintains the vast population in a state of quiescent hibernation. The issue was, however, rarely isolated thereafter, save for carefully focused low-key satires like John Hersey's *My Petition for More Space* (1974). The notion that an increase in environmental pollution was an inevitable concomitant of increasing population was the first significant complication to be introduced into the pattern of expectation, but others followed swiftly in its train, including the possible exhaustion of fossil fuels and—eventually—global warming due to industrial carbon dioxide emissions.

Anxieties regarding the effects of environmental pollution were dramatically reinforced by Rachel Carson's best-selling *Silent Spring* (1962), whose influence reinforced Malthusian anxieties and encouraged their elaboration. The boom year of 1971 was followed by another in 1972, which saw the publication of a large number of compound ecological dystopias and disaster stories. In John Brunner's *The Sheep Look Up* and Philip Wylie's *The End of the Dream* pollution becomes a crucial Malthusian check, as Western civilization drowns ignominiously in its own wastes. In Gordon R. Dickson's *The Pritcher Mass* and William Jon Watkins and Gene Snyder's *Ecodeath*, mutations caused by pollution produce new parasitic organisms, whose spread forces survivors into sealed environments—which, like the similar retreats featured in Andrew J. Offutt's *The Castle Keeps*, soon become unendurable as well as indefensible.

Throughout the 1970s and the subsequent decades of the twentieth century, ecological anxieties played a central role in futuristic fiction, both within and without the generic ghetto of labelled science fiction. The notion that the twenty-first century would be an era of unprecedented ecological crisis, highly likely to lead to a temporary or permanent collapse of civilization, became so firmly entrenched in speculative fiction as virtually to be taken for granted.

ENVIRONMENTALISM AND POSTHUMANISM

The anxieties fostered in the aftermath of *Silent Spring*'s publication lent considerable impetus to a burgeoning environmental protection movement, whose advocates relegated overpopulation to the status of a single aspect of a broader problem. The ideology of the movement was summarized in *The Environmental Handbook* (1970), edited by Garett de Bell, and propagandized by such works as Richard Lillard's *Eden in Jeopardy: Man's Prodigal Meddling with His Environment* (1966), J. Clarence Davis's, *The Politics of Pollution* (1970), and James Ridgeway's *The Politics of Ecology* (1971). Green Parties were founded in several European countries, and such pressure groups as Friends of the Earth (founded in 1969) and Greenpeace (launched in 1971) became significant as lobbyists. Greenpeace also sponsored direct action for publicity purposes, often undertaken by its first naval vessel, *Rainbow Warrior*.

Garrett Hardin, the editor of *Population, Evolution, and Birth Control: A Collage of Controversial Ideas* (1964) went on to sketch out a new discipline of "ecological economics" in a classic essay published in *Science*, "The Tragedy of the Commons" (1968). "Classical" economists had always regarded population growth as a good thing, because it encouraged economic growth, and had also argued that the collective effect of the individual pursuit of personal advantage was an increase in the wealth of the whole society, but Hardin turned those arguments on their head. Wherever people were granted free access to a natural resource, he argued—as in the "commons" where all and sundry had once been entitled to graze their herds—the pursuit of individual advantage would inevitably lead to the overexploitation, spoliation and eventual annihilation of the resource.

The more obvious corollaries of Hardin's argument included the propositions that because the oceans are treated as a commons by fishermen, and the atmosphere is treated as a commons by producers of carbon dioxide, then the oceans are doomed to be denuded of fish and the atmosphere will be subject to catastrophic warming. In this perspective, the whole earth is bound to become dystopian as it lurches towards terminal disaster. As Hardin's essay was widely reprinted and its ideas circulated, the notion that a world ruled by the principles of classical economics was doomed to spoliation, and ultimately to self-destruction, became increasingly common in futuristic fiction, even though the dominant political culture of the U.S.A. came increasingly under the influence of "economic fundamentalists" zealously devoted to the free-market principles of Classical economics.

Hardin's hard-headed alarmism was complemented by a dramatic resurgence of ecological mysticism. The notion that the entire ecosphere could be regarded as a single entity possessed of homoeostatic systems akin to those regulating conditions within an individual body, first broached by Vladimir Vernadsky in *The Biosphere* (1926; tr. 1986), was popularized in spectacular fashion by James Lovelock's "Gaia hypothesis," elaborated in *Gaia: A New Look at Life on Earth* (1973). Although not mystical in itself, the language in which the Gaia hypothesis was couched lent tremendous encouragement to those who desired to construe it as if it were; Gaia displaced Pan as the most popular repersonification of Nature, although the *frisson* of panic remained.

The case for an actual technological retreat as the only viable means of averting a dystopian Tragedy of the Commons was forcefully made in Ernest Callenbach's Millennarian tract *Ecotopia: A Novel About Ecology, People and Politics in 1999* (1978). Its future history describes the secession from the U.S.A. of the western seaboard states, whose new masters establish a new low-tech society based on the principle of ecological sustainability. The unofficial religion of the new state is a species of Gaian mysticism—whose rituals helped to license the popular description of environmentalists as "tree-huggers"—and its folkways gladly embrace the principles of "alternative technology" laid out in such texts as Ernst Schumacher's *Small Is Beautiful* (1973).

Callenbach's new term caught on more widely, to the extent that Kim Stanley Robinson eventually produced a showcase sf anthology entitled *Future Primitive: The New Ecotopias* (1994), which collected works operating on the assumption that contemporary "megacities" cannot serve as models for future development but are, instead, "demonstrations of a dysfunctional social order"—a prospectus that condemns all images of future urban life to the status of dystopias. This supposition is dramatically illustrated by the imagery of the most flamboyant subgenre of late-twentieth-century sf, "cyberpunk" fiction, in which megacities like the Sprawl featured in William Gibson's *Neuromancer* (1984) and its sequels become the ultimate urban jungles, relative to which the wide-open virtual plains of cyberspace become a kind of Heavenly frontier, complete with a nascent God as well as exotic gunslingers.

Although such Gaia-conscious dystopian novels as David Brin's *Earth* (1990) tried hard to maintain a note of optimism in depicting global attempts to cope with ongoing problems of pollution and induced climate change, there was a near-universal consensus among literary commentators that any envisaged "solutions" to Hardin's cold equations—including heroic escapes into virtual reality—could only be local and temporary. *Neuromancer*'s alternative term for cyberspace was adopted as the title of a trilogy of films begun with *The Matrix* (1999) in which a manufactured virtual reality maintains a semblance of contemporary life in a future whose "actual" landscapes attempted a visual summation of dystopian nightmares—imagery replicated to a lesser degree in numerous other movies produced in the wake of Ridley Scott's highly influential *Bladerunner* (1982).

By the time that cyberpunk fiction made its debut, the myth of the Space Age—the notion that the future of humankind would consist of a gradual but illimitable colonization of the universe—had foundered on the realization that the 1969 moon landing really was just one small step, impotent in the short term to facilitate a second. It was obvious by that time that the construction and maintenance of mini-ecospheres required for any expansion into orbital space would be far more problematic than earlier images of spaceships, space stations and space colonies had imagined.

The cyberpunk writers who paid more attention than William Gibson to the possible terms of a human expansion into actual space, most notably Bruce Sterling—in the Shaper/Mechanist series launched in 1982, which culminated in *Schismatrix* (1985)—presumed that such colonization would be as rich in eutopian experimentation as the colonization of the Americas, but with no better result. Indeed, the didactic conclusion of the Shaper/Mechanist series is that effective space colonization is an inherently posthuman project—a conclusion so compelling in its logic that it formed the fundamental assumption of the next subgeneric boom within sf: a "new space opera" whose spacefaring characters are, by necessity, subjected to genetic engineering and/or cyborgization, except for those whose intelligence is purely artificial.

Although most posthumanist fiction is resolutely, flamboyantly and disingenuously upbeat, the fact that J. B. S. Haldane's observation about the initial imaginative impact of "biological inventions" still holds true ensures that the entire spectrum of such fiction retains a curious "dystopian glamour", in which the vicissitudes of ultra-mechanized urban life tend to be transformed into healthy challenges akin to those provided by Nature to S. Fowler Wright's exiles from the sterile eutopia of comforts. Genetic engineering and cyborgization may be regarded as processes of ecological adaptation or ecological defiance, according to one's point of view—taken, in either case, towards a new logical extreme—but in either case, their invocation in futuristic fiction changes the rules of the utopian game.

Although early commentators on the possibility of a posthuman future were felt free to be straightforwardly horror-stricken by such imagery, after the fashion of David Bunch's depiction of a cyborg dystopia in *Moderan* (1971), the majority of post-cyberpunk commentators adopted a calculatedly ironic ambiguity, as they had to do. Sciencefictonal attempts to describe mature posthuman societies, such as those contained in Damien Broderick's *The White Abacus* (1997), Karl Schroeder's *Permanence* (2002), Robert Reed's *Sister Alice* (2003), and Justina Robson's *Natural History* (2003) defy classification as eutopias or dystopias precisely because the societies they describe *are* posthuman, and therefore exceed the capacity of terms designed to reflect the extremes of human ambition and anxiety. Where posthuman possibilities are extravagantly displayed—the most extravagant example to date is the story-sequence collected in Charles Stross's *Accelerando* (2005)—nineteenth-century anxieties about the creeping "mechanization" of human life and the "alienation" of human existence from Nature are inevitably overturned, lost in a fetishistic celebration of mechanization and alienation, which regard the merely human with casual contempt.

DYSTOPIA NOW

As the twentieth century drew to a close, anxieties about environmental pollution—which had broadened out by degrees from vulgar smoke and slag to embrace heavy metals, radioactive wastes, non-biodegradable organic compounds preserved and concentrated within the food chain, and aerosol propellants depleting the ozone layer—became increasingly focused again on a single problem: the threat of global warming caused by emissions of carbon dioxide.

Although many politicians maintained a state of denial for some time after the issue was first raised, a 1992 Earth Summit issued a resolution calling for world carbon dioxide levels to be stabilized at 1990 levels by the year 2000. The Berlin Mandate of 1995, renewed by the Kyoto Protocol of 1997, adopted a higher target and a longer deadline, but were still reduced to futility by the refusal of the U.S.A. to ratify the agreement and the non-involvement of China, whose ultra-rapid programme of industrialization had already become a major source of accelerating carbon dioxide emissions. While these developments were under way, however, reportage of the problem changed its tone markedly, as a tendency developed for every item of inclement weather to be interpreted as a sign that global warming was already under way, and that its momentum was gathering apace.

As with other ecological problems, global warming was something for which every human individual was to some degree responsible, although some individuals and organizations were obviously guiltier than others. This unequal sharing of guilt was dramatized in the notion of a "carbon footprint": the dark dystopian stain left on the earth's surface by the passage through life of every human being and industrial endeavor. Although endeavors of all kinds contributed to an individual's carbon footprint, censure became concentrated on those seen to be the most sinful, in particular the habit of driving "gas-guzzling" cars and the custom of using cheap air travel to take foreign holidays: present indulgences assisting in the precipitation of a present crisis.

The carbon footprint was not the only stigma of ecological sin widely attributed to human individuals in the early twenty-first century, nor was it the one that generated the most anxiety and shame; that dubious honour was given to the phenomenon of obesity, which was subject to a similar quasi-scientific formulation in the "body mass index". While a carbon footprint was only something figuratively left behind, body fat was something people carried around inside them. It thus became the most visible manifestation of the hedonistic over-indulgence—further exemplified by the cheap foreign holidays that were popularly considered to be a key contributor to carbon footprints—that seemed both to constitute and to be hastening the dystopian degradation and ecocatastrophic destruction of the world.

Hedonism always had a bad press in dystopian fiction, since Odysseus first encountered the listless Lotus Eaters; its seductive but destructive appeal underlies the essential irony of "The City of the Living Dead", *Brave New World* and many other twentieth-century accounts of the siren song of technology. The argument obtained a particularly explicit summary in James E. Gunn's *The Joy Makers*

(1961), whose first part describes the acquisition of political power by Hedonics, Inc—a corporation whose slogan is "Your Happiness is Our Business", which persuades individuals to sign over all their wealth in return for a guarantee of permanent happiness. In the novel's second part, a Hedonic Council that has inherited absolute political power plans to sweep away all humankind's Natural dissatisfactions by means of drugs and psychosurgery—with the result that the third part finds the entire race cocooned in the foetal bliss of artificial wombs, attended by a dutiful Mechanism that is in no danger of stopping, but is instead ambitious to export this paradigm of paradise throughout the universe. Arguments of this sort, which became increasingly common as the century progressed, not only endorsed and re-emphasized Malthus's suspicion that human beings would never be willing to pay the cost of achieving eutopia in the currency of moral restraint, but suggested strongly that the battle was already lost, and that dystopia had come to stay.

Although dystopian dramas of environmental spoliation by overpopulation and pollution had not been reluctant to point out that the enemy was not so much an implacable external force as our own lack of moral restraint, the addition of perceptible global warming to the list of the world's political problems and the drastic exaggeration of individual anxieties about obesity played a major role in switching the emphasis of popular rhetoric to the magnification of individual responsibility and the careful cultivation of an individual sense of ecological sin. When the drafters of the American constitution had added the pursuit of happiness to life and liberty as an inalienable human right they had assumed that the pursuit of happiness was, on the whole, a good thing, and an essential component of the eutopian quest. As the twentieth century drew towards its close, however, hedonism had been redefined as a road to dystopia and obesity, the latter being construed not as a sign of wealth and jollity but as the epitome of morbid dysfuctionality.

Literary attempts to anticipate the adaptations that global civilization might yet have to make in order to cope with the "greenhouse effect" induced by carbon dioxide emissions began to appear in some profusion as the twentieth century ended and the twenty-first century began. Notable examples tending towards political fantasy rather than straightforward disaster stories include Bruce Sterling's *Distraction* (1998), Norman Spinrad's *Greenhouse Summer* (1999), William Sanders' "When This World Is All on Fire" (2001), and Kim Stanley Robinson's *Forty Signs of Rain* (2004). What is primarily notable about all these works, as well as the temper of almost all reportage of the unfolding ecocatastrophe, is the absence of the slightest vestige of trust in the possibility that the exercise of moral restraint might slow the catastrophe down, let alone prevent it proceeding to its climax.

The placement of dreams of future eutopia with an ecological perspective has wrought a gradual but inexorable transformation in the significance of dystopian imagery. Such dystopian imagists as Ray Bradbury and John Brunner were fond of arguing that they were not trying to predict the future but trying to prevent it, updating images of Stahlstadt in the hope of evoking a reaction that would favour the development of Frankville. By the end of the twentieth century, however, such arguments had lost their force, because the recognition that the unfolding ecocatastrophe could not be halted, or even slowed down, put Frankville out of reach, at least until the catastrophe had run its course. Dystopian images of the near future can no longer avoid the burden of their own inevitability; Orwellian fears of future tyranny can no longer make more than a marginal difference to the tenor of contemporary pessimism.

Insofar as twenty-first-century futuristic fiction set on Earth retains a eutopian component, its eutopias are necessarily postponed until the aftermath of an environmental collapse. The near-universal assumption of such fiction is that dystopia has already arrived, in embryo, and that its progress to maturity is unavoidable. Having calculated the amount of landbound ice that might eventually be melted into the oceans, we know that the impending Deluge will not be as all-consuming as its mythical prototype, but that will not make it very much easier to endure. Nor does the knowledge that we have brought dystopia upon ourselves by our pursuit of material comforts provide much imaginative solace, even to the kind of people who relish opportunities to say "I told you so".

COSMIC HORROR

Introduction

The notion of "cosmic horror" is closely associated with H. P. Lovecraft and the school of weird fiction associated with him. Lovecraft's fascination with the adjective "cosmic" is clearly evident in his essay on *Supernatural Horror in Literature*, which was initially written in 1924 and published in *The Recluse* in 1927 before undergoing the thorough revision that led to the version published in the Arkham House collection *The Outsider and Others* in 1939 and reprinted as a booklet by Dover in 1973. The adjective is, however, used there in a sense that is rather different from the connotations eventually acquired by "cosmic horror."

In the first chapter of the revised essay, in which Lovecraft defines his field, speaks of a "literature of cosmic fear" that is to be distinguished from the literature of "physical fear and the mundanely gruesome." At first glance "cosmic" seems to be used here merely as a replacement term for "supernatural," but the substitution also implies a particular psychological attitude to the supernatural. The text refers to "that most terrible conception of the human brain—a malign and particular suspension of those fixed laws of Nature which are our only safeguards against the assaults of chaos and the daemons of unplumbed space."

Much of the subsequent argument of the essay is devoted to the establishment of a canonical set of texts in which supernatural phenomena are conceived and represented in these terms, while many other works featuring standard motifs such as ghosts and witches are excluded from that canon on the grounds that the figures in question have become stereotyped, and hence returned to a kind of mundanity. Lovecraft complains at a later stage about the "tedious, artificial and melodramatic" tendencies of much vulgar Gothic fiction.

It is possible, given Lovecraft's inclinations, that the reference to "daemons" in the cited passage is merely a pretentious spelling of "demons." It is more probable, though, that Lovecraft had in mind the kind of daemon featured in Platonic and neo-Platonic thought, which is a kind of raw supernatural power that has far more to do with knowledge than with evil. Lovecraftian fiction is, in essence, a kind of fiction in which horror arises from knowledge that is too much to bear; the ultimate knowledge of that kind is, indeed, related to "unplumbed space" rather than the shallows of human evil, and to "assaults of chaos" rather than the pedestrian traffic of commonplace apparitions and curses. In his own work, Lovecraft was not content merely to continue the existing tradition of supernatural fiction; he attempted to take it to a new extreme, in which the specific element of "cosmic horror" would be carefully focused and extrapolated to its ultimate; by the time it became feasible to talk of *the* cosmic horror as a kind of entity, the adjective had been considerably refined.

The second section of Lovecraft's essay argues that the roots of "cosmic terror" are very ancient. He finds its echoes in a good deal of ancient folklore, associating it with a hypothetical pagan cult of "nocturnal worshippers" whose "revolting fertility-rites" had been driven underground by more elevated and organized religions even before Christianity completed the process. The history and anthropology of this part of his argument—derived from the speculations set out in James Frazer's *The Golden Bough*—are questionable, but the scholarly fantasy in question had become a central element of the mythic past from which most late nineteenth- and early twentieth-century horror fiction drew its imagery. The fundamental thesis that Lovecraft developed in the cultivation of cosmic horror is that technological and social progress since Classical times have facilitated the repression of an awareness of the magnitude and malignity of the macrocosm in which the human microcosm is contained—an awareness that our remoter ancestors could not avoid.

In Lovecraft's argument, *all* organized religion, pagan or Christian—he specifically mentions Druidism and Graeco-Roman religion—is part and parcel of this repressive process: a calculated denial of the essential awfulness of cosmic truth by means of the invention and attempted invocation of gods which, if not actually benign, can at least be flattered and palliated. Lovecraft's argument is that the most artistic and effective works of modern weird fiction are recovering something of a more ancient sensitivity, not in the form of committed belief but in the form of an aesthetic response. In this respect, his argument echoes one that had earlier developed within the context of formal aesthetic philosophy, although it had condemned to the margins of debate by the establishment of a sharply contrasted orthodoxy. The argument in question concerned the supplementation of the notion of beauty with a second kind of aesthetic sensation, more closely akin to awe: "the sublime."

THE SUBLIME, ROMANTICISM, AND THE GOTHIC

The notion of the sublime originated in the first century AD, but the treatise in which it was introduced—by a Sicilian Jew named Cecilius—has been lost, and the earliest surviving work on the subject is a slightly later essay by Longinus. Although Longinus had a considerable influence on sixteenth- and seventeenth-century Italian aesthetic theory, the notion of the sublime remained esoteric elsewhere in Europe, where a very different kind of aesthetic theory developed, which not only remained centered on the notions of beauty, order and harmony but conceived their artistic reproduction in naturalistic terms. Alexander Baumgarten, who popularized the term "aesthetics" in its modern meaning, was a follower of Gottfried Leibniz, and his summary *Aesthetika* (1750-58) makes much of Leibniz's representation of literature as a mode of cognition aspiring to "perceptual clarity." In consequence, Baumgarten's theory focuses attention on matters of order, pattern and symmetry.

Although Leibniz's philosophical consideration of "possible worlds" allowed that works of art might contain worlds markedly different from the world of experience, he had argued in his *Theodicy* (1710) that ours must be the best of all possible worlds (a supposition ruthlessly parodied by Voltaire in the character of Doctor Pangloss in *Candide*). In consequence of this argument, Baumgarten argued that the highest ideal of artistic "secondary creation" must be to produce simulacra of the world of experience rather than to venture into the innately-inferior practice of "heterocosmic" creativity.

In spite of the popularity of Voltaire's mockery of the Leibnizian argument, Baumgarten's stress on naturalistic representation—especially insofar as it detected and celebrated beauty and harmony—fit in very well with the dominant trend in contemporary literature. It did not, however, go entirely unopposed. In Britain, Mark Akenside produced a poetic celebration of *The Pleasures of the Imagination* (1744), which was wholeheartedly committed to the cause of heterocosmic creativity. Akenside's reputation as a poet soon went into a sharp decline, but his ideas were taken up, refined and further extrapolated by Edmund Burke's *Philosophical Enquiry into the Origin of Our Ideas of the Sublime and Beautiful* (1757), which reintroduced the notion of the sublime into English aesthetic theory.

Burke's aesthetic theory was rooted in the emotions rather than the Leibnizian notion of "perceptual clarity." Instead of construing beauty in terms of symmetry and organization he connects it with loving emotions. The sublime, on the other hand, he derives from the fundamental emotion of "astonishment." According to Burke, sublimity is associated with danger, power, vacuity, darkness, solitude, silence, vastness, potential, difficulty and color—and it always has an element of horror. Although this is not disconsonant with Longinus' account of the sublime, Burke's particular emphasis on the horrific component was new. Superficially, at least, it was also rather surprising, in that he associated it with the additional powers of insight lent to the rapt contemplation of nature by contemporary natural philosophy. He was not alone in this; many of his contemporaries found the revelations of scientific Enlightenment innately horrific, although others considered their response more akin to exaltation.

This division of opinion was very obvious in literary reflections of scientific progress, particular those responsive to the conception of the universe developed by Isaac Newton, whose infinite scope, lack of any definable centre and mechanical regularity contrasted very strongly with the narrowly-confined, geocentric and divinely-organized Aristotelian cosmos that had long been accepted into the dogmas of orthodox Christian faith. Although early accounts of the heliocentric solar system had only slightly displaced the centre of the universe, without having much effect on the conception of the peripheral realm of the "fixed stars," eighteenth-century extrapolations of Newton's cosmos took aboard the awareness that our sun was, after all, merely one star among many, and that even the entire sidereal system of which it was an inconspicuous element might be one among many.

Two years before Burke published his thesis, Immanuel Kant had published *Allegemeine Naturgeschichte und Theorie des Himmels* (1755; tr. as *Universal Natural History and Theory of the Heavens*), which included the contention that the Milky Way is merely one lenticular aggregation of stars among a sequence of "island universes"—a notion that had already obtained some empirical support from William Herschel's studies of nebulae. Herschel's observations—which had led him to conclude that the Milky Way consisted of some three hundred million stars, most of them invisible, arranged in a lens-shaped system measuring some 8,000 light-years by 1,500—had considerably increased the prevailing notion of the size of the universe, and the possibility that at least some nebulae were "island universes" added a further order of magnitude to that estimation. The first measurements of stellar parallax, published in 1838-40, fitted neatly enough into the vastness of this imagined scale. The imaginative impact of these measurements was considerable, although Edward Young's *The Complaint; or, Night Thoughts* (1742-45) had already observed of the Newtonian system that "At once it quite engulfs all human thought; / 'Tis comprehension's absolute defeat" before relieving the sense of sublime astonishment with a residue of pride in being able to conceive of such things: "How glorious, then, appears the mind of man, / When in it all the stars, and planets, roll!"

This kind of ambivalence is clearly reflected in much subsequent fiction. Fiction enthusiastic about the discoveries of science tended to focus on the element of exaltation, while fiction sympathetic to the mythological imagery that science seemed to be devastating and displacing was ore likely to concentrate on the horrific, but the most interesting effect was on writers who retained the ambivalence within themselves and their work. Burke's aesthetic theory became a key influence on the English Romantic Movement, several of whose key figures were keenly interested and to some degree educated in science—Samuel Taylor Coleridge had been tutored by the proto-anthropologist J. F. Blumenbach and Percy Shelley by the proto-meteorologist Adam Walker.

The roots of Romanticism were various; its rebellion against a perceived "Classicism" took several different forms, of which the most prominent, in retrospect, are its nostalgic interest in the fantastic and the folkloristic, and its championship of the spontaneity of psychological and aesthetic responses against the imposed order and discipline of formal representation. What philosophers like Walker contributed to the movement was, however, the notion that the world of ordinary sensory experience, mundane time-calculation and social interaction was merely a network of appearances, behind which lay the arcane realities of cosmology, physics and geological time. Walker, by virtue of his meteorological interests, was particularly fascinated by the notion of "atmospheric electricity," and the notion that electricity might provide the key to the phenomenon of life was very fashionable in the late eighteenth century, garishly reflected in the medical theories of such fashionable quacks as James Graham and Anton Mesmer.

Such ideas were a distinctly subsidiary component of Romantic aesthetics, overshadowed and almost overwhelmed by other components. The passage quoted from Young's *Night Thoughts* is a momentary digression from that poem's chief concerns, which are much more intimate, and the Romantic poets who extrapolated the mission of the graveyard school were similarly preoccupied, first and foremost, with meditations on mortality. In the same way, the school of Gothic horror fiction, which was one of Romanticism's two chief extensions into prose fiction—the other being what the German Romantics called *kunstmärchen*, or "art fairy tales"—is primarily preoccupied with death and darkness, and only peripherally concerned with the further reaches of Burkeian sublimity. Even so, Romanticism was fertile ground for the development of a kind of cosmic horror that was not merely supernatural but possessed of a newly-exaggerated sensation of sublimity in its attitude—a sublimity that derives from, although it is not usually explicitly associated with, the imagery of the new cosmos of post-Newtonian science.

This kind of attitude can be found in some atypical Gothic novels—most obviously William Beckford's *Vathek* (1786) and Mary Shelley's *Frankenstein* (1818)—and in such poems as Coleridge's "Rime of the Ancient Mariner" (1798) and Percy Shelley's "Queen Mab" (1813), but the work in which the sensibility that subsequently came to be central to "cosmic horror" is most elaborately and explicitly developed is Thomas De Quincey's *Confessions of an Opium-Eater* (1821). The key passage is one that attempts to define the altered state consciousness induced by opium, in which "a theatre seemed suddenly opened and lighted up within my brain, which presented nightly spectacles of more than earthly splendour":

> "As the creative state of the eye increased, a sympathy seemed to arise between the waking and sleeping states of the brain in one point,—that whatsoever I happened to call up and to trace by a voluntary act upon the darkness was very apt to transfer itself to my dreams; so that I feared to exercise this faculty; for, as Midas turned all things to gold, that yet baffled is hopes and defrauded his human desires, so whatsoever things capable of being visually represented I did but think of in the darkness, immediately shaped themselves into phantoms of the eye; and, by a process apparently no less inevitable, when thus once traced in faint and visionary colours, like writings in sympathetic ink, they were drawn out, by the fierce chemistry of my dreams, into insufferable splendour that fretted my heart.

"For this, and all other changes in my dreams, were accompanied by deep-seated anxiety and gloomy melancholy, such as are wholly incommunicable by words. I seemed every night to descend—not metaphorically, but literally to descend—into chasms and sunless abysses, depths below depths, from which it seemed hopeless that I could ever reascend. Nor did I, by waking, feel that I *had* reascended. This I do not dwell upon; because the state of gloom which attended these gorgeous spectacles, amounting at least to utter darkness, as of some suicidal despondency, cannot be approached by words." (*Essays*, p. 55)

Having described these primary effects of an increase in "the creative state of the eye" De Quincey notes that his sense of space and time were "powerfully affected" by opium: "Space swelled, and was amplified to an extent of unutterable infinity. This, however, did not disturb me so much as he vast expansion of time: I sometimes seemed to have lived for 70 or 100 years in one night; nay, sometimes had feelings representative of a millennium passed in that time, or, however, of a duration far beyond the limits of any human experience." He also notes the effect that opium appears to have on the phenomenon of memory, which lead him to draw the conclusion that nothing is ever, or ever can be, entirely forgotten. No matter what veils are employed by the conscious mind to conceal or bury memories, he asserts, they can always be withdrawn in the correct state of mind to reveal the hidden memory in all its awful clarity.

The role played by opium in De Quincey's account of the perfection of sublime sensibility is a crucial one, echoed in many subsequent literary accounts of cosmic horror. It is a central tenet of the argument that everyday consciousness is blind—conveniently if not willfully—and that it requires some extraordinary intervention to reveal the reality behind appearances (or, in Kantian terms, the noumenal world beyond the phenomenal one). The everyday mind working through the five senses, and the imagination to which it gives rise, cannot comprehend the true implication of the infinity of cosmic space and the depth of cosmic time, nor the extremes of anxiety and melancholy inevitably associated with their perception—which are, in De Quincey's estimation, "wholly incommunicable by words."

The entire tradition of cosmic horror fiction can be regarded as a heroic but doomed attempt to rise to that challenge: to communicate the uncommunicable, by suggesting—in the absence of any possibility of explicit description—the sheer enormity of the revelation that would be vouchsafed to us, were we ever granted permission to see and conceive of the world as it really is, rather than as it appears to our senses: deflated, diminished and domesticated. It is for this reason that "the cosmic horror," conceived as an entity, is by far the most elusive of all the icons of horror fiction, almost definable by its indescribability. Its presence can be felt, but only the merest glimpses an ever be caught of its form. Its description and definition can be tentatively approached in various ways—one may observe that it is daemonic rather than demonic, and that it is more akin to the alien than the traditionally supernatural—but can never be completed or clarified.

Discussion of "comic horror" is, in consequence, bound to consist primarily of a series of contrasts, incessantly stating what it is *not*—because what it *is* remains intrinsically beyond the reach of ordinary experience, potentially accessible only by means of some hypothetical transcendental experience. Even hallucinogenic drugs give no more than a hint of the possibility; De Quincey's highly idiosyncratic response to opium proved unrepeatable by many others who followed his example. Coleridge, who solicited—and obtained—various different hallucinogenic drugs from the botanist Joseph Banks, the President of the Royal Society, never managed to complete the interrupted "Kubla Khan," let alone discover further imaginary worlds that he could explore and describe in detail. Subsequent literary representations of hallucinatory experience bear no more resemblance to actual experiences of that kind than literary dreams do to actual dreams; the literary mind inevitably pursues meaning, even in mazy experiences whose procedure is destructive of meaning.

Cosmic Pessimism and Its Antidotes

As Edward Young's two couplets illustrate, one of the most common—and perhaps most natural—responses to the sensation of cosmic horror is the rapid substitution of a more uplifting sense of wonder. The neo-Platonists and their intellectual descendants, who attempted to retain, refine and complicate the essential holism of their world-view by assiduously searching out all manner of occult connections and correspondences, encapsulated their supposed wisdom in the dictum "as above, so below," asserting that the microcosm and the macrocosm were reflections of one another. When the revelation arrived that the scales of cosmic space and time were much vaster than the schemes of human visual experience and the human lifetime, its horrific component could be resisted by several means, including the conviction that the human mind might be capable of far more than it routinely achieved.

Although there were significant works of Romantic and post-Romantic fiction that embraced various shades of cosmic pessimism—Mary Shelley's *The Last Man* (1826) and Robert Browning's "Childe Roland to the Dark Tower Came" (1855) are among the more conspicuous examples—the more typical literary response was to search for antidotes to that threat. One writer who took a good deal of inspiration from his brief acquaintance with the Shelleys, Edward Bulwer—who adopted his mother's surname into his own before becoming famous as Edward Bulwer-Lytton—found his antidote in the notion of Rosicrucianism: an imaginary "occult science" whose teaching might equip a man, intellectually and spiritually, to apprehend the cosmos as it was without cowering in terror. The operative word was, however, *might*. His two great occult romances, *Zanoni* (1842) and *A Strange Story* (1862)—which proved a great inspiration to subsequent lifestyle fantasists as well as literary fantasists—place a heavy emphasis on the difficulty of that attainment and the dangers of hastening towards it without adequate preparation.

The eponymous Zanoni has already made significant progress in his occult studies under the tutelage of his associate Mejnour, but eventually turns away from that path in order to enjoy the mundane love of the story's heroine. The young Englishman Glyndon, rejected by the heroine, attempts to take Zanoni's place as Mejnour's pupil, but impatience brings him into confrontation with the Dweller of the Threshold, the symbolic guardian of the path to superhumanity and the first tentative step in the direction of equipping "the comic horror" with a perceptible mask. Nothing can be discerned of its face by a pair of demonic eyes, whose stare penetrates its shrouding veil:

> "All fancies, the most grotesque, of Monk or Painter in the early North, would have failed to give to the visage of imp or fiend that aspect of deadly malignity which spoke to the shuddering nature in those eyes alone. All else so dark—shrouded—veiled and larva-like. But that burning glare so intense, so livid, yet so living, had in it something that was almost *human*, in its passion of hate and mockery—something that served to show that he shadowy Hor-

ror was not all a spirit, but partook of matter enough, at least, to make it more deadly and fearful an enemy to material forms." (p. 172)

In the more explicitly Faustian *A Strange Story* Mejnour is replaced by the seductively handsome Margrave and Glyndon by the materialistic physician Fenwick, and the crucial confrontation scene is delayed until the end of the story. This time the threshold between this world and the macrocosm is guarded by a veritable host of entities initially discernible as an array of terrible eyes—but when a single entity coalesces from the swirling confusion of demonic forms, all that can be seen of it is a gigantic foot. Although Margrave is destroyed, Fenwick withdraws from the uncrossed threshold in a much better condition than Glyndon, morally and spiritually rearmed and confident of the vale of incurious human faith.

A more complex path to a similar destination was followed by Edgar Allan Poe, whose earliest publications included the visionary poem "Al Aaraaf" (written c1820), which echoed Akenside's *Pleasures of the Imagination* in some respects but set a significant precedent of its own. Titled for Tycho Brahe's New Star, which heralded the reconstruction of the cosmos by John Kepler, Galileo and Isaac Newton, it details a visionary odyssey through a universe undergoing a crucial conceptual metamorphosis. Poe's prose fiction gave more explicit voice to his early cosmic pessimism, which seems to be at its height in "Shadow—A Parable" (1835), "Silence—A Fable" (1838) and the apocalyptic "The Conversation of Euros and Charmion" (1839). By the time he wrote the more elaborate "Memeric Revelation" (1844), he had found an antidote of sorts to "the substantive vastness of infinity," in the notion that the present life of humankind is merely "rudimental," limited by the inadequacy of the sense organs, whose eventual transcendence is inevitable.

"The multitudinous conglomeration of raw matter into nebulae, planets, suns and other bodies, which are neither nebulae, suns, nor planets," Poe's mesmerized subject laconically reports, "is for the sole purpose of supplying *pabulum* for the indiosycrasy of the organs of an infinity of rudimental beings. But for the necessity of the rudimental, prior to the ultimate life, there would have been no bodies such as these." In other words, although the vast cosmos of modern science could not have been conceived for the use and convenience of man—as the geocentric cosmos was—it is nevertheless a mere contrivance, whose vastness and complexity merely reflects the abundance and variety of "rudimental beings."

Poe expanded this perspective to its conceptual limits in *Eureka* (1848), which concludes with a vision of a Kantian cosmos in which island universes follow a complex life-cycle, eventually collapsing under the influence of gravity so that its matter re-achieves a primal "unity" from which a new island universe might be reborn giving rise to an eternal sequence that is the pulsation of the "Heart Divine," By this means, the matter made for the containment and generation of rudimental beings is endlessly recycled, in order that it might continue to serve its purpose, while the beings themselves move on to some (unimaginable) further phase of existential evolution.

While Bulwer-Lytton and Poe were engaged in these and other literary experiments, several attempts were made in continental Europe to make more productive use of the altered state of consciousness described by de Quincey. In Paris, opium had recently been supplemented by the importation of hashish, which was fed to Théophile Gautier and other members of the self-styled *Club de Haschichins* by the proto-psychologist Joseph Moreau, who liked to style himself "Moreau de Tours." Moreau's scientific treatise on *Hashish and Mental Alienation* (1845), based in these experiments, reprinted the whole of an article on "Hashish" that Gautier had published in 1843.

Gautier describes the effects of hashish in more generous terms than Coleridge's description of the effects of opium, alleging that his body appeared to become transparent, allowing him to see the drug he had consumed as an emerald within his breast "emitting millions of little sparks". These began to spin around, joining with other precious stones in a kaleidoscopic dance, while his companions appeared to be disfigured, becoming chimerical figures with vegetal or avian characteristics. He began laughing and juggling with cushions, while one of his companions spoke to him in Italian, which the hashish translated into Spanish. Subsequently, he experienced a further series of visions, involving swarms of butterflies and amazing flowers, when his sense of hearing became so "acute" that he could "hear the very sounds of the colours" and was set adrift on an ocean of sounds.

He claims:

> "Never had such beatitude flooded me with its waves. I had so melted into the indefinable, I was so absent, so free from myself (that detestable witness ever dogging one's footsteps) that I realised for the first time what might be the way of life of elemental

spirits, of angels, and of souls separated from their bodies. I was like a sponge in the midst of the ocean: at every moment floods of happiness penetrated me... my whole being had been transfused by the colour of the medium into which I had been plunged."

There is no cosmic horror here, but rather a sense of comfort and belonging—a blitheness reproduced in most of Gautier's tales of the supernatural, in which momentary anxieties always tend to be blotted out by erotic ecstasy. His experiences were, however, not matched by those of a writer whose tenure in Moreau's club was much briefer and far less satisfactory. Charles Baudelaire's essay "Du vin et du hashish" (1851) similarly represents itself as a quasi-scientific study, but its treatment of the supposed delights of alcoholic intoxication moves swiftly on to a sarcastic description of the "supersublime" ignominies of drunkenness, and the shorter account of hashish follows much the same pattern.

Baudelaire advises that one should submit oneself to the action of hashish only in "favourable circumstances and environments", because its effect is to magnify *all* subjective sensations, including negative ones. "From time to time," he concedes, "your personality vanishes. The sense of objectivity that creates pantheistical poets and great actors becomes so powerful that you are confounded with external objects. Now you are a tree moaning in the wind and murmuring vegetal melodies to nature. Now you hover in the azure of an immensely expanded sky. Every sorrow has disappeared.... Soon the very idea of time will disappear." He is, however, pessimistic about the prospect of reproducing such sensations in literary form. He attempted to do it in such prose-poems as "Le Chambre double" (1862), in which an opium dream briefly transforms the viewpoint-character's drab room into a kind of paradise, but the major trend in his work was in the opposite direction, visionary transformations producing such horrific images as those detailed in "Les Métamorphoses du vampire" (1857) and his whole attitude to the world being infected and permeated by the allegedly unbearable effects of *spleen*—a kind of inescapable anguish born of an unusually clear-sighted sensitivity to the vicissitudes of existence.

Baudelaire found his antidote to *spleen* in a paradoxical readjustment of his attitude. Rather than settling for the consolations of faith, as his spiritual brother Poe had done, he elected to re-evaluate horror as a positive sensation, to be welcomed for its preferability to the corrosive tedium of *ennui*. In one of his longest poems, "Le voyage" (1859), he offers the perversely triumphant lament: "Amer savoir, celui qu'on tire du voyage! / Le monde, monotone et petit, aujourd'hui, / Hier, demain, toujours, nous fait voir image: / Une oasis d'horreur dans un désert d'ennui!" [Bitter is the knowledge we obtain from traveling. Yesterday, today and tomorrow, the monotonous and tiny world confronts us with our own image: an oasis of horror in a desert of ennui.]

The notion that horror itself—or, at least, the ability to derive aesthetic satisfaction from horror—might constitute an antidote to cosmic pessimism was taken up by the writers inspired by Baudelaire who came to constitute the Decadent Movement, who were provided with a Bible of sorts by Joris-Karl Huysmans' black comedy *À rebours* (1884). Huysmans' novel offers a darkly ironic guide to the ultimate Decadent lifestyle fantasy, as undertaken by Jean Des Esseintes, whose health has been ruined by syphilis—a disease which, for him, takes on the key attributes of cosmic horror:

> "He had a sudden vision, then, of humankind in its entirety, ceaselessly tormented since time immemorial by that contagion. From the beginning of the world, all living creatures had handed down from father to son the everlasting heritage: the eternal malady which had ravaged the ancestors of man, whose disfigurations could be seen on the recently-exhumed bones of the most ancient fossils! Without ever weakening in its destructive power it had descended through the centuries to the present day, cunningly concealing itself in all manner of painful disguises, in migraines and bronchial infections, hysterias and gouts. From time to time it clambered to the surface, preferentially assaulting those who were badly cared for and malnourished, exploding in lesions like nuggets of gold, ironically crowning the poor devils in its grip with diamond-studded head-dresses, compounding their misery by imprinting upon their skin the image of wealth and well-being." ("Des Esseintes' Dream (from *À rebours*)" p. 42)

Des Esseintes' conscious vision is followed by another, which takes the form of a nightmare that confronts him with the incarnate specter of the "Great Plague": a horridly diseased rider. In fleeing from the rider he experiences various bizarre visions, eventually finding himself confronted by a woman who undergoes a progressive metamorphosis, the parts of her body being replaced and consumed by features of exotic plants he had earlier been studying. At the climax of the dream, he sees the woman's sexual organs as a huge Venus fly-trap: a "bloody maw surrounded by sword-blades"; a vegetal *vagina dentata*. Far from being downcast by this dream, however, Des Esseintes revels in its reportage, appreciating both the keenness and the lurid quality of its associated sensations. The horrific element of the sublime is here explicitly represented as something to be concentrated and savored. It had, of course, been *tacitly* savored in the earlier works of Beckford, de Quincey, Bulwer-Lytton and Poe, but none of those writers had been prepared to acknowledge the perversity of their own tastes, and all of them had taken refuge in some form of consolatory retreat. In the wake of Baudelaire and Huysmans, however, such retreats became unnecessary; the problem of representing cosmic horror, and the search for a means of depicting *the* cosmic horror, was transformed by its connoisseurs into a curious kind of perverse literary grail-quest.

THE DECADENT WORLD-VIEW

Baudelaire was not the only writer of his era to achieve an alchemical transmutation of cosmic horror into perverse delight. He would not have been the first had not Gustave Flaubert, who completed the first version of *La Tentation de Saint-Antoine* on 12 September 1849, been persuaded by the two friends to whom he read it aloud—Maxime Du Camp and Louis Bouilhet—not to publish it According to Du Camp's memoirs, Bouilhet advised the author to "throw it in the fire and never speak of it again". He did not, but it was not until 1874 that he finally published a revised version.

Flaubert's direct inspiration for the *Tentation* was a famous painting by Pieter Brueghel that he had seen in Genoa, although Flaubert's account of the phantasmagoric contest between Satan and the ascetic saint was far less orthodox than Brueghel's. Satan is the real central character of the first version of the drama; he delivers the novel's last triumphant speech and departs leaving the stage echoing with his laughter, clearly believing that the dawn that has banished his apparitions cannot deliver Anthony's salvation. The Devil's confidence is based on the final sequence of his temptations, consequent upon his carrying Anthony away from the Earth into the infinite realm of the stars, in order to deliver final proof of the utter irrelevance of the Earth—and hence of humankind—within the universe.

The final version of the text offers a much more elaborate account of this part of the narrative than the first, and adds a further aspect to the visionary odyssey, which is only briefly trailed in the original as a speech made by "Science". When Anthony returns to his hovel after his flight through time and space he is assailed in both versions by the phantoms of his imagination, but where pagan deities and personalizations of the seven deadly sins raise a clamor in the first, they are replaced in the final version by a parade of bizarre monsters. Satan is not even on stage during this final act of the final version, having quit the scene after challenging Anthony with the philosophical possibility that the phenomenal world might be an "illusion of...intellect". The final parade of monsters is thus presented without any diabolical commentary; Anthony is left to draw his own, rather surprising, conclusion:

"Oh bliss! bliss! I have seen the birth of life," Anthony says, in his final speech. "I have seen the origin of motion. The blood beats so powerfully in my veins that it seems set to burst out. I feel the urge to fly, to swim, to bark, to bellow, to howl. I would that I had wings, a turtle's shell, a rind; that I were able to blow out vapour, possess a trunk, coil my body; to spread myself out, encompassing every place and every thing, emanating all odours; to flow like water, vibrate like sound, radiate like light; to be outlined in every form, penetrate every atom, descend into the very depths of matter—to *be* matter!" The horror implicit in the cosmos of science and the parade of monsters is not set aside in favor of commitment to an old or new faith, but transformed into a kind of exaltation.

Flaubert's exemplar presumably prompted the production of one of the most striking nineteenth-century accounts of an existential breakthrough to the realm of cosmic horror, Jules Richepin's "La machine à métaphysique" (tr. As "The Metaphysical Machine"), which appeared in the collection *Les Morts bizarres* (1877), but its revelation remains tantalizingly elusive. Many of the writers who subsequently embraced the Decadent world-view did not find it so easy to achieve the kind of transfiguration contrived by Flaubert. Jean Lorrain, who provided a dramatized record of his own experiences under the influence of ether in a sequence of *contes d'un buveur d'éther* written in the early 1890s (translated in *Nightmares of an Ether-Drinker*) was much more severely afflicted, physically as well as psychologically, and yet he persisted in reveling in the horrific imagery he produced. His novel *Monsieur de Phocas* (1900) includes one of the most elaborate literary accounts of a nightmarish hashish-dream. Remy de Gourmont found it hard to write further stories in the delightedly perverse vein of *Histoires Magiques* (1894; tr. as "Studies in Fascination" in *Angels of Perversity*) when he was horribly disfigured by the effects of lupus, but he maintained his steadfast critical championship of Decadent style and Decadent pretensions.

The notion of decadence had started out as a form of cosmic pessimism, based in the hypothesis that cultures or civilizations have a natural life-cycle akin to that of human individuals, and that the phase corresponding to an individual's senescence would manifest analogous symptoms of decrepitude and disorientation, as its jaded and morally-anaesthetized aristocrats indulged sybaritic lifestyles, hyperconscious of their own futility. The idea had been given quasi-scientific expression by the Baron de Montesquieu in *Considérations sur les causes de la grandeur des Romains et de leur décadence* (1734), but the supposition that the glories of imperial Rome had given way to the Dark Ages because its rulers had embraced debauchery rather than cultivating ambition had been commonplace even while the process was in train.

The decision by Baudelaire and his followers to celebrate Decadence rather than decrying it was itself a source of horror to those who persisted in their horrified response to the scientific revelation. Max Nordau's *Entartung* (1893; tr. as *Degeneration*) assaulted all forms and analogues of Decadent art as morbid symptoms of a cultural twilight. This German antithesis to the French idea of progress was further extrapolated by Oswald Spengler's *Der Undertang des Abendlandes* (1918; tr. as *The Decline of the West*), which looked gloomily forward to the inevitable eclipse of the Faustian culture that had traded its soul for scientific enlightenment and technological enrichment. Ideological opposition to the idea of progress also found support in physics, when the formulation of the concept of entropy drew a swift response from Sir William Thomson (subsequently ennobled as Lord Kelvin), whose essay "On a Universal Tendency in Nature to the Dissipation of Mechanical Energy" (1852) concluded that the Earth must one day become uninhabitable because of the effects of entropy. Kelvin attempted to put a date on this inevitable extinction in "On the Age of the Sun's Heat" (1862), which assumed (falsely) that the sun's heat is produced by the energy of gravitational collapse.

Kelvin's calculations exercised a considerable influence on the literary imagination, providing the ideative underpinnings of a school of far-futuristic fantasy whose products included Camille Flammarion's *La fin du monde* (1893-94; tr. as *Omega: The Last Days of the World*), H. G. Wells' *The Time Machine* (1895), and William Hope Hodgson's *The House on the Borderland* (1908). Although the first two titles adopted an elegiac tone, finding the prophesied end of the world to be too far distant in time to be worth overmuch worry, Hodgson took a different view, embracing Kelvin's cosmic pessimism much more intimately, and integrating it into an unprecedentedly elaborate account of cosmic horror.

The House on the Borderland is a threshold fantasy, like *Zanoni*, but it reverses the earlier work's narrative scheme. While Bulwer's protagonists were willing, and sometimes able, to cross the threshold separating the phenomenal and noumenal worlds in order to come to terms with the latter, Hodgson's lives in mortal dread of that threshold breaking down and allowing the entities native to the noumenal world to cross over into ours. As in *A Strange Story*, those entities are vague and demonic, and the forms that they assume, in dreams or materially, are attributed to them by the particular phobias of the beholder. In Hodgson's work they are invariably swinish; one of its key manifestations was in the posthumously-published "The Hog" (1947, in the Mycroft and Moran edition of *Carnacki the Ghost-Finder*).

By the time Hodgson published *The House on the Borderland* he had already written the first version of his masterpiece, *The Night Land* (1912), in which a dreamer devastated by loss transforms the nourishment of his grief into a vision of a Kelvinesque end of the world, when the barriers separating the phenomenal and noumenal worlds begin to break down and the Earth's surface is invaded by all manner of monstrous entities, whose sum constitutes the burden of cosmic horror. In both these novels, as well as *The Ghost Pirates* (1909), Hodgson offers tentative pseudoscientific explanations of these entities, but has no authoritative spokesman among his characters. In the short story initially published as "The Baumoff Explosive" (written 1912; published 1919) and reprinted with a fully-restored text as "Eloi, Eloi, Sabachthani" (1975), however, the scientist Baumoff offers a more detailed account of matter as "a localised vibration [in the Aether], traversing a closed orbit" whose vibration is capable of modification by alien vibrations. When Baumoff attempts to recapitulate the experience of Christ on the cross he exposes himself to such an alien vibration, and the revelation he receives is very different from the kind of revelation that underlies the Christian faith. (Hodgson, like many other writers of scientific romance, was the freethinking son of a dogmatic clergyman.)

"The Hog" also contains an attempted explanation of the nature of its eponymous entity, this time delivered by the psychic detective Carnacki, who suggests that planetary atmospheres are stratified in a whole series of zones, the outermost of which is psychic as well as physical, and which is home to "million-mile-long clouds of monstrosity." The final pages of the story elaborate on this thesis considerably: "The monstrosities of the Outer Circle are malignant towards all that we consider desirable.... They are predatory—as all positive force is predatory. They have desires regarding us which are incredibly more dreadful to our minds when comprehended than an intelligent sheep would consider our desires towards its own carcass."

Although this comes close to relegating the cosmic horror to the status of a mere alien—the intelligent product of an alternative process of material evolution—that was not Hodgson's intention; the difference between the inner circles of matter and the psychic circle is one of kind as well as magnitude. The cosmic horror belongs to a different order of existence, which lies beyond the phenomenal world of ordinary perception, separated from it by a threshold that the human mind can breach in dreams with relative safety, although the consequences of a crossing in the other direction would be dire.

This kind of notion had been tacitly or explicitly reflected in various other works connected with the English extension of the French Decadent Movement. The central pillar of the British Movement—whose downfall virtually killed it off—was Oscar Wilde, whose incorrigible flippancy stifled the horror element in such stories as "Lord Arthur Savile's Crime" and "The Canterville Ghost" (both 1887), although the visionary odyssey contained in the early poem "The Sphinx" (1874) attributes some of the menace of Hodgson's hoggish monstrosities to its eponymous chimera. Here too, however, the eventual movement is one of revulsion and rejection, as the narrative voice wonders "What snake-tressed fury fresh from Hell, with uncouth gestures and unclean, / Stole from the poppy-drowsy queen, and led you to a student's cell?" and eventually bids the apparition "Get hence, you loathsome mystery!... Go thou before, and leave me to my crucifix."

While Decadence flourished briefly in Britain, Arthur Machen developed a kind of cosmic horror in "The Great God Pan" (1890) and the belatedly-published "The White People" (1899) but drew back thereafter from the nastier implications of his sublime vision; his later fantasies found a powerful antidote to cosmic horror in the form of the Celtic Grail featured in "The Great Return" (1915) and *The Secret Glory* (1922). The closest parallel to Hodgson's fiction in Britain was contained in Algernon Blackwood's story "The Willows" (1907), in which a small island in the Danube serves as an interdimensional gateway similar to *The House on the Borderland*. Like Machen, however, Blackwood countered the horror element of his subsequent metaphysical fantasies with a powerful positive force. In *The Human Chord* (1910) and *The Centaur* (1911) sensitivity to slightly different versions of cosmic reality provide creative inspiration, ecstatic experience and a potential route to superhumanity, while much of his other fiction developed a complex and rather elusive theory of elemental spirits.

Although there was no place on Earth less hospitable to the ideas and ideals of the Decadent Movement than the U.S.A., fugitive echoes can be found in the work of some of the self-styled Bohemians who clustered in New York and San Francisco. The most striking early manifestation of Decadent horror were contained in the early stories in Robert W. Chambers' *The King in Yellow* (1895), written during or shortly after his sojourn in Paris as an art student, but Chambers soon went native in his own land and turned to more commercial work. The imagery of the horror stories in *The King in Yellow* borrows some motifs from the work of one of the West Coast Bohemians, Ambrose Bierce, but Bierce's own horror fiction has no significant cosmic component. Another of Bierce's associates, however, was the poet George Sterling, whose continuation of the tradition of *The Pleasures of the Imagination*, "Al Aaraaf," "Le Voyage", and "The Sphinx" was "A Wine of Wizardry" (1907), which is more indulgent than any of its predecessors.

The visionary odyssey undertaken by the poet's Fancy in "A Wine of Wizardry"—whose publication in *Cosmopolitan* amazed and appalled many of that periodical's readers—not only takes her into realms of bizarre Decadence but revels in her experience thereof. The poem overflows with references to such entities as "the bleeding sun's phantasmagoric gules," "tiger-lilies known to silent ghouls," "unresting hydras wrought of bloody light" and "red alembics whence [Circe's] gleaming broths obscenely fume" even before Fancy reaches Satan's Hell—which cannot satisfy her lust for exotic sensation, and from which she soon moves on to the substance of Asiatic mythologies before returning home to her grateful host. It was Sterling's friend and protégé, Clark Ashton Smith, who took up the torch of this tradition and took it to its furthest extreme, and whose correspondence with H. P. Lovecraft assisted Lovecraft to move on from the relatively crude conception of "cosmic fear" contained in his essay to a more elaborate and fully-fledged notion of cosmic horror.

THE LOVECRAFT SCHOOL

Clark Ashton Smith was a more dedicated student of French Decadence than any other American Bohemian; he learned French in order to savor the works of Baudelaire, and produced numerous translations and pastiches of Parnassian and Decadent verse. His most elaborate poem, "The Hashish-Eater; or, The Apocalypse of Evil," first published in *Ebony and Crystal* (1922) crosses the visionary extravagance of "A Wine of Wizardry" with the splenetic attitude of Baudelaire's most aggravated works. Smith subsequently referred to it in a letter to Sam Sackett, written in 1950, as "a much misunderstood poem, which was intended as a study in the possibilities of cosmic consciousness," adding: "It is my own theory that, if the infinite worlds of the cosmos were opened to human vision, the visionary would be overwhelmed by horror in the end, like the hero of this poem."

This is, in capsule form, the manifesto of the cosmic horror story, and "The Hashish-Eater" is a striking extrapolation of the contention made in de Quincey's *Confessions of an Opium-Eater*. It begins with the arrogant declaration "Bow down: I am the emperor of dreams" and proceeds to follow an extraordinarily elaborate "trail of terror" through a syncretic amalgam of mythologies, whose climax is another confrontation that attempts to equip the indescribable with a suggestive mask, in the form of a rapidly-expanding star: "and floating up through gulfs and glooms eclipsed, / It grows and grows, a huge white eyeless Face, / That fills the void and fills the universe, / And bloats against the limits of the world / With lips of flame that open...."

In another account of "the argument" of "The Hashish-Eater," reproduced as a preface to the 1989 edition of the poem issued as a pamphlet by Necronomicon Press, Smith describes this final image as "the face of infinity itself, in all its awful blankness." In the prose fiction that he wrote for the pulp magazines *Weird Tales* and *Wonder Stories* when he was in desperate need of money to support his aged and ailing parents, Smith made numerous attempts to paint suggestive features on the blank face of infinity. In the Hyperborean fantasy "The Seven Geases" (1934) he reversed Hodgson's notion of stratified circles surrounding the Earth by obliging its protagonist to descend through a series of subterranean circles until he finally reaches the innermost cavern of the Archetypes (the word being used here in a Platonic rather than a Jungian sense). The various hypothetical past milieux he employed eventually proved inadequate to his needs, however, and his most extravagant Decadent fantasies were developed against the far-futuristic background of the Earth's last continent, Zothique, in which a terminal corrosion of barriers of possibility, similar to that afflicting Hodgson's Night Land, has restored the power of black magic and malign miracle. Such stories as "The Empire of the Necromancers" (1932), "Xeethra" (1934), and

"Necromancy in Naat" (1936) replaced the irony of "The Seven Geases" with a more intensely splenetic narrative voice and an unprecedentedly wholehearted cosmic pessimism.

Although Smith's supernatural fiction was more successful in purely literary terms than his science fiction, it was in the stories he contributed to the science fiction pulps that he made his most concerted attempts to make cosmic horror incarnate. Initially, in such stories as "Marooned in Andromeda" (1930) and "The Amazing Planet" (1931), he adopted the simple strategy of envisaging cosmic horror in terms of a plethora of repulsive alien life-forms, but he embarked on more adventurous endeavors in a group of metaphysical fantasies, most notably "The Eternal World" (1932), in which a traveler in four-dimensional space-time breaches the boundary of perceived space to enter a timeless milieu, one of whose native inhabitants is drawn back into the material universe. "The Dimension of Chance" (1932) similarly attempts to describe a parallel universe in which the physical constants underlying the order of the material world are mercurial, giving rise to a world of chaotic change. The element of horror in these stories is, however, overtaken and subsumed by the intellectual challenge of the project. A further group of relatively modest tales of altered states of consciousness, including "The Light from Beyond" (1933) and "The Visitors from Mlok" (1933), similarly moves the focus away from horror in the direction of more detached cerebration—a movement characteristic of the genre.

H. P. Lovecraft's early poetry has little of the depth and flair of Smith's, and such imitations of Poe as "Astrophobos" (written 1917) are unconvincing. The prose fiction he began to publish in 1919 is, however, much more enterprising in its attempts to develop the kind of cosmic fear that his historical essay had identified as the most interesting aspect of supernatural fiction. This quest was initially alleviated by a much more optimistic fascination with the lure of the exotic derived from the works of Lord Dunsany, but once he began writing for *Weird Tales*—which was founded in 1923—he began to concentrate much more intently on the horrific component of his hallucinatory fantasies. Before then, in "The Music of Erich Zann" (1922), he had broached the idea of breaching the kind of cosmic barrier that Hodgson had envisaged, with similarly disastrous consequences.

As with Hodgson, there was an idiosyncratic aspect to way in which Lovecraft went about constructing the imagery of the noumenal world and the manner in which its produce might be transferred into phenomenal reality. The notion of "nocturnal worshippers" engaged in "revolting fertility-rites" always retained a special resonance in Lovecraft's consciousness; such imagery recurred continually in his work from "Dagon" (1919) through "The Horror a Red Hook" (1927) and "The Call of Cthulhu" (1928) to *The Shadow over Innsmouth* (1936). The objects of suh cultish worship in Lovecraft's fiction are, however, even more chimerical than Hodgson's swine-creatures; the key elements of their confused nature tend to be batrachian, vermiform and cephalopodan, although reanimated corpses already much-ravaged by decay also crop up repeatedly. The early glimpses of the multitudinous faces of cosmic horror caught in such stories as "The Outsider" (1926), "Pickman's Model" (1927), and the barrier-breaching "The Dunwich Horror" (1929), became much more elaborate in later novellas that produced a new hybrid form of horror-science fiction.

Less tolerant of Hugo Gernsback's idosyncrasies than Smith, Lovecraft only appeared once in the Gernsback pulps, with "The Color out of Space" (1927), a subtle story that makes cosmic horror manifest as a kind of animate parasitic sheen, whose appearance recalls Baudelaire's professed fascination with "the phosphorescence of putrescence." In "The Whisperer in Darkness" (1931), which appeared in *Weird Tales*, the careful hybridization of horror and science fiction was more clearly manifest, but in this novella—to a greater extent than any other of his stories—Lovecraft confined the manifestations of cosmic horror to indirect hints. The climactic revelation is content to reveal the existence of a mask, while teasingly refusing to describe that which it had concealed.

One of the two novellas that Lovecraft subsequently published in *Astounding Stories of Super-Science*, "At the Mountains of Madness," was considerably rewritten by the editor, but a version closer to the original was included in *The Outsider and Others* and subsequently reprinted as the title-story of a collection. Cast as an archaeological fantasy, with deliberate echoes of Poe's *Narrative of Arthur Gordon Pym* (1838), the story facilitates the gradual revelation of the Earth's prehistory, specifically its invasion and long occupation by the Old Ones, the creators and engineers of Earthly life, whose eventual destruction by glaciation has kept various relics and residues capable of dangerous reanimation, leading to a climactic revelation that is one of Lovecraft's own summations of cosmic horror:

> "Danforth was totally unstrung, and the first thing I remember of the rest of the journey was hearing him light-headedly chant an hysterical formula in

which I alone of mankind could have found anything but insane irrelevance....

"South Station Under—Washington Under—Park Street Under—Kendall—Central—Harvard—" The poor fellow was chanting the familiar stations of the Bostn-Cambridge tunnel that burrowed through our peaceful native soil thousands of miles away in New England, yet to me the ritual had neither irrelevance nor home feeling. It had only horror, because I knew unerringly the monstrous, nefandous analogy that had suggested it. We had expected, upon looking back, to see a terrible and incredible moving entity if the mists were thin enough; but of that entity we had formed a clear idea. What we did see—for the mists were indeed all too malignly thinned—was something altogether different, and immeasurably more hideous and detestable. It was the utter, objective embodiment of the fantastic novelist's "thing that should not be"; and its nearest comprehensible analogue is a vast, onrushing subway train as one sees it from a station platform—the great black front looming colossally out of infinite subterranean distance, constellated with strangely colored lights and filling the prodigious burrow as a piston fills a cylinder.

"But we were not on a station platform. We were on the track ahead as the nightmare, plastic column of fetid black iridescence oozed tightly onward through its fifteen-foot sinus, gathering unholy speed and driving before it a spiral, rethickening cloud of the pallid abyss vapor. It was a terrible, indescribable thing vaster than any subway train—a shapeless congeries of protoplasmic bubbles, faintly self-luminous, and with myriads of temporary eyes forming and unforming as pustules of greenish light all over the tunnel-filling that bore down upon us, crushing the frantic penguins and slithering over the glistening floor that it and its kind had swept so evilly free of all litter." (p. 95)

The accommodation within this secret history of the substance of numerous earlier stories allowed them to be retrospectively reconfigured as a semi-coherent series, usually dubbed the Cthulhu Mythos—a process of syncretic fusion that also absorbed Lovecraft's other *Astounding* story, "The Shadow out of Time" (1936). In this novella, a different company of alien masters—whose empery spanned a later period of prehistory than that of the Old Ones—is called the Great Race. The Great Race is not a manifestation of cosmic horror, but it is pursued and harassed by enigmatic semi-material enemies, which are.

The aggregation, consolidation, and further elaboration of the Cthulhu Mythos was largely carried out by Lovecraft's disciples and imitators, who began such work in response to an open invitation to his correspondents to make use of motifs he had invented—particularly the imaginary library of "forbidden books," centered on the *Necronomicon*, that he had invented to serve as a continual source of awful revelations. The hybridization of horror and science fiction pioneered by Lovecraft and Smith in the interests of invoking the sensation of cosmic horror was quickly and enthusiastically taken up by two of the coterie, Donald Wandrei and Frank Belknap Long.

Wandrei produced a short series of far-futuristic fantasies that looked far beyond Smith's tales of Zothique, to the end of the entire cosmos. In "The Red Brain" (1927) the Cosmic Dust is in the process of consuming everything, and the vast Brains that are the last representatives of material intelligence gather in the Hall of the Mist to debate their future. The Red Brain offers them a ray of hope, but it turns out to be the illusory product of madness. The climactic work in the series, "On the Threshold of Eternity" was presumably written at the same time as the earlier items, but remained unpublished until 1944. It describes the reverie of the last surviving Great Brain as it bears rapt witness to "the supreme triumph of Death", watching "the final play and march of mighty color," while "out of its being welled a silent response to the greatest music, to the greatest anthem of them all."

Wandrei, the co-founder with August Derleth of Arkham House, subsequently wrote a Lovecraftian archaeological fantasy for that project, which helped to summarize the syncretic progress of the Cthulhu Mythos, *The Web of Easter Island* (1948), but in the meantime he contributed a series of flamboyant melodramas to the science fiction pulps. Most turned away from cosmic horror in order to contrive the positive endings favored by sf editors, or clichéd climactic retrogressions into inchoate slime, but there are significant attempts to give phantom form to cosmic horrors in "Blinding Shadows" (1934), "Finality Unlimited" (1936), and the apocalyptic "Infinity Zero" (1936).

Long's early attempts at cosmic horror fiction, "The Space Eaters" (1928), "The Hounds of Tindalos" (1929), and "The Horror from the Hills" (1931) were relatively straightforward Lovecraftian pastiches, but he made more ingenious use of sciencefictional melodrama in a sequence of far-futuristic fantasies comprising "The Last Men" (1934), "Green Glory" (1935), and "The Great Cold" (1935), in which the Earth has fallen under the dominion of land-based insects and ocean-based giant barnacles, which have reduced humankind's descendants to the status of loyal servitors. Long's subsequent science fiction, however, became increasingly orthodox and its horror elements became much more mundane. A similar fate overtook the collaborative development of the Cthulhu mythos, as its materials became increasingly familiar and stories employing it increasingly mechanical in their operation. August Derleth, both as a writer and as Arkham House's presiding genius, played a considerable role in this routinization, although his novel based on a Lovecraft fragment, *The Lurker at the Threshold* (1945), is a reasonably effective story of an interdimensional barrier whose threatened breakage is eventually prevented.

Although the productions of subsequent generations of the Lovecraft school became increasingly profuse, most of the innovative work done within the tradition moved away from cosmic horror towards more intimate forms of psychological stress. Attempts to describe the indescribable inevitably came to seem a trifle pointless, especially when the suggestive motifs adopted by Bulwer-Lytton, Hodgson, Lovecraft and Smith were eroded by frequent repetition. Such belated pastiches as the fragments making up Brian Lumley's *The Transition of Titus Crow* (1975) added little to the initial quest, and ex-Lovecraftian writers like Fritz Leiber and Robert Bloch tended to be more effective when they moved away from Lovecraftian templates. Leiber's "Smoke Ghost" (1941) and Bloch's "The Funnel of God" (1960) aim for horrific essences of an ambitious but markedly different kind. Writers more specifically influenced by Clark Ashton Smith—including Jack Vance, who updated Zothique in his accounts of *The Dying Earth* (1950)—also found it difficult to carry forward the cosmic horror component of their model's work, although Vance took far-futuristic Decadence to a more elaborate extreme in *The Last Castle* (1966).

Although Leiber's *Our Lady of Darkness* (1977)—which pays explicit homage to Clark Ashton Smith—is the best of all late Lovecraftian novels it follows the example of "Smoke Ghost" in anchoring its horror to the specific vicissitudes of city life. Leiber's most adventurous attempt at cosmic horror fiction, "A Bit of the Dark

World" (1962), founders on the rock of its own discipline, unable in the end to penetrate the darkness in which its horrors are scrupulously hidden. The surreal gloss added to his materials by the most stylish of all the late-twentieth-century Lovecraftian writers, Thomas Ligotti, was not well adapted to the pursuit of cosmic horror, although such stories as "The Tsalal" (1994) move suggestively in that direction. More concerted and flamboyant attempts were made by Michael Shea, under the marked influence of Clark Ashton Smith and Jack Vance, in a graphic series of far-futuristic fantasies; many of them make abundant use of a bizarrely exotic underworld, which is brought into the foreground in some of the stories in *Nifft the Lean* (1982) and *The Mines of Behemoth* (1997).

In spite of the intense commitment of many of Lovecraft's and Smith's disciples to the ideals of their fiction, keys to the effective evocation of cosmic horror proved very elusive, and there is a sense in which the attempts they and their contemporaries made were essentially products of their particular time. They were not entirely confined to *Weird Tales*—Lovecraft called attention in the revised version of *Supernatural Horror in Literature* to Leonard Cline's novel *The Dark Chamber* (1927), which offers an account of drug-induced of psychosomatic metamorphosis that gropes in the same direction as many of his own tales of retrogression—but they did not extend much further. *Weird Tales* became inhospitable to such work when it changed proprietors in 1940—three years after Lovecraft's death—and Dorothy McIlwraith was installed as editor with a brief that specifically excluded the kind of literary extravagance that Clark Ashton Smith had introduced to its pages. *Wonder Stories* and *Astounding Stories*, which had played host to many attempts to evoke cosmic horror, had also changed proprietors and editors, and had similarly struck out in different directions.

The temporal restriction of attempts to reproduce the sensation of cosmic horror was not simply a matter of the obliteration of its marketplace, however. The new cosmos whose magnitude had first been revealed by Herschel a century before had continued to evolve within the scientific imagination—the fact of its expansion, which was to provide the foundation-stone of Big Bang cosmology was first discovered in the 1920s—but it no longer seemed as intimidating as it once had. The argument of Smith's "Hashish-Eater," that a clear imaginative vision of the cosmos must ultimately be overwhelmed by the horror, became less plausible as time went by, and the advent of pulp science fiction generated a powerful ideological force in favor of the supposition that the component of wonder, rather than that of horror, was the more important aspect of the modern experience of the sublime. Genre sf soon marginalized the kinds of hybrid pioneered by Lovecraft and Wandrei, and made robust attempts to discover and amplify new antidotes to cosmic pessimism—but in so doing, it sometimes contrived to re-emphasize the attitude it was opposing.

COSMIC HORROR IN SCIENCE FICTION

The champion who emerged to carry the cause of science fiction forward when pulp sf threatened to decay into a stereotyped form of futuristic costume drama was John W. Campbell Jr., one of the pioneers of the "space opera" that took action-adventure fiction on to a galactic stage. Campbell was eventually forced to give up writing when he became editor of *Astounding Stories* (which he renamed *Astounding Science Fiction*, and then *Analog*) but there was a brief interim between his career as a space opera writer and the cessation of his writing activity when he adopted the pseudonym Don A. Stuart for work of a more sophisticated kind, including far-futuristic fantasies.

Campbell had begun dabbling in far-futuristic fantasy in "The Voice of the Void" (1930), in which beings of "pure force" attack the ultimate descendants of humankind ten billion years in the future, and "The Last Evolution" (1932), which sketches out a future history in which a decadent human species threatened by a war for survival is replaced by intelligent machines designed to fight that war, which are superseded in their turn by similar "beings of force." The notion of future human decadence induced by over-dependence on machines, leading inevitably to supersession by the machines in question, is more elaborately dramatized in two Don A. Stuart stories, "Twilight" (1934) and "Night" (1935).

Subsequent Stuart stories elaborated various alternative scenarios for humankind's future evolution, all of which searched for an antidote to this impasse and the pessimism associated with it. The one that seemed to Campbell to provide the most satisfactory solution—a solution that subsequently became central to the image of the future synthesized by his magazine—was "Forgetfulness" (1937), in which the pattern of technological dependence is conclusively interrupted by the development of parapsychological powers. This breakthrough was closely akin to that credited by Edward Bulwer-Lytton to his Rosicrucian sages, and also to the future humankind whose mastery of the primal force of *vril* is described in his Utopian novel *The Coming Race* (1971). In spite of the success of this antidote, however, the cosmic horror it was intended to combat was not entirely vanquished. "Don A. Stuart" went on to write one of the most effective of all horror-sf stories in "Who Goes There?" (1938), in which a group of humans is confronted with a protean alien menace capable of mimicking any living form. In the face of such potential opposition, human presence—even augmented by parapsychological armor—seemed simply inadequate, in spite of the narrative fix contrived in the story.

The vast majority of alien menaces envisioned by science fiction writers posed straightforwardly mundane threats, and they were usually defeated in the end, but the notion of humans as conquerors and colonists of infinite space was always subject to the suspicion that *Homo sapiens* was simply not up to the job, which would have to be taken over in the long run by creatures better-designed to accomplish it. Inevitably, this sensibility was most obvious in far-futuristic fantasies, which routinely imagined the supersession of humankind on Earth, and frequently took that supersession for granted on a cosmic time-scale.

Scientific estimates of the likely future duration of the Earth took a great leap forward when Arthur Eddington proposed in 1926 that the sun's radiation was produced by a nuclear fusion reaction, rendering Lord Kelvin's nineteenth-century estimates obsolete. The reflection of the new timetable in such accounts of future human and post-human evolution as J. B. S. Haldane's "The Last Judgment" (1928), J. D. Bernal's *The World, the Flesh and the Devil: An Enquiry into the Future of the Three Enemies of the Rational Soul* (1929), and Olaf Stapledon's *Last and First Men* (1930) found this a cause for optimism, but Stapledon's account of the superhumanity of the ultimate descendants of *Homo sapiens* also served to highlight the inadequacies of the current model, resulting in a splenetic resentment of contemporary existential restriction whose bitterness was considerably magnified in *Last Men in London* (1932), *Odd John* (1934), and *Star Maker* (1937). The last-named integrates a distinct note of cosmic horror into its climactic vision of the kind of creator who might be responsible for a universe like ours—which, in Stapledon's estimation, falls far short of being the best possible.

Star Maker was published in the year of H. P. Lovecraft's death, which became a watershed in the history of cosmic horror in Britain as well as the U.S.A. The Lovecraftian school of horror fiction continued to make attempts to exploit the resource, but the writers of British scientific romance and American science fiction who followed in the footsteps of Olaf Stapledon and John W. Campbell were swimming with a different tide. In their work, the element of cosmic horror was not only counterbalanced but ultimately overwhelmed by the exaltatory aspects of the sublime. This imaginative thrust was by no means restricted to fictional analyses of the macrocosmic context; the most determined attempt to put an optimistic gloss on the prospect of a future evolution that would render humankind obsolete was made by the French evolutionist Pierre Teilhard de Chardin, who began to formulate his Omega Point thesis in the 1920s but was forbidden to publish by the Society of Jesus, of which he was a member.

The first published version of Teilhard's Omega Point hypothesis eventually appeared posthumously, in *Le Phénomène humain* (1955; tr. as *The Phenomenon of Man*), which argues that the Earth's evolving ecosphere is supplemented by an equivalent intellectual entity, the noösphere, whose future evolution will involve its progressive integration into a coherent whole, until a climactic "concurrence of human monads" brings Earthly evolution to its terminus. The local Omega Point described in *The Phenomenon of Man* had already been extrapolated to a universal stage in a 1945 lecture that was reprinted in *L'Avenir de l'homme* (1959; tr. as *The Future of Man*), which suggested that the Earthly noösphere might detach itself from the planet in order to join a universal collective, comprising all the intelligences in the universe.

The notion of the Omega Point was eventually taken up, and dramatically reconfigured, by the physicist Frank Tipler in *The Physics of Immortality: Modern Cosmology, God and the Resurrection of the Dead* (1994), which combined Teilhard's model with ideas drawn from Freeman Dyson's "Time Without End: Physics and Biology in an Open Universe" (1979) and inspiration borrowed from the strong version of Brandon Carter's "anthropic cosmological principle," which points out that if the fundamental physical constants were even slightly different, the universe would be incapable of harboring life as we know it. Building on the assumption that any space-traveling species ought to be able to take eventual control of the entire universe, Tipler suggested that such a civilization would undoubtedly want to deploy some of the resources of the universe to the purpose of recapitulating its entire history, contriving the resurrection of every entity that has ever existed within the cyberspace of an ultimate computer, thus fulfilling the most ambitious dreams of theology.

Teilhard's Omega Point had been mirrored in a good deal of science fiction, but Tipler's sparked a more immediate and prolific response. Some of the works that followed in its train had elements of horror within them, but it was not cosmic horror; in making the Omega Point imaginatively available for philosophical and literary development, Teilhard and Tipler drastically reduced its power to generate shock and awe; although the scale of the ideas involved was still capable of making minds boggle, it was not capable of inducing the kind of reflexive reaction that Clark Ashton Smith had integrated into the climax of "The Hashish-Eater." The notion had become graspable, and it was no longer inherently intimidating.

There were many other developments in the science fiction of the latter half of the twentieth century that were conducive to the production of horror stories. The popularization of the idea of genetic engineering had a built-in "yuck factor" that generated a whole school of horror-sf, and the notion of nanotechnological "assemblers"—molecule-sized machines—that would be capable of processing any raw materials into object of desire rapidly gave rise to melodramatic accounts of "grey goo catastrophes" and monstrous reconstructions of the environment perpetrated by out-of-control nanotechnology. Even at their most extreme, however, such horror stories could not strike the note of cosmic horror that had served as a siren song for the Lovecraft school when it was in its heyday.

The Lovecraftian idea of cosmic horror is founded in the supposition that the human mind is, ultimately, the helpless prisoner of the macrocosm, the futility of all its microcosmic ambitions and self-delusions being illustrated and defined by the magnitude and strangeness of a cosmos to which the principle of "as above, so below" is flatly inapplicable. The imaginative thrust of scientific romance and science fiction, however, challenged the assumption that the vastness of the cosmos can only be made imaginatively tolerable by making it correspond in some fashion to the sphere of human life. Early science fiction did try to maintain such a correspondence, by developing such motifs as the galactic empire, in which the vast cosmos of contemporary astronomy was filled up with an infinite array of Earth-clone worlds and human-clone aliens—but it was not a forced move. Sophisticated science fiction was not intimidated by the notion that *Homo sapiens* is an ephemeral species, or the notion that the evolving universe will ultimately change out of all recognition.

If human beings are infinitely adaptable, and can not only be unintimidated by, but might willingly play midwife to, a new era of post-human diversification, then the threshold between the phenomenal and noumenal worlds can no longer be protected by anything as crude as a Dweller of the Threshold. That kind of cosmic horror is impotent to resist the imaginative antidotes offered by contemporary science fiction. Although the prospect of wholesale transfiguration is not without its own horrific potential, the horror in question is not cosmic—indeed, it is more intimate than the traditional sources of horror.

There have always been horrors lurking within actual and potential human nature; that is where the great majority of the icons of horror fiction originated, and where most of them remain confined. In the past, they have been arbitrary and accidental aspects of that nature, conceivable as unlucky afflictions of fate. In the future, that will not be the case; the horrors luring within future human nature will be products—or, at least, by-products—of human design. That prospect generates many discomfiting possibilities, but the one possibility it denies absolutely is that humans are prisoners of their own nature, doomed to suffer the slings and arrows of outrageous fortune without any means of fighting back. The kinds of terrors that might have motivated the kinds of fertility-cults that figured in H. P. Lovecraft's nightmares—whether or not any such institutions ever really existed—have not been uneasily repressed but permanently exorcized; they cannot come back.

This does not mean, however, that cosmic horror is redundant as an aesthetic experienced or as an object of literary ambition. Nor has it been reduced to a mere matter of nostalgic amusement. It is useful, now that we can no longer be horrified by mere matters of spatial and temporal magnitude, or by the consciousness that the cosmos was not constructed for our benefit, to be able to remember and appreciate what a privilege that freedom is. There is a definite imaginative utility in continuing to test its limits. An ability to remain unhorrified by the fact that the entire universe, outside the fragile envelope of the Earth's biosphere, is extremely and unremittingly hostile to human existence, ought to amplify rather than diminish the horror implicit in the fact that we are more than sufficiently hostile to one another, and to the human microcosm in its worldly entirety, not to need any cosmic assistance.

GROWING UP AS A SUPERHERO

Teenage superheroes come in all the traditional varieties. Some, like Clark Kent of Krypton, Smallville, and Metropolis, were born super. Some, like Harry Potter at Hogwarts Academy, must graft their way to superiority. The rest, like Buffy the Vampire-Slayer when she became the Chosen One and Peter Parker after his fateful meeting with a genetically-modified spider, have superiority unexpectedly thrust upon them.

One might expect superheroes of the last kind to find it hard to adjust, but sudden transformation is a commonplace of teenage experience. The worst existential difficulty that will afflict them as they grow older is the necessity of living in the world of series melodrama. As their adventures multiply, the inexorable process of melodramatic inflation will force their adversaries to become weirder, more destructively ambitious, and far more ingenious in finding terrible ways to place them in mortal danger.

This process is evident in the history of superheroism as well as individual biographies. Comic-book superheroes are direct descendants of the superheroes who featured in the American pulp magazines of the 1930s, but evolution has given them greater powers and gaudier plumage. Superman, the Man of Steel, is a linear descendant of Doc Savage, the Man of Bronze. As a technologically-sophisticated haunter of the dark, Batman is an extrapolation of The Shadow. Spider-Man is a modernized version of The Spider, whose main claim to fame was that he was even more screwed-up than all the other secret-identity-nursing masked vigilantes commissioned to thwart the terrorist activities of criminal masterminds in the Great Depression.

Spider-Man has been hyped as the first conspicuously post-September 11 superhero movie, but September 11s have always been routine business for American superheroes. The January 1935 issue of *The Spider* pitted the eponymous hero against "The City Destroyer"; the story's blurb, juxtaposed with a picture of a crumbling skyscraper, began: "Thousands of busy persons bent over their desks in the tallest building in the world—conducting the commerce of the nation—when suddenly the steel girders began to creak and twist, and the gigantic edifice swayed giddily in the wind...." Unfettered by the Comic Book Code, the Spider—who usually contented himself with burning a spidery brand into the foreheads of his deserving victims after shooting them dead with his twin Magnum .45s—eventually trapped the skyscraper-felling Murder Master in a tank full of acid, reassuring himself while listening to the felon's screams of agony that: "It was horrible.... But it was necessary, and it was just. God knows it was just!"

When this melodramatic tradition is traced back to its origins in the French *roman feuilleton*, we find that it was the supervillains rather than their law-abiding adversaries who initially bagged the titles and cultivated the big reputations. The unsung pioneer of melodramatic crime fiction was Paul Féval, who was a prolific inventor of criminal secret societies run by exotic and charismatic masterminds between 1843, when *Les Gentilhommes de la Nuit* featured in *Les Mystères de Londres*, and 1875, when the eighth and last novel chronicling the evil exploits of *Les Habits Noirs* appeared. The English "penny dreadful" serials that ran in parallel to the early *romans feuilletons* in the 1840s and 1850s produced *Varney the Vampyre*, *Wagner the Wehr-Wolf*, and—in *The String of Pearls*—Sweeney Todd, the Demon Barber of Fleet Street, but not a single hero whose name became legend.

When Catwoman's ultimate ancestress, *La Vampire* (tr. as *The Vampire Countess*), hit Paris in a Féval serial published in 1855 (but set in 1804) the main opposition to the eponymous femme fatale was provided by the seemingly-unassuming Jean-Pierre Sévérin, the keeper of the Paris Morgue—but Jean-Pierre only needed a broken fishing-rod in his hand and a change of stance to be revealed as master swordsman Gâteloup, the ultimate ancestor of all dual-personality superheroes. The mysterious masked swordsman in the luxuriously-caped all-scarlet costume who had earlier featured in Féval's *Le Fils du diable* [The Devil's Son] (1846) was only able to appear in several places at once because there were three of him, and nobody much cared who they were when they were not in fancy dress, but they provided the ultimate model for America's first caped crusader, Johnston McCulley's Zorro. By the time Zorro arrived on the scene, though, charismatic villains had enjoyed half a century of hero-eclipsing celebrity.

The fact that superheroism had evolved as a belated response to escalating supervillainy was carefully noted by the first philosophical advocate of superheroism, Friedrich Nietzsche, who wisely advised the would-be *übermensch* that: "Whoever fights monsters should see to it that in the process he does not become a monster." In the game of melodrama, it is villains who define the moral magnitude of the tasks facing heroes, thus licensing the lengths to which they may go in heroic opposition; by threatening and perpetrating horrors, villains invite the visitation of similar horrors upon themselves. Any hero who responds wholeheartedly to such an invitation runs the risk of becoming more and more like his adversaries as his career progresses.

The dangers of superheroism evolving to mirror supervillainy are compounded by an opposite process. The alchemy of melodrama often makes extravagant villainy look suspiciously like heroism, as William Blake observed when commenting that Milton was "of the Devil's party without knowing it". Morally disreputable characters like Rocambole and Fantômas became the stars of ever-extending series of nineteenth- and early twentieth-century *romans feuilletons*, plotting a course subsequently followed by the likes of Fu Manchu and Count Dracula. The modern glut of school-set fantasies in which the problems of adolescence are modelled in the imaginative clay of horror movies began in 1957 with *I was a Teenage Werewolf* and was cleverly sophisticated in the 1970s by Stephen King and Brian de Palma in *Carrie*. In stories of this kind victims freed from their inhibitions and given the power to strike back become monsters with whom it is perilously easy to sympathize.

A dramatic demonstration of these problems was provided by the most recent series of Buffy the Vampire-Slayer to be aired in the UK [in August 2002, when this aetricle was written]. While Buffy sulked her way through the series, so resentful of her recall from heaven that she eventually left the climactic salvation of the world to Xander's care-bear impression, Spike the vampire was driven to such extremes by unrequited love that the last episodes found him valiantly undergoing a terrible trial by ordeal in order to recover his old pure-evil self, only to end up with a soul instead. Having had lots of practice, Spike would doubtless have made a far more convincing über-adversary in the following series than the temporarily-demonized Willow did in the one in question, but moral distinctions that are already blurred can hardly help becoming even more confused as such series progress.

In the meantime, while Harry Potter has yet to sit his GCSEs, Lord Voldemort is patiently gathering the forces and armaments he will need to precipitate the apocalypse in volume seven of J. K. Rowling's series. Unlike Luke Skywalker, Harry will probably be spared the awkward discovery that his arch-enemy is actually his father, but the peculiar relationship between their wands has already generated some suspicious convolutions in the climax of *Harry Potter and the Goblet of Fire*. The plots of all the novels so far making up the series [again, in 2002] turn on the extreme difficulty of figuring out which of the seemingly good guys is actually bad, and *vice versa*.

Given that superheroes are mere phantoms of melodrama, produced by the extrapolation of the principles of poetic justice to outlandish extremes, it may seem that none of this matters very much. As Oscar Wilde pointed out, however, life imitates art more often and more assiduously than art imitates life. *Spider-Man* was allegedly delayed in production by the necessity of removing a scene in which Spider-Man strung a web between the Twin Towers, whose actual destruction generated exactly the kind of horror that provided the imaginative fuel of "The City Destroyer". No superheroes are available to hunt down the Murder Master responsible for the authentic atrocity, but there is a superstate, which must formulate its own response—and whose collective conscience must decide what is ultimately to take the place of The Spider's lethal tankful of acid.

Although few contemporary Americans are likely to take much inspiration from Nietzsche, no matter how apt his observations may have been, they do have other models of superheroism available than spectacular deliveries of retributive justice. Canadian band Crash Test Dummies suggested in their debut single "Superman's Song" (1991) that it was actually Clark Kent, not Superman, who was the real hero, because—even though nobody could stop him from simply taking anything he wanted—he put his suit and glasses on, got a job and earned his daily crust just like any ordinarily virtuous person.

Bearing in mind that movie superheroes actually have triple identities, we can take a further step behind this particular example. Who could think of Christopher Reeve as an authentic superhero when, having made his own giant leap to superstardom, he allowed his Superman to dump Lois Lane because poor Margo Kidder had grown a little older between movies? Who, on the other hand, can doubt that he is an authentic superhero now, when he requires courage and endurance even to draw breath and pours millions of dollars into research into technologies that might one day restore to him, or at least to many others, the ability to put on their suits and glasses and go to work?

While planning the further extrapolation of their superheroic careers, Peter Parker and his audience might do well to consider these issues, no matter what plans Hollywood may have for Spider-Man's next adversary.

BIBLIOGRAPHY

PRIMARY SOURCES

Aeschylus. *Prometheus Bound*. New York: Dover, 1995. [Original publication in Greek, 6th century BC.]

Ainsworth, W. Harrison. *Auriol: Fragment of a Romance*. London: Chapman and Hall, 1850. [Original publication 1844.]

Andrezel, Pierre (Karen Blixen). *The Angelic Avengers*. New York: Random House, 1946.

Anon. "Tam Lin" in *Reliques of Ancient English Poetry* ed. Thomas Percy. London: J, Dodsley, 1765.

-------. "Thomas the Rhymer" in *Reliques of Ancient English Poetry* ed. Thomas Percy. London: J, Dodsley, 1765.

Arnold, Edwin Lester. *The Wonderful Adventures of Phra the Phoenician*. London: Chatto and Windus, 1891.

Asimov, Isaac. *The Caves of Steel*. Garden City, N.Y.: Doubleday, 1954

-------. *The Rest of the Robots*. Garden City, N.Y.: Doubleday, 1964.

-------. "Strange Playfellow" *Super Science Stories* September 1940; reprinted as "Robbie" in *I, Robot*. Garden City, N.Y.: Doubleday, 1950.

Atherton, Gertrude. *Black Oxen*. New York: Boni and Liveright, 1923.

Austin, William. *Peter Rugg, the Missing Man*. Worcester, Mass.: F. P. Rice, 1882. [Original publication 1824; exp. 1827.]

Babbitt, Natalie. *Tuck Everlasting*. New York: Farrar, Straus & Giroux, 1975.

Ballard, J. G. "Billenium." *New Worlds* November 1961.

-------. "The Lost Leonardo" *The Magazine of Fantasy & Science Fiction* March 1964.

-------. *Memories of the Space Age*. Sauk City, Wisconsin: Arkham House, 1988.

Balzac, Honoré de. "The Elixir of Life" and "Melmoth Reconciled" in *The Unknown Masterpiece and Other Stories*. London: J. M. Dent, 1896. [Original pulications in French as "L'elixir de longue vie," 1830 and "Melmoth Réconcilié, 1835.]
Baring-Gould, Sabine. "Margery of Quether." *Cornhill Magazine* April-May 1884.
Barr, Robert. "The Doom of London." *The Idler* November 1892.
Barrie, J. M. *Peter Pan*. London: Hodder & Stoughton, 1904. [Novelization as *Peter and Wendy*. London: Hodder & Stoughton, 1911.]
-------. *Mary Rose*. London: Hodder & Stoughton, 1924.
Bass, Thomas J. *Half Past Human*. New York: Ballantine, 1971.
Baudelaire, Charles. "Le Chambre double" *La Presse* August 27, 1862.
-------. "Les Métamorphoses du vampire" in *Les fleurs du mal*. Paris: Pulet-Malassis et de Broise, 1857.
-------. "Le Voyage" Revue Française March 20, 1859.
-------. "Wine and Hashish" in *Hashish Wine Opium* by Théophile Gautier and Charles Baudelaire, tr. Maurice Stang. *Signature* 14. London: Calder and Boyars, 1972. [Original publication in French as "Du vin et du hashish," 1851.]
Bayley, Barrington J. "The Remembrance" in *Tales of the Wandering Jew* ed. Brian Stableford. Sawtry, Cambs.: Dedalus, 1991.
Beauclerk, Helen. *The Love of the Foolish Angel*. London: Collins, 1929.
Beckford, William. *An Arabian Tale*. London: J. Johnson, 1786. [Usually known as *Vathek*.]
Bernal. J. D. *The World, the Flesh and the Devil: An Enquiry into the Future of the Three Enemies of the Rational Soul*. London: Kegan Paul, Trench & Trubner, 1929.
Besant, Walter. *The Inner House*. Bristol: Arrowsmith, 1888.
Bien, H. M. *Ben-Beor: A Story of the Anti-Messiah*. Baltimore: Friedenwald, 1894.
Bishop, Michael. *Brittle Innings*. New York: Bantam, 1994.
Blackwood, Algernon. *The Centaur*. London: Macmillan, 1911.
-------. *The Human Chord*. London: Macmillan, 1910.
-------. "The Willows" in *The Listener and Other Stories*. London: Eveleigh Nash, 1907.
Blish, James, with Norman L. Knight. *A Torrent of Faces*. Garden City, N.Y.: Doubleday, 1967.
Bloch, Robert. "The Funnel of God." *Fantastic* January 1960.
-------. "Slave of the Flames" *Weird Tales* June 1938.
-------. "Yours Truly, Jack the Ripper" *Weird Tales* July 1943.

Bodin, Félix. *Le Roman de l'avenir*. Paris: Lecointe et Poucin, 1834; preface derived from an article first published in the *Gazette Littéraire* on 17 février 1831. English translation as *The Novel of the Future*, Encino, Cal.: Black Coat Press, 2008.
Boothby, Guy. *A Bid for Fortune*. London: Ward Lock, 1895.
-------. *Pharos the Egyptian*. London: Ward Lock, 1899.
Bradbury, Ray. *Fahrenheit 451*. New York: Ballantine, 1953.
Brin, David. *Earth*. New York: Bantam, 1990.
Browning, Robert. "Childe Roland to the Dark Tower Came" in *Men and Women*. London: Chapman and Hall, 1855.
Brunner, John. *The Sheep Look Up*. New York: Harper, 1972.
-------. *Stand on Zanzibar*. Garden City, N.Y.: Doubleday, 1969.
Buchanan, Robert *The Wandering Jew: A Christmas Carol*. London: Chatto and Windus, 1893.
Bulwer-Lytton, Edward. *The Coming Race*. Edinburgh: Blackwood, 1871. [Early editions anonymous.]
-------. *Falkland and Zicci*. London: Routledge, 1876. [Original publication of Zicci 1841.]
-------. *The Haunters and the Haunted*. London: Simpkin Marshall. [Original publication in Blackwood's Magazine, 1859.]
-------. *A Strange Story*. London: Sampson Low, 1862. [Early editions anonymous.]
-------. *Zanoni*. London: Chapman and Hall, 1853. [Original publication London: Saunders & Otley, 1842; early editions anonymous.]
Bunch, David. *Moderan*. New York: Avon, 1971.
Callenbach, Ernst. *Ecotopia: A Novel about Ecology, People and Politics in 1999*. Berkeley, Cal.: Banyan Tree, 1978.
Campbell, John W. Jr. "The Last Evolution." *Amazing Stories* August 1932.
-------. "The Voice of the Void". *Amazing Stories Quarterly* Summer 1930.
Capes, Bernard. "The Accursed Cordonnier" in *Plots*. London: Methuen, 1902.
Čapek, Karel. *The Macropoulos Secret: A Comedy* tr. by Paul Selver. London: Robert Holden, 1927.
-------. *R. U. R., A Fantastic Melodrama*. Garden City, N.Y.: Doubleday Page, 1923.
Carlyle, Thomas. "Signs of the Times." *Edinburgh Review* June 1829.
Carson, Rachel. *Silent Spring*. Boston: Houghton Mifflin, 1962.
Chambers, Robert W. *The King in Yellow*. New York: F. T. Neely, 1895.

Chousy, Didier, Comte de. *Ignis*. Paris: Berger-Levrault, 1883. English tr. as *Ignis: The Central Fire*, Encino: Cal: Black Coat Press, 2009.

Cline, Leonard. *The Dark Chamber*. New York: Viking Press, 1927.

Cobban, J. Maclaren Cobban. *Master of his Fate*. Edinburgh: Blackwood, 1890.

Coleridge, Samuel Taylor. "The Rime of the Ancient Mariner" in *Lyrical Ballads*. London: Arch, 1798.

Constantine, Murray. *The Devil, Poor Devil!* London: Boriswood, 1934.

Corelli, Marie. *The Sorrows of Satan*. London: Methuen, 1895.

-------. *The Young Diana: An Experiment of the Future*. London: Hutchinson, 1915.

Cousin de Grainvllle, Jean-Baptiste. *Le Dernier home*. Paris: Deterville, 1805.

Cowper, Richard. "The Tithonian Factor" in *Changes* ed. Michael Bishop and Ian Watson. New York: Ace, 1983.

Crawford, F. Marion. *The Witch of Prague*. London: Macmillan, 1891.

Croly, George. *Salathiel: A Story of the Past, Present, and the Future*. London: Henry Colburn, 1827. [Early editions anonymous.]

Cyrano de Bergerac, Savinien. *Fragment d'histoire comique contenant les états et empires du soleil*. Paris: Charles de Sercy, 1662; tr. with following item by Richard Aldington in *Voyages to the Moon and Sun*. London: Routledge & New York: Dutton, 1923; tr. by Geoffrey Strachan in *Other Worlds: The Comic History of the States and Empires of the Moon and Sun*. London: Oxford University Press, 1963.

-------. *Histoire comique contenant les états et empires de la lune*. Paris: Charles de Sercy, 1657.

Daniels, Jonathan. *Clash of Angels*. New York: Brewer and Warren, 1930.

De Bell, Garret. *The Environmental Handbook*. New York: Ballantine, 1970.

Del Rey, Lester. *The Eleventh Commandment*. Evanston, Ill.: Regency, 1962.

De Quincey, Thomas. "Confessions of an Opium-Eater" in *Essays*. London: Ward Lock, 1878. pp. 1-70. [Original publication London: Taylor, 1822.]

Derennes, Charles. *Le peuple du pôle*. Paris: Mercure de France, 1907. Tr. by Brian Stableford as *The People of the Pole*, Encino: Cal.: Black Coat Press, 2008.

Derleth, August, and H. P. Lovecraft. *The Lurker at the Threshold*. Sauk City, Wisc.: Arkham House. 1945.

Dickson, Gordon R. *The Pritcher Mass*. Garden City, N.Y.: Doubleday, 1972.

-------. *Sleepwalker's World*. Philadelphia: Lippincott, 1971.

Donnelly, Ignatius (as Edmund Boisgilbert, M.D.). *Caesar's Column: A Story of the Twentieth Century*. Chicago: F. J, Schulte, 1890.

Douglas, Theo. *Iras: A Mystery*. Edinburgh: Blackwood, 1896.

Dumas, Alexandre. *Isaac Laquedem*. Brussels: Lebègue, 1853.

-------. *Memoirs of a Physician*. London: George Peirce, 1846. [Originally published in French as *Joseph Balsamo*, 1846.]

-------. *The Return of Lord Ruthven*. Encino, Calif.: Black Coat Press, 2005. [Original publication in French as *Le vampire*, 1851.]

Eekhoud, Georges. "Le coeur de Tony Wandel" in *Kermesses*. Brussels: Henry Kistemaeckers, 1884.

Egan, Greg. *Permutation City*. London: Millennium, 1994.

Ehrlich, Paul R. "Ecocatastrophe." *Ramparts* 8 (1969): 24-28.

Emerson, Ralph Waldo. *Nature*. Boston: James Munroe, 1836.

England, George Allan. "The Elixir of Hate" *Cavalier* August-November, 1911.

Erskine, John. *Venus, the Lonely Goddess*. New York: Morrow, 1949.

Farrère, Claude [Charles Bargone]. *Les Condamnés à mort*. Paris: Édouard Joseph, 1920.

-------. *The House of the Secret*. New York: Dutton, 1923. [Original publication in French as *La maison des hommes vivants*, 1911.]

Féval, Paul. *Le Fils du Diable*. Paris: Meline, Cans, 1847

-------. *Les Mystères de Londres*. Paris: Comptoir des Imprimeurs Réunis, 1844

-------. *La Vampire* in *Les Drames de la Mort*. Paris: Charlieu & Huillery, 1856. English tr. as *The Vampire Countess*, Encino: Cal,: Black Coat Press, 2003.

--------. *The Wandering Jew's Daughter*. Tr. by Brian Stableford. Encino, Calif.: Black Coat Press, 2005. [Original publication in French as *Vicomte Paul*, 1864.]

Field, Eugene. "The Holy Cross" in *The Holy Cross and Other Tales*. New York: Scribner's, 1896. pp. 3-23. [Original publication Chicago: Stone & Kimball, 1893.]

Flammarion, Camille. *Omega: The Last Days of the World*. New York: Cosmpolitan, 1894. [Tr. of *La fin du monde*. Paris: Flammarion, 1893.]

Flaubert, Gustave. *La première tentation de Saint-Antoine*. Paris: Charpentier, 1908.

-------. *La Tentation de Saint-Antoine*. Paris: Charpentier, 1874.

Flecker, James Elroy. *The Last Generation: A Story of the Future*. London: New Age, 1908.

Fletcher, George U. *The Well of the Unicorn*. New York: Sloane, 1948.

Forster, E. M. "The Machine Stops." *Oxford and Cambridge Review*, Michaelmas Term, 1909.

Foster, George C. *The Lost Garden*. London: Chapman and Hall, 1930.

France, Anatole "Saint Satyr" in *The Second Dedalus Book of Decadence: The Black Feast* ed. Brian Stableford, Sawtry, Cambs.: Dedalus, 1992. [Original publication in French in *Le puits de Sainte Claire*, 1895.]

--------. *The Revolt of the Angels*. London: John Lane, 1914. [Original publication in Fench as *La révolte des anges*, 1914.]

Garnett, Richard. "The Twilight of the Gods" in *The Twilight of the Gods and Other Tales*. London: T. Fisher Unwin, 1888.

Gautier, Théophile. "Hashish" in *Hashish Wine Opium* by Théophile Gautier and Charles Baudelaire, tr. Maurice Stang. *Signature* 14. London: Calder and Boyars, 1972. [Original publication in French, 1843.]

Gayton, Bertram. *The Gland Stealers*. London: Herbert Jenkins, 1922.

Gerhardi, William, and Brian Lunn. *The Memoirs of Satan*. London: Cassell, 1932.

Gibson, William. *Neuromancer*. New York: Ace, 1984.

Godwin, William. *St Leon: A Tale of the Sixteenth Century*. London: C.C.J. and J. Robinson, 1799.

Gourmont, Remy de. *Angels of Perversity*. Tr. by Francis Amery. Sawtry, Cambs.: Dedalus, 1992. [Original versions as *Histoires magiques* 1894, and "Le fantôme," 1891]

Gunn, James E. *The Joy Makers*. New York: Bantam, 1961.

Haggard, H. Rider. *She: A History of Adventure*. New York: Harper, 1886.

Haldane, J. B. S. *Daedalus; or, Science and the Future*. London: Kegan Paul, Trench & Trubner, 1923.

-------. "The Last Judgment" in *Possible Worlds and Other Essays*. London: Chatto & Windus, 1927.

Hales, E. E. Y. *Chariot of Fire*. London: Hodder & Stoughton, 1977.

Hardin, Garrett, ed. *Population, Evolution and Birth Control: A Collage of Controversial Ideas.* San Francisco: W. H. Freeman, 1964.
-------. "The Tragedy of the Commons" *Science* 162 (1968): 1243-8.
Harrison, Harry. *Make Room! Make Room!* Garden City, N.Y.: Doubleday, 1966.
Hawkins, Willard. "The Dwindling Sphere." *Astounding Stories* March 1940.
Hawthorne, Nathaniel. "Doctor Heidegger's Experiment" in *Twice-Told Tales*. Boston, Mass.: American Stationers Co, 1837.
-------. "Ethan Brand" in *The Snow-Image and Other Twice-Told Tales*. Boston: Ticknor, Reed and Field, 1852. [Original publication 1851.]
-------. "A Virtuoso's Collection" in *Mosses from an Old Manse*. New York: Wiley and Putnam, 1846. [Original publication 1842.]
Hawthorne, Nathaniel, and Julian Hawthorne. *Doctor Grimshawe's Secret*. Boston: Houghton Mifflin, 1882.
Hay, W. D. *The Doom of the Great City*. London: Newman, 1880.
Heine, Heinrich. "The Memoirs of Herr von Schnabelewopski." in *The Works of Heinrich Heine*. London: Dutton, 1906. [Original publication in German 1834.]
Henry, O. "The Door of Unrest" in *Sixes and Sevens*. New York: Doubleday Doran, 1911.
Hersey, John. *My Petition for More Space*. New York: Knopf, 1974.
Heym, Stefan. *The Wandering Jew*. New York: Holt, Rinehart and Winston, 1984. [Original publication in German as *Ahasver: Der Ewige Jude*, 1981.]
Hichens, Robert. *Dr Artz*. London: Hutchinson, 1929.
Hilton, James. *Lost Horizon*. London: Macmillan, 1933.
Hix, J. Emile. *Can a Man Live Forever?* Chicago: Western News Co, 1898.
Hodgson, William Hope. "The Baumoff Explosive" *Nash's Weekly* September 17, 1919. [written 1912; restored text as "Eloi, Eloi, Sabachthani" in *Out of the Storm* ed. Sam Moskowitz. West Kingston, R.I.: Donald M. Grant, 1975.]
-------. "The Hog" in *Carnacki the Ghost-Finder*. Saunk City, Wisc.: Mycroft & Moran, 1947.
-------. *The House on the Borderland*. London: Chapman and Hall, 1908.
-------. *The Night Land*. London: Eveleigh Nash, 1912.
Hoffman, David. *Chronicles Selected from the Originals of Cartaphilus*. 3 vols. London: T. Bosworth, 1853-54.

Holland, Clive. *An Egyptian Coquette*. London: C. Arthur Pearson, 1898.
Holt-White, William. *Helen of All Time*. London: T. Fisher Unwin, 1905.
Hudson, W. H. *A Crystal Age*. London: Fisher Unwin, 1887
-------. *Green Mansions: A Romance of the Tropical Forest*. London: Duckworth, 1904.
Hugo, Victor. "Plein ciel" in *La Légende des siècles.* Paris: Michel Levy frères & Hetzel et cie, 1859.
Huxley, Aldous. *After Many a Summer Dies the Swan*. London: Chatto and Windus, 1939.
-------. *Ape and Essence*. New York: Harper, 1948.
-------. *Crome Yellow*. London: Chatto & Windus, 1921.
-------. *Brave New World*, London: Chatto & Windus, 1932.
Huxley. Julian. "The Tissue-Culture King." *Amazing Stories* October 1927.
Huysmans, Joris-Karl. *À rebours*. Paris, Charpentier, 1884.
-------. "Des Esseintes' Dream (from *À rebours*)") tr. by Francis Amery, in *The Second Dedalus Book of Decadence: The Black Feast* edited by Brian Stableford. Sawtry, Cambs: Dedalus, 1992. pp. 35-47.
Hyams, Edward. *The Astrologer*. London: Longmans Green, 1950.
Hyne, C. J. Cutcliffe. *Abbs: His Story Through Many Ages*. London: Hutchinson, 1929.
Jaeger, Muriel. *Retreat from Armageddon*. London: Duckworth, 1936.
Jarry, Alfred. "Commentaire pour servir à la construction patique de la machine à explorer le temps." *Mercure de France* Février 1899.
-------. *Les Jours et les nuits*. Paris: Gallimard, 1897.
-------. *Le surmâle*. Paris: Fasquelle, 1902. English tr. as *The Supermale*. London: Jonathan Cape, 1964.)
Jefferies, Richard. *After London; or, Wild England*. London: Cassell, 1885.
Jones, Diana Wynne. *The Homeward Bounders*. London: Macmillan, 1981.
Kast, Pierre. *The Vampires of Alfama*. London: W. H. Allen, 1976. [Original publication in French as *Les vampires d'Alfama*, 1975.]
Kerby, Susan Alice. *Mr Kronion*. London: Werner Laurie, 1949.
Knight, Damon. "Natural State." Galaxy, January 1954; reprinted as *Masters of Evolution*. New York: Ace, 1959.
Kornbluth, C. M. "Reap the Dark Tide." *Vanguard* June 1958 [reprinted as "Shark Ship"]

Lagerkvist, Pär. *The Sibyl*. London: London: Chatto and Windus, 1958. [Original publication in Swedish as *Sibyllan*, 1956.]

-------. *The Death of Ahasuerus*. London: Chatto and Windus, 1962. [Original publication in Swedish as *Ahasverus' död*, 1960.]

Langford, David. "Waiting for the Iron Age" in *Tales of the Wandering Jew* ed. Brian Stableford. Sawtry, Cambs.: Dedalus, 1991.

Lawrence, C. E. "Spikenard" *Cornhill Magazine* 1930.

le Breton, Thomas. *Mr. Teedles, the Gland Old Man*. London: Werner Laurie, 1927.

Leland, Charles Godfrey. *Flaxius: Leaves from the Life of an Immortal*. London: P. Welby, 1902.

Lee, Edgar. *Pharaoh's Daughter*. Bristol: Arrownsmith, 1889.

Leiber, Fritz. "A Bit of the Dark World" *Fantastic* February 1962.

-------. *Our Lady of Darkness*. New York: Putnam, 1977.

-------. "Smoke Ghost" *Unknown* October 1941.

Lewis, C. S. *The Great Divorce*. London: Geoffrey Bles, 1945.

Lewis, Matthew Gregory. *The Monk*. London: J. Bell, 1796.

Ligotti, Thomas. "The Tsalal" in *Noctuary*. London: Robinson, 1994.

Long, Frank Belknap. "The Great Cold." *Astounding Stories* February 1935.

-------. "Green Glory." *Astounding Stories* January 1935.

-------. "The Horror from the Hills" *Weird Tales* January-February 1931.

-------. "The Hounds of Tindalos" *Weird Tales* March 1929.

-------. "The Last Men." *Astounding Stories* August 1934.

-------. "The Space-Eaters" *Weird Tales* July 1928.

Lorrain, Jean. *Monsieur de Phocas*. Tr. Francis Amery. Sawtry, Cambs: Dedalus, 1994. [Original publication in French, 1900.]

-------. *Nightmares of an Ether-Drinker*. Carlton-in-Coverdale, North Yorks.: Tartarus Press, 2002.

Louÿs, Pierre. *The Adventures of King Pausole*. New York: William Godwin, 1933.

Lovecraft, H. P. "Astrophobos" in *Collected Poems*. Sauk City, Wisc.: Arkham House, 1963.

-------. "At the Mountains of Madness" in *At the Mountains of Madness and Other Novels of Terror*. Sauk City, Wisc.: Arkham House, 1964. pp. 1-101. [Originally published in abridged form in *Astounding Stories* February-April 1936.]

-------. "The Call of Cthulhu." *Weird Tales* February 1928.

-------. "The Color out of Space." *Amazing Stories* September 1927.

-------. "Dagon." *Weird Tales* October 1923.

-------. *Dagon and Other Macabre Tales*. Sauk City, Wisc.: Arkham House, 1965.
-------. "The Dunwich Horror." *Weird Tales* April 1929.
-------. *The Dunwich Horror and Others*. Sauk City, Wisc.: Arkham House, 1963.
-------. "The Music of Erich Zann." *Weird Tales* May 1925. [Originally published 1922.]
-------. "The Outsider." *Weird Tales* April 1926.
-------. *The Outsider and Others*. Sauk City, Wisc.: Arkham House, 1939.
-------. "Pickman's Model." *Weird Tales* October 1927.
-------. *The Shadow over Innsmouth*. Everett, Penn.: Visionary Press, 1936.
-------. "The Shadow out of Time." *Astounding Stories* June 1936.
-------. "The Horror at Red Hook." *Weird Tales* January 1927.
Lovelock, James. *Gaia: A New Look at Life on Earth*. Oxford: Oxford University Press, 1973.
Lumley, Brian *The Transition of Titus Crow*. New York: DAW Books, 1975.
McCarthy, Justin Huntly. *The Dryad*. London: Methuen, 1905.
MacDonald, George. *Thomas Wingfold, Curate*. London: Hurst and Blackett, 1876.
Machen, Arthur. *The Great God Pan and The Inmost Light*. London: John Lane, 1894. [Original publication of "The Great God Pan" 1890.]
-------. *The Great Return*. London: Faith Press, 1915.
-------. *The Secret Glory*. London: Martin Secker, 1922.
-------. "The White People" in *The House of Souls*. London: Grant Richards, 1906. [Original publication 1899.]
McKenna, Stephen. *The Oldest God*. London: Thornton Butterworth, 1926.
Mann, Jack. *Maker of Shadows*. London: Wright & Brown, 1938.
-------. *The Ninth Life*. London: Wright & Brown, 1939.
Manning, Laurence, with Fletcher Pratt. "The City of the Living Dead" *Science Wonder Stories* May 1930.
Marriott-Watson, H. C. *Erchomenon; or, The Republic of Materialism*. London: Sampson Low, 1879) [published anonymously]
Marryat, Frederick. *The Phantom Ship*. London: Henry Colburn, 1839.
Martyn, Wyndham. *Stones of Enchantment*. London: Herbert Jenkins, 1948.

Maturin, Charles. *Melmoth the Wanderer: A Tale*. Oxford: Oxford University Press, 1968. [Originally published London: Hurst and Robinson, 1820].
Mercier, Luois-Sébastien. *L'an deux mille quatre cent quarante.* Paris: [no publisher indicated] 1771; definitive ed. Paris, 1786.
Miller, Walter M. *A Canticle for Leibowitz*. Philadelphia: Lippincott, 1960.
Mitchison, Naomi. *Not By Bread Alone*. London: Marion Boyars, 1983.
-------. *Solution Three*. London: Dennis Dobson, 1975.
Moorcock, Michael. *An Alien Heat*. New York: Harper and Row, 1972.
-------. *The End of All Songs*. New York: Harper and Row, 1976.
-------. *The Hollow Lands*. New York: Harper and Row, 1974.
Morrow, James. *The Eternal Footman*. Harcourt Brace, 1999.
-------. *Only Begotten Daughter*. Harcourt Brace, 1990.
Neele, Henry "The Magician's Visiter" in *The Literary Remains of the Late Henry Neele*, London: Smith Elder, 1829.
Nesbit, E. *Dormant*. London: Methuen, 1911.
Newman, Kim, and Eugene Byrne. "The Wandering Christian" in *Tales of the Wandering Jew* ed. Brian Stableford. Sawtry, Cambs.: Dedalus, 1991.
Nodier, Charles. "Hurlubleu grand Manifafa d'Hurlubière ou la perfectibilité." *Revue de Paris* août 1833.
-------. "Léviathan le long Archikan des Patagons de l'île savante ou la perfectibilité." *Revue de Paris* novembre 1833.
Nodier, Charles, with Achille de Jouffroy and Jean-Toussaint Merle. *The Vampire* in *Lord Ruthven the Vampire* ed. Frank J. Morlock, Encino, Calif.: Black Coat Press, 2005. [Original production in French as *Le Vampire*, 1820].
Norton, Caroline *The Undying One, and Other Poems*. London: Henry Colburn, 1830.
Offutt, Andrew J. *The Castle Keeps*. New York: Berkley, 1972.
O'Leary, Patrick. *The Impossible Bird*. New York: Tor, 2002.
Orwell, George. *Nineteen Eighty-Four*. London: Secker & Warburg, 1949.
Phillpotts, Eden. *The Girl and the Faun*. London: Cecil Palmer, 1916.
Poe, Edgar Allan. *Al Aaraaf*. New York: The Facsimile Text Society, 1933. [Original publication 1829.]
-------. "The Conversation of Eiros and Charmion" in Tales of the Grotesque and Arabesque. Philadelphia: Lea and Blanchard, 1840. [Original publication 1839.]

-------. *Eureka: A Prose Poem*. New York: Putnam, 1848.
-------. "Mesmeric Revelation" in *Tales of Edgar A. Poe*. New York: Wiley and Putnam, 1845. [Original publication 1844.]
-------. *The Narrative of Arthur Gordon Pym of Nantucket*. New York: Harper, 1838. [First edition anonymous.]
-------. "Shadow—A Parable" in *Tales of the Grotesque and Arabesque*. Philadelphia: Lea and Blanchard, 1840. [Original publication 1835.]
-------. "Silence—A Fable" in *Tales of the Grotesque and Arabesque*. Philadelphia: Lea and Blanchard, 1840. [Original publication 1838.]
Pohl, Frederik. "The Census Takers." *The Magazine of Fantasy & Science Fiction* February 1956.
Polidori, John *The Vampyre: A Tale*. London: Sherwood, Neeley & Jones, 1819. [Early editions anonymous.]
Potocki, Jan. *The Manuscript found at Saragossa*. London: Viking, 1995.
Powers, Tim. *On Stranger Tides*. New York: Ace, 1987.
Powys, T. F. *Unclay*. London: Chatto and Windus, 1931.
Q (Arthur Quiller-Couch) "The Mystery of Joseph Laquedem" in *Old Fires and Profitable Ghosts*. London: Cassell, 1900.
Quinet, Edgar. *Ahasvérus*. Paris: Bureau de la Revue des Deux-Mondes, 1834.
Reed, Robert. *Sister Alice*. New York: Tor, 2003.
Renard, Maurice. "Depuis Sinbad" *L'Ami des livres* 15 Juin 1923.
-------. *Le Docteur Lerne, sous-dieu*. Paris: Mercure de France 1908.
-------. *Un Homme chez les microbes*. Paris: Crès, 1928.
-------. "L'Homme truqué". *Je sais tout*, Mars 1921.
-------. *Le Maître de la lumière*. *L'Instransigeant* 8 Mars-2 Mai 1933.
-------. *Les Mains d'Orlac*. Paris: Nilsson, 1920.
-------. *Le Péril bleu*. Paris: Louis Michaud, 1911.
-------. "Le Roman d'hypothèse" *A.B.C.* 15 Decembre 1928.
-------. "Du Roman merveilleux-scientifique et de son action sur l'intelligence du progrès". *Spectateur* 6 (Octobre 1909).
-------. *Le Singe* (with Albert Jean). Paris: Crès, 1925.
-------. "Les Vacances de Monsieur Dupont"in *Fantômes et Fantoches* {as by Vincent St. Vincent]. Paris: Plon 1905.
-------. *Le Voyage Immobile suivi d'autres histoires singulières*. Paris: Mercure de France 1909.
Rice, Anne. *Interview with the Vampire*. London: Raven, 1976.
Richepin, Jules "La machine à métaphyqique" in *Les morts bizarres*. Paris: Georges Decaux, 1877.

Robinson, Kim Stanley. *Forty Signs of Rain*. New York: Bantam Spectra, 2004.
-------. ed. *Future Primitive: The New Ecotopias*. New York: Tor, 1994.
Robson, Justine. Natural History. London: Macmillan, 2003.
Rosny, J. H. aîné. "Un Autre Monde" *Revue Parisienne* 1895.
-------. *La Force Mystérieuse*. Paris: Plon, 1914.
-------. *La Guerre du feu*. Paris: Fasquelle, 1911.
-------. *La Mort de la Terre*. Paris: Plon, 1910.
-------. *Les Xipéhuz*. Paris: Savine, 1887.
Russell, W. Clark. *The Death Ship*. London: Hurst & Blackett, 1888.
Sampson, Ashley. *The Ghost of Mr Brown*. London: Fortune Press, 1941.
Sauer, Rob, ed. *Voyages: Scenarios for a Ship Called Earth*. New York: Ballantine, 1971.
Scarborough, Harold. *The Immortals*. London: T. Fisher Unwin, 1924.
Schachner, Nathan. "Sterile Planet." *Astounding Stories* July 1937.
Schroeder, Karl. *Permanence*. New York: Tor, 2002.
Schumacher, Ernst. *Small is Beautiful: A Study of Economics as if People Mattered*. London: Bond and Briggs, 1973.
Shaw, George Bernard. *Back to Methuselah: A Metabiological Pentateuch*. London: Constable, 1921.
Shea, Michael. *Nifft the Lean*. New York: DAW, 1982.
-------. *The Mines of Behemoth*. New York: Baen, 1997.
Sheckley, Robert. "The People Trap." *The Magazine of Fantasy & Science Fiction* June 1968.
Shelley, Mary. *Frankenstein; or, The Modern Prometheus*. London: Lackington, Hughes. 1818.
-------. *The Last Man*. London: Henry Colburn, 1826.
-------. "The Mortal Immortal" in *Tales and Stories*. London: W. Paterson, 1891. [Original publication 1834.]
Shelley, Percy Bysshe. *Hellas: A Lyrical Drama*. London: Charles & James Ollier, 1822.
-------. "Queen Mab: A philosophical Poem" in *Poetical Works*. London: Milner and Sowerby, 1867. [Original publication by the author, 1813.]
Sherrill, Stephen. *The Minotaur Takes a Cigarette Break*. Winston Salem, N.C.: John F. Blair, 2000.
Shiel, M. P. *This Above All*. New York: Vanguard, 1933.
Silverberg, Robert. *The Book of Skulls*. New York: Signet, 1972.
-------. "Born with the Dead" *The Magazine of Fantasy & Science Fiction* April 1974.

———. *Master of Life and Death*. New York: Ace, 1957.
———. "Sailing to Byzantium" *Isaac Asimov's Science Fiction Magazine* February 1985.
———. *Son of Man*. New York: Ballantine, 1971.
———. *The World Inside*. Garden City, N.Y.: Doubleday, 1971.
Smith, Clark Ashton. "The Amazing Planet." *Wonder Stories Quarterly* Summer 1931.
———. "The Dimension of Chance." *Wonder Stories* November 1932.
———. "The Empire of the Necromancers" *Weird Tales* September 1932.
———. "The Eternal World." *Wonder Stories* March 1932.
———. *The Hashish-Eater; or, The Apocalypse of Evil*. West Warwick, R.I.: Necronomicon Press, 1989. [Original publication in *Ebony and Crystal*. Auburn, Calif.: Auburn Journal, 1922.]
———. "The Light from Beyond." *Wonder Stories* April 1933.
———. "Marooned in Andromeda." *Wonder Stories* October 1930.
———. "Necromancy in Naat." *Weird Tales* July 1936.
———. "The Seven Geases." *Weird Tales* October 1934.
———. "The Visitors from Mlok." *Wonder Stories* May 1933.
———. "Xeethra." *Weird Tales* December 1934.
Southey, Robert. *The Curse of Kehama*. London: Longman, Hurst et al, 1810.
Souvestre, Émile. *Le Monde tel qu'il sera*. Paris: W. Coquevert, 1846.
Spinrad, Norman. *Greenhouse Summer*. New York: Tor, 1999.
Stableford, Brian, ed. *The Germans on Venus and Other French Scientific Romances*. Encino, Cal.: Black Coat Press, 2009.
———. *Tales of the Wandering Jew*. Sawtry, Cambs.: Dedalus, 1991.
Stapledon, Olaf. *Last and First Men*. London: Methuen, 1930.
———. *Last Men in London*. London: Methuen, 1932.
———. *Odd John*. London: Methuen, 1934.
———. *Star Maker*. London: Methuen, 1937.
Sterling, Bruce. *Distraction*. New York: Bantam, 1998.
———. *Schismatrix*. New York: Arbor House, 1985.
Sterling, George. *A Wine of Wizardry, and Other Poems*. San Francisco: A. M. Robertson, 1909. [Original publication in *Cosmopolitan*, 1907.]
Stewart, Fred Mustard. *The Mephisto Waltz*. New York: Coward-McCann, 1969.
Stockton, Frank R. *The Vizier of the Two-Horned Alexander*. New York: Century, 1899.
Stong, Phil. *The Other Worlds*. New York: Funk, 1941.

Stonier, G. W. *Memoirs of a Ghost*. London: Grey Walls Press, 1947.
Street. A. G. *Already Walks Tomorrow*. London: Faber & Faber, 1938.
Strieber, Whitley. *The Hunger*. London: Bodley Head, 1981.
Stross, Charles. *Accelerando*. New York: Tor, 2005.
Stuart, Don A. (John W. Campbell Jr). "Forgetfulness." *Astounding Stories* June 1937.
-------. "Night." *Astounding Stories* October 1935.
-------. "Twilight." *Astounding Stories* November 1934.
-------. "Who Goes There?" *Astounding Stories* August 1938.
Sue, Eugène. *The Mysteries of Paris*. London: Chapman and Hall, 1844-45. [Original punblication in French as *Les mystères de Paris*, 1842-43.]
-------. *The Wandering Jew*. London: Chapman and Hall, 1844-5. [Original publication in French as *Le juif errant*.]
Swayne, Martin. *The Blue Germ*. New York: Doran, 1918.
Swift, Jonathan. *Travels into Several Remote Nations of the World in Four Parts...by Lemuel Gulliver*. London: Bliss, Sands & Foster, 1896. [Facsimile of first edition published in 1726-7; usually reprinted as *Gulliver's Travels*].
Teilhard de Chardin, Pierre. *The Future of Man*. London: Collins, 1964. [Original publication in French as *L'avenir de l'homme*. 1959.]
--------. *The Phenomenon of Man*. London: Collins, 1959. [Original publication in French as *Le phénomène humain* 1955].
Tennyson, Alfred, Lord. In Memoriam A.H.H. London: Edward Moxon, 1850.
Thurston, E. Temple. *The Wandering Jew*. London: Putnam, 1920.
Teilhard de Chardin, Pierre. *The Future of Man*. London: Collins, 1964. [Original publication in French as *L'avenir de l'homme*. 1959.]
--------. *The Phenomenon of Man*. London: Collins, 1959. [Original publication in French as *Le phénomène humain* 1955].
Tipler, Frank *The Physics of Immortality: Modern Cosmology, God and the Resurrection of the Dead*. New York: Doubleday, 1994.
Tolkien, J. R. R. *The Lord of the Rings*. 3 vols. London: Allen & Unwin, 1954-55.
Tsiolkovsky, Konstantin. *Vne zemli* [1916]; tr. as "Outside the Earth" in *The Call of the Cosmos*. Moscow: Foreign Languages Publishing House, 1963.
Twain, Mark. *The Innocents Abroad*. New York: Hartford, Conn.: American Publishing Co, 1869.

Upton, Smyth. *The Last of the Vampires*. Weston-Super-Mare, Somerset: J. Whereat, 1845.

Vance, Jack. *The Dying Earth*. New York: Hillman, 1950.

-------. *The Last Castle*. New York: Ace, 1967. [Original pubication 1966.]

Vansittart, Peter. *The Death of Robin Hood*. London: Peter Owen, 1981.

-------. *Parsifal*. London: Peter Owen, 1988.

Vernadsky, Vladimir. *The Biosphere*. Oracle, Ariz.: Synergiustic Press, 1986. [Originally published in Russian, 1926]

Verne, Jules [with Paschal Grousset], *Les cinq cents millions de la begum*, Paris: Hetzel, 1879; tr. as *The Begum's Fortune*, London: Sampson Low, Marston, Searle and Rivington, 1880.

-------. *Paris au XXe siècle*. Paris: Hachette, 1994; tr. as *Paris in the Twentieth Century*. New York: Random House, 1996.

-------. *Robur le conquérant*. Paris: Hetzel, 1886; tr. as *The Clipper of the Clouds*. London: Sampson Low, Marston, Searle and Rivington, 1887.

-------. *Vingt mille lieues sous les mers*. Paris: Hetzel, 1870; tr. as *Twenty Thousand Leagues Under the Sea*. London: Sampson Low, Marston, Searle and Rivington, 1873 [actually 1872].

-------. *Voyage au centre de la terre* (Paris, Hetzel, 1864.

Viereck, George S. *Gloria*. London: Duckworth, 1952.

Viereck, George S., and Paul Eldridge. *The Invincible Adam*. New York: Liveright, 1932.

-------. *My First Two Thousand Years*. New York: Macaulay, 1928.

-------. *Salome, the Wandering Jewess*. New York: Liveright, 1930.

Villiers de l'Isle Adam, Comte de. *L'Ève Future*. Paris: Brunhoff, 1886.

Vinge, Vernor. *True Names*. New York: Dell, 1981.

Voltaire. *Candide, ou l'optimisme*. Geneva: Cramer, 1759.

-------. *Le Micromégas de mr. de Voltaire*. Londres [actually Berlin], 1752.

Vonnegut, Kurt Jr. "The Big Trip Up Yonder." *Galaxy* January 1954.

Wandrei, Donald. "Blinding Shadows." *Astounding Stories* May 1934.

-------. "Finality Unlimited." *Astounding Stories* September 1936.

-------. "Infinity Zero." *Astounding Stories* October 1936.

-------. "On the Threshold of Eternity" in *The Eye and the Finger*. Sauk City, Wisc.: Arkham House, 1944.

-------. "The Red Brain." *Weird Tales* October 1927.

-------. *The Web of Easter Island*. Sauk City, Wisc.: Arkham House, 1948.
Webb, Catherine. *Webwalkers*. London: Atom, 2003.
Wells, H. G. "In the Abyss." *Pearson's Magazine* August 1896.
-------. The Invisible Man. London: Pearson, 1897.
-------. *The First Men in the Moon*. London: Newnes, 1901.
-------. *The Food of the Gods and How it Came to Earth*. London: Macmillan, 1904.
-------. "A Story of the Days to Come" *Pall Mall Magazine* June-October 1897; revised version in *Tales of Space and Time*. London: Harper, 1899.
-------. *The Time Machine: an Invention*. London: Heinemann, 1895.
-------. *The War of the Worlds*. London: Heinemann, 1898.
Wilde, Oscar. "The Canterville Ghost" and "Lord Arthur Savile's Crime" in *Lord Arthur Savile's Crime and Other Stories*. London: Osgood, McIlvaine, 1891. [Original publications 1887.].
-------. *The Picture of Dorian Gray*. London: Ward Lock, 1891.
-------. *The Sphinx*. London: Elkin Matthews, 1894. [Original publication 1874.]
Watkin, L. E. *On Borrowed Time*. New York: Knopf, 1937.
Watkins, William Jon, with Gene Synder. *Ecodeath*. Garden City, N.Y.: Doubleday, 1972.
Wilkins, Vaughan. *Valley Beyond Time*. London: Jonathan Cape, 1955.
Williamson. Jack *Golden Blood*. New York: Lancer, 1964. [Original publication in Weird Tales, 1933.]
Woolf, Virginia. *Orlando: A Biography*. London: L. and V. Woolf, 1928.
Wright, S. Fowler. *The Adventure of Wyndham Smith*. Jenkins, 1938
-------. *The New Gods Lead*. London: Jarrolds, 1932.
-------. "The Rat" *Weird Tales* March 1929.
Wylie, Philip. *The End of the Dream*. Garden City, N.Y.: Doubleday, 1972.
Yarbro, Chelsea Quinn. *Hotel Transylvania*. New York: St Martin's Press, 1978,
Young, Edward. *The Complaint; or, Night Thoughts*. London: R. Dodsley, 1742-45.
Zamiatin, Eugene. *We*. New York: Dutton, 1924.
Zelazny, Roger. *Isle of the Dead*. New York: Ace, 1969.
-------. *Lord of Light*. New York: Doubleday, 1967.
-------. *This Immortal*. New York: Ace, 1966.

SECONDARY SOURCES

Akenside, Mark. *The Pleasures of the Imagination*. London: R. Dodsley, 1744.
Aldiss, Brian W. *Billion Year Spree*. London: Gollancz, 1973; rev., with David Wingrove, as *Trillion Year Spree*. London: Gollancz, 1986.
Anderson, George K. *The Legend of the Wandering Jew*. Providence, R.I.: Brown University Press, 1965.
Baumgarten, Alexander. *Aesthetica*. New York: Georg Olms, 1986. [Original publication in German, 1750-58.]
Burke, Edmund. *A Philosophical Enquiry into the Origin of Our Ideas of the Sublime and Beautiful*. London: R. and J. Dodsley, 1757.
Butor, Michel. "On Fairy Tales" in *Inventory*. London: Jonathan Cape, 1970. pp. 211-223.
Clute, John, and John Grant. *The Encyclopedia of Fantasy*. London: Orbit, 1997.
Galaxy October 1950, back cover.
Conway, Moncure Daniel. *The Wandering Jew*. London: Chatto and Windus, 1881.
Dyson, Freeman "Time Without End: Physics and Biology in an Open Universe" *Reviews of Modern Physics* 51 (1979): 452-4.
Frazer, James G. *The Golden Bough: A Study in Comparative Religion*. 2 vols. London: Macmillan, 1890. rev. as *The Golden Bough: A Study in Magic and Religion*. 13 vols. London: Macmillan, 1932.
Jones, Diana Wynne. *The Tough Guide to Fantasyland*. London: Vista, 1996.
Kant, Immanuel. *Universal Natural History and Theory of the Heavens*. Tr. Stanley K. Jaki. Edinburgh: Scottish Academic Press, 1981. [Original publication as *Allegemeine Naturgeschichte und Theorie des Himmels*, 1755].
Leibniz, Gottfried. *Theodicy*. New York: Wipf and Stock, 2001. [Original publication in German, 1710.]
Longinus. *On the Sublime*. Tr. by A. O. Prickard. Oxford: Clarendon Press, 1926. [Original version 1st century AD.]
Lovecraft, H. P. *Supernatural Horror in Literature*. New York: Dover, 1973. [Originally published 1927; revised version 1939.]
Malthus, T. R. *An Essay on the Principle of Population; or, a View of its Past and Present Effects on Human Happiness; with an Inquiry into our Prospects Respecting the Future Removal or Miti-

gation of the Effects which it Occasions. A New Edition, very much Enlarged. London: Printed for J. Johnson by T. Bensley, 1803. [First edition 1798.]

Mendlesohn, Farah. "Towards a Taxonomy of Fantasy". *Journal of the Fantastic in the Arts* vol. 13, no.2 (2002). pp. 173-87.

Montesquieu, Charles le Secondat, Baron de. *Considérations sur les causes de la grandeur des Romains et de leur décadence*. Amsterdam: Jacques Desbordes, 1734.

Moreau, Joseph. *Hashish and Mental Illness*. New York: Raven Press, 1973. [Original publication in French, 1845.]

Nordau, Max Simon. *Degeneration*. London: Heinemann, 1895. [Original publication in German as *Entartung*, 1893.]

Shelley, Percy Bysshe. "A Defence of Poetry" in *Shelley's Poetry and Prose* ed. Mary Shelley. London: Edward Moxon, 1840.

Silverstein, Alvin. *Conquest of Death: The Prospects for Emortality in Our Time*. New York: Macmillan, 1979.

Spengler, Oswald. *The Decline of the West*. London: Allen and Unwin, 1918. [Original publication in German as *Der Undertang des Abendlandes*, 1918.]

Thomson, Sir William (Lord Kelvin). "On a Universal Tendency in Nature to the Dissipation of Mechanical Energy" *Proceedings of the Royal Society of Edinburgh* April 19, 1852.

--------. "On the Age of the Sun's Heat" *Macmillan's Magazine* March 5, 1862: 288-93.

Wollheim, Donald A. *The Universe Makers: Science Fiction Today*. New York: Harper, 1971.

Yanarella, Ernest J. *The Cross, the Plow and the Skyline: Contemporary Science Fiction and the Ecological Imagination*. Parkland, Fl.: Brown Walker, 2001.

FILMOGRAPHY

Bladerunner. Dir. Ridley Scott, 1982.
Carrie. Dir. Brian de Palma, 1976.
Death Becomes Her. Dir. Robert Zemeckis, 1992.
I Was a Teenage Werewolf. Dir. Gene Fowler, 1957.
Lost Horizon. Dir. Frank Capra, 1937.
Mad Love. Dir. Karl Freund, 1935.
The Matrix. Dir. 1999
Metropolis. Dir. Fritz Lang, 1926.
On Borrowed Time. Dir. Harold S. Bucquet, 1939.
The Wandering Jew. Dir. Maurice Elvey, 1933.
Z.P.G. Dir. Michael Campus, 1972.

DISCOGRAPHY

Crash Test Dummies "Superman's Song" *The Ghosts That Haunt Me*. Arista, 1991.

INDEX

A.B.C. 97
Abbs: His Story Through Many Ages 47
About, Edmond 89
Accelerando 120
"Accursed Cordonnier, The" 40
Adams, John Quincy 104
Adventure of Wyndham Smith, The 110, 112
Aeschylus 31
Aesop 65
Aesthetika 126
After London; or, Wild England 109
After Many a Summer Dies the Swan 47
Ahasver, der Ewige Jude 51
Ahasvérus 36
Ahasverus död 51
Ainsworth, W. Harrison 43-44
Akenside, Mark 126, 133
"Al Aaraaf" 133, 142
Albertus Magnus 40
Aldiss, Brian W. 14, 19
Alien Heat, An 58
Allais, Alphonse 86
Allegemeine Naturgeschichte und Theorie des Himmels 127
Already Walks Tomorrow 114
"Amazing Planet, The" 144
Amazing Stories 99
Ami des livres, L' 94
Analog 150
Anderson George K. 34, 39
An deux mille quatre cent quarante, L' 78, 106
Andreae, J. V. 40
Angelic Avengers, The 50

Angels of Perversity 138
Ape and Essence 113
Apollinaire, Guillaume 87
Apollonius of Tyana 37
À rebours 136-137
Aristotle 61-62, 66, 127
Arkham House 124, 147-148
Arnold, Edwin Lester 45
Arthur [King] 50, 56
Asimov, Isaac 16, 26, 115
Astounding Science Fiction 22, 150
Astounding Stories of Super-Science 145, 149-150
Astrologer, The 114
"Astrophobos" 144
Atherton, Gertrude 47
"At the Mountains of Madness" 145-146
Auriol 43
Austin, William 44
Avenir de l'homme, L' 152
Babbitt, Nathalie 58
Back to Methuselah 47
Bacon, Francis 69
Ballard, J. G. 23, 57, 115
Balzac, Honoré de 43
Banks, Joseph 104, 131
Baring-Gould, Sabine 43
Barr, Marleen 7
Barr, Robert 109
Barrie, J. M. 46
Bass, T. J. 116
Baudelaire, Charles 135-137, 139, 142-143, 145
Baumgarten, Alexander 7, 9, 12, 126
"Baumoff Explosion, The" 140
Bayley, Barrington J. 58
Beauclerk, Helen 53
Beckford, William 129, 137
Begum's Fortune, The 106-107
Ben-Beor: A Story of the Anti-Messiah 39
Béranger, Pierre de 36
Bergson, Henri 86
Bernal, J. D. 151
Besant, Walter 46, 109
Bid for Fortune, A 45

Bien, H. M. 39
Bierce, Ambrose 142
"Big Trip Up Yonder, The" 115
"Billennium" 115
Billion Year Spree 14
Biosphere, The 118
Bishop, Michael 56
"Bit of the Dark World, A" 148-149
Black Oxen 47
Blackwood, Algernon 141-142
Bladerunner 119
Blake, William 53, 105, 157
Blavatsky, Madame Helena 45
Bligh, William 104
Blind Circle 100
"Blinding Shadows, The" 147
Blish, James 115
Blixen, Karen 50
Bloch, Robert 49, 148
Blue Germ, The 47
Blue Peril, The 93
Blumenbach, J. F. 128
Bodin, Félix 74-75, 77-82
Boisgilbert, Edmund 107
Book of Skulls, The 58
Boothby, Guy 45
"Born with the Dead" 58
Bouilhet, Louis 137
Bradbury, Ray 113, 123
Brave New World 110-113, 121
Brentano, Clemens 35
Brin, David 119
Brittle Innings 56
Broderick, Damien 120
"Brouillard de 26 Octobre, Le" 100
Browning, Robert 132
Brueghel, Pieter 137
Brunner, John 115-116, 123
Buchanan, Robert 38
Buffy the Vampire-Slayer 155, 157
Bulwer-Lytton, Edward 44-45, 132-133, 137, 140, 148, 150
Bunch, David 120
Burke, Edmund 126-127, 129

Butor, Michel 12
Byrne, Eugene 58
Cabinet des fées 85
Caesar's Column 107
Cagliostro 40
Cain 32-33
Callenbach, Ernest 118
"Call of Cthulhu, The" 145
Campbell, John W. Jr. 150-151
Can a Man Live Forever? 46
Candide 126
"Canterville Ghost, The" 141
Canticle for Leibowitz, A 57
Čapek, Karel 47-48, 108
Capes, Bernard 40
Capital 108
Capra, Frank 44
Carlyle, Thomas 107
Carnacki the Ghost-Finder 140
Carrie 157
Carroll, Lewis 67
Carson, Rachel 116
Carter, Brandon 152
Castle Keeps, The 117
Caves of Steel, The 115
Cecilius 126
"Census Takers, The" 115
Centaur, The 141
Chambers, Robert W, 142
"Chambre Double, Le" 135
Chariot of Fire 56
"Childe Roland to the Dark Tower Came" 132
Chousy, Didier, Comte de 85-86
Chronicles Selected from the Originals of Cartaphilus 38
Cinq cent millions de la bégum, Le 106-107
"City of the Living Dead, The" 112, 121
Claeys, Gregory 8
Clash of Angels 54
Cline, Leonard 149
Clipper of the Clouds, The 17
Clute, John 12, 52
Cobban, J. Maclaren 43
Cobbett, William 105, 109

"Coeur de Tony Wandel, Le" 46
Colette 86-87
Coleridge, Samuel Taylor 128-129, 131, 135
"Color Out of Space, The" 145
Coming Race, The 150
Complaint, The; or, Night Thoughts 128
Condamnés à mort, Les 108
Condorcet, Marquis de 76, 103-104
Confessions of an English Opium-Eater 129-130, 143
Conquest of Death 41
Considérations sur les causes de la grandeur des Romains et de leur décadence 139
Constantine, Murray 53
"Conversation of Eiros and Charmion, The" 133
Conway, Moncure Daniel 38
Corelli, Marie 47, 53
Corpus Hermeticum 40
Cosmopolitan 142
Cousin de Grainville, Jean Baptiste 74
Cowper, Richard 58
Crawford, F. Marion 45
Critias 66
Croly, George 38
Crome Yellow 110
Crystal Age, A 109
Curie, Pierre and Marie 99
Curse of Kehama, The 41
Cyrano de Bergerac, Savinien 85, 89
Daedalus; or, Science and the Future 111
"Dagon" 145
Daniels, Jonathan 54
Dark Chamber, The 149
Darwin, Charles 63, 85
Daudet, Léon 87
Davis, J. Clarence 117
Davray, Henri 84, 87
Days and Nights 86
Death Becomes Her 59
Death of Ahasuerus, The 51
Death of Robin Hood, The 56
Death Ship, The 44
De Bell, Garrett 117
Debussy, Claude 96

Decline of the West, The 139
Dedalus [publisher] 58
Dee, John 40
Degeneration 139
del Rey, Lester 115
De Palma, Brian 157
"Depuis Sinbad" 94-95, 97
De Quincey, Thomas 129-131, 134, 137, 143
Derennes, Charles 87, 89
Derleth, August 147-148
Dernier Homme, Le 74
Descartes, René 70-72
Devil, The 40, 42, 53-54
Devil, Poor Devil, The 53
Dickson, Gordon R. 116
"Dimension of Chance, The" 144
Distraction 122
Doc Savage 155
Docteur Lerne, sous-dieu, Le 87, 92-93, 100
"Doctored Man, The" 93
Doctor Grimshawe's Secret 44
"Doctor Heidegger's Experiment" 44
Doctor Jekyll and Mister Hyde 89
Doctor Lerne, Subgod 87
Dominik, Hans 99
Donnelly, Ignatius 107
"Doom of London, The" 109
Doom of the Great City, The 109
"Door of Unrest, The" 40
Doré, Gustave 36
Dormant 47
Douglas, Theo 45
Dover [publisher] 124
Dr. Artz 47
Dryad, The 53
Du Camp, Maxime 137
Dumas, Alexandre 36-37, 43, 45, 63
Dunsany, Lord 144
"Dunwich Horror, The" 145
"Dwindling Sphere, The" 114
Dying Earth, The 148
Dyson, Freeman 152
Earth 119

Ebony and Crystal 143
Ecclesiastes 113
"Ecocatastrophe" 114
Ecodeath 116
Ecotopia: A Novel about Ecology, People and Politics in 1999 118
Eddington, Arthur 151
Eden in Jeopardy: Man's Prodigal Meddling with his Environment 117
Edict, The 116
Edison, Thomas Alva 99
Eekhoud, Georges 46
Egan, Greg 59
Egyptian Coquette, An 45
Ehrlich, Max 116
Ehrlich, Paul 114
Einstein, Albert 63
Eldridge, Paul 48-51
Eleventh Commandment, The 115
"Elixir de longue vie, Le" 43
"Elixir of Hate, The" 47
"Elixir of Long Life, The" 43
"Eloi, Eloi, Sabachthani" 140
Emerson, Ralph Waldo 102
"Empire of the Necromancers, The" 143
Encyclopedia of Fantasy, The 12
End of All Songs, The 58
End of the Dream, The 116
England, George Allan 47
Entartung 139
Environmental Handbook, The 117
Eos 29
Erchomenon; or, the Republic of Materialism 108
Erckmann-Chatrian 95
Erskine, John 53
Essay on the Principle of Population as it Affects the Future Improvement of Society 103
Eternal Footman, The 59
"Eternal World, The" 144
"Ethan Brand" 38
Ève future, L' 85
Ewers, Hanns Heinz 95
"Exploits and Opinions of Dr. Faustroll, 'Pataphysician" 86
Fahrenheit 451 113

Farrère, Claude 43, 108
Faust 35, 40-42, 44, 55, 139
Faust (Goethe) 35
Fawcett, Edgar 83
Féval, Paul 37-38, 156
Field, Eugene 39
Fille de juif errant, Le 37
Fils du diable, Le 156
"Finality Unlimited" 147
Fin du monde, La 139
First Men in the Moon, The 17, 99
"Five After Five" 100
Flammarion, Camille 89, 139
Flaxius: Leaves from the Life of an Immortal 45
Flaubert, Gustave 137-138
Flecker, James Elroy 109-110
Flight of the Aerofix, The 100
Flying Dutchman, The 44
Food of the Gods and How it Came to Earth, The 17-18, 26, 99
Force Mystérieuse, La 97-98
"Forgetfulness" 150
Forty Signs of Rain 122
Forster, E. M. 111-112
Foster, George C. 47
France, Anatole 53
Frankenstein 15, 129
Frazer, James 125
"Funnel of God, The" 148
Future of Man, The 152
Future Primitive: The New Ecotopias 118
Gaia: A New Look at Life on Earth 118
Galaxy 22
Galileo Galilei 63, 133
Galland, Antoine 84
Garnett, Richard 53
Gautier, Théophile 134-135
Gayton, Bertram 47
Genesis 103
Gerhardi, William 53
Germans on Venus and Other French Scientific Romances, The 75
Gernsback, Hugo 83, 99-100, 112, 145
Gestes et opinions du Docteur Faustroll, 'pataphysicien 86
Ghost of Mr. Brown, The 56

Ghost Pirates, The 140
Gibson, William 119
Gilbert, W. S. 67
"Girl and the Faun, The" 53
Gland Stealers, The 47
Gloria 53
Godwin, William 41, 43, 104
Goethe J. W. von 35
Golden Blood 49
Golden Bough, The 125
Goncourt, Edmond 87
Gounod, Charles 36
Gourmont, Remy de 138
Graham, James 128
"Great Cold, The" 148
Great Divorce, The 56
"Great God Pan, The" 141
"Great Return, The" 141
"Green Glory" 148
Greenhouse Summer 122
Green Mansions 109
Greenwood Press 8
Gregory, Owen 108
Grousset, Paschal 106-107
Gunn, James 7, 121-122
Haeckel, Ernst 102
Haggard, H. Rider 45
Haldane, J. B. S. 111, 120, 151
Hales, E. E. Y. 56
Halévy, Fromentin 38
Half Past Human 116
Hands of Orlac, The 93
Hardin, Garrett 117-118
Harris, Thaddeus William 104
Harrison, Harry 115-116
Harry Potter and the Goblet of Fire 158
"Hashish" 134
Hashish and Mental Alienation 134
"Hashish-Eater, The; or, The Apocalypse of Evil" 143, 149, 153
"Haunters and the Haunted, The" 44
Hawking, Stephen 63
Hawkins, Willard E. 114
Hawthorne, Nathaniel 38, 44

Hay, W. D. 109
Heine, Heinrich 44
Helen of All Time 45
"Hellas" 38
Henry, O. 40
Hermes Trismegistus 40
Herod 37
Herodias 37
Herschel, William 127-128, 149
Hersey, John 116
Hetzel, P.-J. 16, 81
Heym, Stefan 51
Hichens, Robert 47
Hilton, James 44
Histoire des états et empires de la Lune et Soleil 85
Histoires magiques 128
Hitler, Adolf 113
Hix, J. Emile 46
Hodgson, W. H. 139-141, 143-144, 148
Hoffman, David 38
Hoffmann, E. T. A. 84, 95
"Hog, The" 140-141
Holland, Clive 45
Hollow Lands, The 58
Holt-White, William 45
"Holy Cross, The" 39
Homeward Bounders, The 57
Homme chez les microbes, Un 92-93, 97, 99
Homme truqué, L' 93
"Horror at Red Hook, The" 145
"Horror from the Hills, The" 148
"Hounds of Tindalos, The" 148
"House and the Brain, The" 44
House of the Secret, The 44
House on the Borderland, The 139-140
Hudson, W. H. 109
Hugo, Victor 79
Human Chord, The 141
Hunger, The 57
"Hurlubleu grand Manifafa d'Hurlubière ou la perfectibilité" 75
Huxley, Aldous 47, 110-113
Huxley, Julian 111, 114
Huysmans, Joris-Karl 136-137

Hyams, Edward 114
Hyne, C. J. Cutcliffe 47
"Hypothetical Fiction" 97
Iamblichus 40
Ignis 85-86
Immortals, The 47
Impossible Bird, The 59
"Infinity Zero" 147
In Memoriam 103
Inner House, The 46, 109
Innocents Abroad, The 38
Interview with the Vampire 56
"In the Abyss" 91
Invincible Adam, The 48
Invisible Man, The 91, 98
Iras: A Mystery 45
Isaac Laquedem 36
Island of Doctor Moreau, The 89, 98
Isle of the Dead 58
"Is the Scientific Paper a Fraud?" 64
I Was a Teenage Werewolf 157
Ixion 32
Jaeger, Muriel 111
Jarry, Alfred 84-86, 88-89, 97
Jean, Albert 100
Jefferies, Richard 109
Jefferson, Thomas 104
"Jersualem" 105
Je Sais Tout 93
Jesus Christ 33-34, 37-38, 41, 51, 58
John [Gospel] 34, 51
John the Baptist 37
Jones, Diana Wynne 12, 50, 57
Joseph Balsamo 45
Joshi, S. T. 7
Jouffroy, Achille de 43
Journey to the Center of the Earth 81
Jours et les nuits, Les 86
Joy Makers, The 121-122
Judas 34
Juif errant, Le 36
Jung, Carl 143
Kant, Immanuel 127, 130

Kapital, Das 108
Kast, Pierre 56
Kelvin, Lord 85-86, 139, 151
Kent, Clark 155, 158
Kepler, John 133
Kerby, Susan Alice 53
Kidder, Margot 158
King, Stephen 157
King in Yellow, The 142
Knight, Damon 115
Knight, Norman L. 115
Kornbluth, C. M. 115
"Kubla Khan" 131
Lagerkvist, Pär 51
La Hire, Jean de 86
Lang, Fritz 100, 108
Langford, David 58
Last and First Men 151
Last Castle, The 148
"Last Evolution, The" 150
Last Generation, The 109
"Last Judgment, The" 151
Last Man, The 74, 132
"Last Men, The" 148
Last Men in London 151
Last of the Vampires 43
Lawrence, C. E. 50-51
Lazarus 51
Lear, Edward 67
Le Breton, Thomas 47
Lee, Edgar 45
Légende des siècles, La 79
Legend of the Wandering Jew, The 34
Leiber, Fritz 148-149
Leibniz, Gottfried 9, 126-127
Leland, Charles Godfrey 45
Le Rouge, Gustave, 87
"Léviathan le long Archikan des Patagons de l'île savante ou la perfectibilité" 75
Lewis, C. S. 56
Lewis, Matthew Gregory 38
"Light from Beyond, The" 144
Ligotti, Thomas 149

Lillard, Richard 117
Long, Frank Belknap 147-148
Longinus 126
"Lord Arthur Savile's Crime, The" 141
Lord of Light 58
Lord of the Rings, The 10, 50
Lorrain, Jean 138
Lost Garden, The 47
Lost Horizon 44
"Lost Leonardo, The" 57
Louis-Philippe 75
Lovecraft, H. P. 124-125, 142, 144-151, 153-154
Lovelock, James 118
Love of the Foolish Angel, The 53
Lumley, Brian 148
Lunn, Brian 53
Lurker at the Threshold, The 148
McCarthy, Justin Huntly 53
McCulley, Johnston 156
MacDonald, George 39-40
Machen, Arthur 141
"Machine à métaphysique, La" 138
"Machine Stops, The" 111-112
McIlwraith, Dorothy 149
McKenna, Stephen 53
Macropoulos Secret, The 47-48
Mad Love 100
"Magician's Visiter, The" 38
Mains d'Orlac, Les 93, 100
Maison des hommes vivants, La 43-44
Maître de la lumière, Le 93
Make Room! Make Room! 116
Maker of Shadows 49
Malthus, Robert 103-104, 114
Man Among the Microbes and Other Stories, A 88
Mann, Jack 49
Manning, Laurence 112
"Margery of Quether" 43
"Marooned in Andromeda" 144
Marschner, Heinrich 43
Marriott-Watson, H. C. 108
Marryat, Captain 44
Martyn, Wyndham 49

Marx, Karl 108
Mary Rose 46
Master of His Fate 43
Master of Life and Death 115
Master of Light, The 93
Masters of Evolution 115
Matrix, The 119
Matthew [Gospel] 37
Maturin, Charles 42
Maxwell, James Clerk 67
Meccania 108
Medawar, Peter 64-65
"Melmoth Reconciled" 43
"Melmoth reconcilié" 43
Melmoth the Wanderer 42-43
Memoirs of a Ghost 56
"Memoirs of Herr von Schnabelwopski, The" 44
Memoirs of Satan, The 53
Memoirs of the Year Two Thousand Five Hundred 78, 106
Memories of the Space Age 23
Mendlesohn, Farah 9-10, 13-14, 54-55
Mephisto Waltz, The 57
Mercier, Louis-Sébastien 78, 81, 106
Mercure de France 84, 87, 89
Merle, Jean-Toussaint 43
Merlin 50
Mesmer, Anton 128
"Mesmeric Revelation" 133
"Métamorphoses du vampire, Les" 135
"Metaphysical Machine, The" 138
Metropolis 100, 108
Micromégas 99
Mill, James 112
Mill, John Stuart 102, 112
Mille et une nuits, La 84-85
Miller, Walter M. 57
Milton, John 53, 157
Mines of Behemoth, The 149
Minotaur Takes a Cigarette Break, The 56
Mr. Kronion 53
Mr. Teedles, the Gland Old Man 47
Mitchison, Naomi 111
Moderan 120

Monde tel qu'il sera, Le 81, 106
Monk, The 38
Monsieur de Phocas 138
"Monsieur Dupont's Vacation" 87
Montesquieu, Baron de 139
Montgolfier brothers 79
Moorcock, Michael 58-59
Moreau, Joseph 134
Morrow, James 59
"Mortal Immortal, The" 43
Mort de la Terre, La 98
Morts bizarres, Les 138
Mullem, Louis 87
"Music of Erich Zann, The" 144
Mycroft and Moran 140
My First Two Thousand Years 48, 53
Myi 108
My Petition for More Space 116
Mystères de Londres, Les 156
Mystères de Paris, Les 36
Mysteries of Paris, The 36
"Mystery of Joseph Laquedem, The" 40
Napoléon, Louis (Emperor Napoléon III) 36
Narrative of Arthur Gordon Pym, The 145
Natural History 120
"Natural State" 115
Nature 102
"Necromancy in Naat" 144
Necronomicon, The 147
Necronomicon Press 143
Neele, Henry 38
Nesbit, E. 47
Neuromancer 119
New Bodies for Old 100
New Gods Lead, The 110
New Humanist 8
Newman, Kim 58
Newton, Isaac 63, 72, 127-128, 133
New Worlds 69
New York Review of Science Fiction, The 8
Nietzsche, Friedrich 157
Nifft the Lean 149
"Night" 150

Night Land, The 140, 143
Nightmares of an Ether-Drinker 138
Nineteen Eighty-Four 113
Ninth Life, The 49
Nodier, Charles 43, 74-82
Nordau, Max 139
Norton, Caroline 41
Not by Bread Alone 111
Novel of the Future, The 74
Odd John 151
Offutt, Andrew J. 116-117
Oldest God, The 53
O'Leary, Patrick 59
Omega: The Last Days of the World 139
"On a Universal Tendency in Nature to the Dissipation of Mechanical Energy" 139
On Borrowed Time 30
"On Fairy Tales" 12
Only Begotten Daughter 59
"On Scientific Marvel Fiction and its Effect on the Consciousness of Progress" 87-89
On Stranger Tides 59
"On the Age of the Sun's Heat" 139
"On the Threshold of Eternity" 147
Orlando: A Biography 47
Orwell, George 113-114, 123
Other Worlds 85
Other Worlds, The 20
Our Lady of Darkness 148
"Outsider, The" 145
Outsider and Others, The 124, 145
Outside the Earth 23
Pan 52-53, 110
Paradise Lost 53
Paris au vingtième siècle 81
Paris in the Twentieth Century 16, 81
Paris, Matthew 34
Parker, Peter 155, 158
Parsifal 56
Pawlowski, Gaston de 86
People of the Pole, The 87, 89
"People Trap, The" 116
"Perfectibility" 75

Péril bleu, Le 93
Permanence 120
Permutation City 59
Peter and Wendy 46
Peter Pan 46, 58
Peter Pan 46
"Peter Rugg, the Missing Man" 44
Peuple de la pôle, Le 87, 89
Phantom Ship, The 44
Pharaoh's Daughter 45
Pharos the Egyptian 45
Phénomène humain, Le 152
Phenomenon of Man, The 152
Phillpotts, Eden 53
Philosophical Enquiry into the Origin of Our Ideas of the Sublime and the Beautiful, A 126-127
Philostratus 37
Physics of Immortality, The 59, 152
"Pickman's Model, The" 145
Picture of Dorian Gray, The 45-46
Plato 61-62, 66, 73, 79, 125, 143
Pleasures of the Imagination, The 126, 133, 142
"Plein ciel" 79
Plume, La 84, 86-87
Poe, Edgar Allan 84, 89, 95, 99, 133-135, 137, 144-145
Pohl, Frederik 115
Polidori, John W. 43
Politics of Ecology, The 117
Politics of Pollution, The 117
Popper, Karl 65
"Population Bomb, The" 114
Population, Evolution, and Birth Control: A Collage of Controversial Ideas 117
Potter, Harry 155, 157
Powers, Tim 59
Powys, T. F. 30, 59
Pratchett, Terry 68
Pratt, Fletcher 50, 112
Pritcher Mass, The 116
Prometheus 31-32, 57, 59
Prometheus Bound 31-32
"Queen Mab" 38, 129
"Quelque romans scientifiques, De" 84-85

Quiller-Couch, Arthur 40
Quinet, Edgar 36, 38
Rachilde 87
"Rat, The" 30
Ray, Jean 94, 97
"Reap the Dark Tide" 115
Recluse, The 124
"Red Brain, The" 147
Reed, Robert 120
Reeve, Christopher 158
"Remembrance, The" 58
Renard, Maurice 87-101
Republic, The 66
Rest of the Robots, The 16
Retreat from Armageddon 111
Revelation of St. John 36
Révolte des anges, La 53
Revolt of the Angels, The 53
Rice, Anne 56
Richepin, Jules 138
Ridgeway, James 117
Riley, Charles V. 104
"Rime of the Ancient Mariner, The" 129
Ring Cycle 52
Robida, Albert 90
Robinson, Kim Stanley 118, 122
Robson, Justina 120
Roger of Wendover 34
Roman de l'avenir, Le 74-75
"Roman d'hypothèse, Le" 97-98
"Roman Merveilleux-scientifique et son action sur l'intelligence du progress, Du" 87-89
Rosny, J. H. 86-87, 97-99
Rousseau, Jean-Jacques 105
Rowling, J. K. 157
R.U.R. 108
Russell, W. Clark 44
Sackett, Sam 143
"Sailing to Byzantium" 58
Saint-Germain, Comte de 40, 57
St. Leon: A Tale of the Sixteenth Century 41
"Saint Satyr" 53
Salathiel 38

Salome the Wandering Jewess 48
Sampson, Ashley 56
Sanders, William 122
Santos-Dumont, Alberto 86
Sauer, Bob 116
Scarborough, Harold 47
Scenarios for a Ship Called Earth 116
Schachner, Nathan 114
Schismatrix 119
Schrödinger, Erwin 67
Schroeder, Karl 120
Schubart, Christian 35
Schumacher, Ernst 118
Scientific American 114
Scott, Ridley 119
Scribe, Eugène 38
Secret Glory, The 141
"Seven Geases, The" 143-144
Shadow, The 155
"Shadow—A Parable" 133
"Shadow out of Time, The" 147
Shadow Over Innsmouth, The 145
"Shark Ship" 115
Shaw, George Bernard 47
She 45
Shea, Michael 149
Sheckley, Robert 116
Sheep Look Up, The 116
Shelley, Mary 14-15, 43, 129, 132
Shelley, Percy 27, 38, 53, 128-129
Sherrill, Stephen 56
Shiel, M. P. 51
Sibyl, The 51
Sibyllan 51
"Signs of the Times" 107
"Silence—A Fable" 133
Silent Spring 116-117
Silverberg, Robert 58, 115-116
Silverstein, Alvin 41
"Since Sinbad" 94-95
Singe, Le 100
Sister Alice 120
Sisyphus 32

"Slave of the Flames" 49
Sleepwalker's World 116
Small is Beautiful 118
Smith, Clark Ashton 142-145, 147-149, 153
"Smoke Ghost" 148
Snyder, Gene 116
Socrates 61, 66
Solution Three 111
Son of Man 58
Sorrows of Satan, The 53
Southey, Robert 41
Souvestre, Émile 81, 106
"Space-Eaters, The" 148
Spectateur, Le 87
Spengler, Oswald 139
Spider, The 155-156, 158
Spider-Man 155-156, 158-159
"Sphinx, The" 141-142
"Spikenard" 51
Spinrad, Norman 122
Stableford, Brian 75
Stalin, Josef 113
Stand on Zanzibar 115
Stapledon, Olaf 151
Star Maker 151
"Sterile Planet" 114
Sterling, Bruce 119, 122
Sterling, George 142
Stevenson, Robert Louis 89
Stewart, Frred Mustard 57
Stockton, Frank R. 46
Stones of Enchantment 49
Stong, Phil 20
Stonier. G. W. 56
"Story of the Days to Come, A" 17
"Strange Playfellow" 26
Strange Story, A 44-45, 132-133, 140
Street, A. G. 114
Strieber, Whitley 57
String of Pearls, The 156
Stross, Charles 120
Stuart, Don A. 150-151
"Studies in Fascination" 138

Sue, Eugène 36-38
Supermale, The 84
Superman 155, 158
Supernatural Horror in Literature 124, 149
Surmâle, Le 84
Swayne, Martin, The 47
Swift, Jonathan 32-33, 98-99, 116
Tales of the Wandering Jew 58
"Tam Lin" 55
Tantalus 32, 59
Tarry Thou Till I Come 38
Teilhard de Chardin, Pierre 59, 152-153
Tennyson, Alfred, Lord 103
Tentation de Saint-Antoine, Le 137-138
Theodicy 126
This Above All 51
This Immortal 58
"Thomas the Rhymer" 55
Thomas Wingfold, Curate 39-40
Thomson, Sir William 139
Thoreau, Henry David 102
Thousand-and-One Nights, The 95
Thrilling Wonder Stories 100
Thurston, E. Temple 40
Timaeus 66
Time Machine, The 107, 139
"Time Without End: Physics and Biology in an Open Universe" 152
Tipler, Frank 59, 152-153
"Tissue-Culture King, The" 111
"Tithonian Fator, The" 58
Tithonus 29, 49
Titus 38
Todorov, Tzvetan 84
Tolkien, J. R. R. 10, 50
Tomorrow's Eve 85
"Tony Wandel's Heart" 46
Torrent of Faces, A 115
Tough Guide to Fantasyland 12, 50
"Tragedy of the Commons, The" 117-118
Transition of Titus Crow, The 148
Travels into Several Remote Nations of the World in Four Parts...by Lemuel Gulliver 32-33, 99

Treatise on Some Insects of New England Which are Injurious to Vegetation 104
Trevithick, Richard 79
True Names 59
"Tsalal, The" 149
Tsiolkovsky, Konstantin 23
Tuck Everlasting 58
Turgot, Anne-Robert 76, 103-104
Twain, Mark 38
Twenty Thousand Leagues Under the Sea 17
"Twilight" 150
"Twilight of the Gods, The" 53
Tycho Brahe 133
Unclay 30
Undying One, The 41
Universal History and Theory of the Heavens 127-128
Universe Makers, The 23
Undertang des Abendlandes, Der 139
Upton, Smyth 43
Useless Hands 108
"Vacances de Monsieur Dupont, Les" 87
Vallette, Alfred 87
Valley Beyond Time 50
Vampire, La 156
Vampire Countess, The 156
Vampires d'Alfama, Les 56
Vampires of Alfama, The 56
Vampyr, Der 43
"Vampyre, The" 43
Vance, Jack 148-149
Vansittart, Peter 56
Varlet, Théo 86
Varney the Vampyre 156
Vathek 129
Věc Macropoulos 47
Veidt, Conrad 40
Venus, the Lonely Goddess 53
Verlaine, Paul 87
Vernadsky, Vladimir 118
Verne. Jules 16, 20, 81, 84-85, 90, 106-108
Vernoy de Saint-Georges, Henri 38
Vicomte Paul 37
Viereck, George S. 48-51, 53

Villiers de l'Isle Adam, Comte de 85, 89
"Vin et du hashish, Du" 135
Vinge, Vernor 59
"Virtuoso's Collection. A" 38, 44
"Visitors from Mlok, The" 144
Vizier of the Two-Horned Alexander, The 46
"Voice in the Void, The" 150
Voltaire 98-99, 126
Vonnegut, Kurt Jr. 115
Voronoff, Sergei 46-47
"Voyage, Le" 135-136, 142
Voyage au centre de la terre 81
Voyage Immobile suivi d'autres histoires singulières 87-88, 93
Wagner, Richard 52
Wagner the Wehr-Wolf 156
"Waiting for the Iron Age" 58
Walker, Adam 128
"Wandering Christian, The" 58
Wandering Jew, The 34-42, 44, 46-51, 55, 57
Wandering Jew, The (Conway) 38-39
Wandering Jew, The (Heym) 51
Wandering Jew, The (Thurston) 40
Wandering Jew: A Christmas Carol, The 38
Wandering Jew's Daughter, The 37
Wandrei, Donald 147, 150
War of the Worlds, The 17, 89, 97
Washington, George 104
Watkin, L. E. 30
Watkins, William Jon 116
Watson, James 63
Waywalkers 59
We 108
Webb, Catherine 59
Web of Easter Island, The 147
Weird Tales 143-145, 149
Well of the Unicorn, The 50
Wells, H. G. 16-18, 20, 26, 83-85, 87, 89, 97-99, 107-108, 139
"When This World is All on Fire" 122
White Abacus, The 120
"White People, The" 141
"Whisperer in Darkness, The" 145
"Who Goes There?" 151
Wilde, Oscar 45-46, 141, 158

Wilkins, Vaughan 50
Williamson, Jack 49
"Willows, The" 141
Willy 86-87
"Wine of Wizardry, A" 142-143
Witch of Prague, The 45
Wollheim, Donald A. 23
Wonderful Visit, The 89
Wonder Stories 143, 149
Woolf, Virginia 47
Wonderful Adventures of Phra the Phoenician, The 45
World as It Shall Be, The 106
World Inside, The 116
"World Population" 114
World, the Flesh, and the Devil, The: An Enquiry into the Three Enemies of the Rational Soul 151
Wright, S. Fowler 30, 110, 112, 120
Wylie, Philip 116
"Xeethra" 143
"Xipéhuz, Les" 97
Yarbro, Chelsea Quinn 57
Young, Edward 128, 131
Young Diana, The 47
"Yours Truly, Jack the Ripper" 49
Zamyatin, Evgeny 108
Zanoni 44-45, 132-133, 140
Zelazny, Roger 58
Zeus 32
Zicci 44
Zoroaster 77
Z.P.G. 116

Lightning Source UK Ltd.
Milton Keynes UK
05 August 2010

157977UK00001B/32/P